IFIP Advances in Information and Communication Technology 656

Editor-in-Chief

Kai Rannenberg, Goethe University Frankfurt, Germany

Editorial Board Members

IFIP – The International Federation for Information Processing

IFIP was founded in 1960 under the auspices of UNESCO, following the first World Computer Congress held in Paris the previous year. A federation for societies working in information processing, IFIP's aim is two-fold: to support information processing in the countries of its members and to encourage technology transfer to developing nations. As its mission statement clearly states:

> IFIP is the global non-profit federation of societies of ICT professionals that aims at achieving a worldwide professional and socially responsible development and application of information and communication technologies.

IFIP is a non-profit-making organization, run almost solely by 2500 volunteers. It operates through a number of technical committees and working groups, which organize events and publications. IFIP's events range from large international open conferences to working conferences and local seminars.

The flagship event is the IFIP World Computer Congress, at which both invited and contributed papers are presented. Contributed papers are rigorously refereed and the rejection rate is high.

As with the Congress, participation in the open conferences is open to all and papers may be invited or submitted. Again, submitted papers are stringently refereed.

The working conferences are structured differently. They are usually run by a working group and attendance is generally smaller and occasionally by invitation only. Their purpose is to create an atmosphere conducive to innovation and development. Refereeing is also rigorous and papers are subjected to extensive group discussion.

Publications arising from IFIP events vary. The papers presented at the IFIP World Computer Congress and at open conferences are published as conference proceedings, while the results of the working conferences are often published as collections of selected and edited papers.

IFIP distinguishes three types of institutional membership: Country Representative Members, Members at Large, and Associate Members. The type of organization that can apply for membership is a wide variety and includes national or international societies of individual computer scientists/ICT professionals, associations or federations of such societies, government institutions/government related organizations, national or international research institutes or consortia, universities, academies of sciences, companies, national or international associations or federations of companies.

More information about this series at https://link.springer.com/bookseries/6102

David Kreps · Robert Davison ·
Taro Komukai · Kaori Ishii (Eds.)

Human Choice and Digital by Default: Autonomy vs Digital Determination

15th IFIP International Conference on Human Choice and Computers, HCC 2022, Tokyo, Japan, September 8–9, 2022, Proceedings

Springer

Editors
David Kreps 🆔
University of Galway
Galway, Ireland

Robert Davison 🆔
City University of Hong Kong
Hong Kong, Hong Kong

Taro Komukai 🆔
Chuo University
Tokyo, Japan

Kaori Ishii
Chuo University
Tokyo, Japan

ISSN 1868-4238   ISSN 1868-422X (electronic)
IFIP Advances in Information and Communication Technology
ISBN 978-3-031-17138-3   ISBN 978-3-031-15688-5 (eBook)
https://doi.org/10.1007/978-3-031-15688-5

This Springer imprint is published by the registered company Springer Nature Switzerland AG
The registered company address is: Gewerbestrasse 11, 6330 Cham, Switzerland

Preface

This book contains the proceedings of the 15th International Conference on Human Choice and Computers (HCC 2022), which was held at the Faculty of Global Informatics (iTL), Chuo University, Japan, during September 8–9, 2002. The conference was organized by the International Federation for Information Processing (IFIP) Technical Committee 9 (TC9): Information and Communication Technology (ICT) and Society.

All papers were double-blind reviewed by at least two members of the Program Committee, during a six week review period. In total, 16 full papers were accepted, calculated by review score. Papers submitted by a Program Committee member were managed by the program chairs independently.

The conference co-chairs, Taro Komukai (Japan representative to TC9), David Kreps, (chair of TC9), Robert M. Davison (chair of WG94), and Kaori Ishii (guest program chair), chose the theme for this year's conference: "Human Choice and Digital by Default: Autonomy vs Digital Determination." Tracks were advertised in the call for papers addressing a range of concerns across the working groups of TC9, and the accepted papers coalesced into two groups: ethics and law.

The papers selected for this book are based on both academic research and the professional experience of information systems practitioners working in the field. It is the continued intention of TC9 that academics, practitioners, governments, and international organizations alike will benefit from the contributions of these proceedings.

Details of the activities of IFIP TC9's activities are posted at http://www.ifiptc9.org/

July 2022

David Kreps
Robert M. Davison

Human Choice and Digital by Default: Autonomy vs Digital Determination

Robert Davison[1] and David Kreps[2]

[1] City University of Hong Kong
isrobert@cityu.edu.hk
[2] University of Galway, Ireland
david.kreps@nuigalway.ie

1 Choice

Choice is a wonderful thing to have, and in a booming market of Internet-connected devices, not to mention the millions of apps and programmes that service them, there might appear to be a cornucopia of choices. But if it was that simple, why the need for a conference about Human Choice and Computers? Perhaps the choices are not as widespread as they seem, or perhaps darker forces mean that what goes for choice is actually an illusion.

The first choice is whether to use a computer or not. That seems simple enough, but it is increasingly the case that if you don't have a computer, and an internet connected one at that, it is very hard to survive in the developed economies of the world. Here 'computer' is interpreted quite liberally to mean any device with computer-like processing power, memory, and storage, and thus includes phones, tablets, notebooks and laptops, desktops, mainframes, and even super computers, if you have one at home, as well as everything in between. A recent study from New Zealand [1] documented how difficult it is for rural residents to live without the Internet because so many service providers have moved all their services online, whether it be banking, retail sales, or grocery shopping. Even though many of the people interviewed for this study stated loudly and clearly that they really don't want to be connected to the Internet, nor to use a computer, actually they have very little choice. Even if they grow all their own food, they still have to pay bills and e-banking is the only way. Meanwhile, in Hong Kong under COVID-19 restrictions, access to many buildings, shops, offices, etc. is only possible by scanning a QR code using an app on your phone. If you don't have a phone, clearly you can't scan anything. Perhaps mobile phone ownership is so ubiquitous that this seems strange. Who would NOT want to have a phone? But that's not the point. The point is, do we have a choice? Are we allowed NOT to have (and pay for) a phone if we don't want one? If we don't have a phone, can we still receive the same quality of services as everyone else who does have a phone? The answer is clearly 'no', and thus phone ownership is essentially mandatory.

Meanwhile, there is considerable pressure to upgrade our devices every few years, whether because software is no longer supported or new versions of apps require better hardware and the old versions don't work anymore. Thus, we really don't have either the choice or the non-choice: use is compulsory.

Moving to other realms, those of us who like to read books increasingly find that we have to buy books online as many physical bookshops have closed. Kindle Books is an option, if you are happy with Amazon. For new paper books, Amazon will readily sell them to you, as will Book Depository (owned by Amazon), and for second handbooks, Abebooks (also owned by Amazon) is a good place to look. There are non-Amazon choices (Wordery, Barnes and Noble), but it's not always obvious who is the parent company.

Of course, these examples are selective, and others could be picked. But what about choice? Is choice a right or an illusion? It's been 14 years since The Economist declared that privacy is dead, but perhaps choice is going the same way. Although there are some choices left, they are dwindling in number. The most fundamental choice – to use or not to use a computer – seems to be a relic of the past.

2 Papers

As one of us stated in a recent paper elsewhere, "Ethics is a matter of professionalism, generally understood as being outside the purview of law and regulation. Though law often embodies ethical principles, law and ethics are not co-extensive; laws are created based on a society's ethics, to enforce behaviours we are expected to follow, but ethics suggest what we ought to follow, and help us explore options to improve our decision-making." [2] The papers accepted for this conference fell broadly into two categories: those which dealt with the more ethical side of the dilemma of choice in contemporary society, and those which dealt more with the legal side.

In the first section, Salla Ponkala, Jani Koskinen, Camilla Lähteenmäki, and Antti Tuomisto begin the proceedings with research into worker well-being in the era of the data economy: if we have no choice but to adapt to digital transformation, the least our employers can do is help us upskill and pay attention to our well-being needs in the face of increasing technostress. Mikko Vermanen, Minna Rantanen, and Jani Koskinen then present a study of employee privacy in Internet of Things ecosystems, trying to establish what the prerequisites must be for ethical data collection and use in such increasingly ubiquitous circumstances: surely, we ought to have some choice in what data such systems can ethically gather about us?

Sticking with contentious issues for the ethics of modern digital technologies, Aimi Ozaki then presents a study of live facial recognition technology use by private companies in public places: here, certainly, there seems little if any choice, for city-dwellers at least, whether or not they are thus surveilled (unless they cover up completely with dark glasses/goggles, hat, balaclava, and more).

Johanna Sefyrin and Mariana Gustafsson then take us into the world of sociomaterial relations, with a study on librarians' and social workers' roles and practices in addressing the needs of vulnerable groups, which is followed by Barbara Nino Carreras and Sisse Finken's research into autonomy alliances and data care practices in the context of the digitalisation of welfare. In the care professions, matters of choice and consent are paramount, and navigating the impact of digital technologies increasingly difficult.

Staying with sociological analysis, Shigenori Ohashi, Noritaka Maeda, Shigeru Fujimura, and Atsushi Nakadaira explore social capital types in Japan through the lens of social networking sites: can bonding and bridging behaviour affect how we tweet?

Moving into eHealth, Mayu Terada presents a study of personal data use in Japanese medical care, and Ryuta Yamashita, Tadaaki Shimizu, Natsuki Yoshinaka, Rintaro Kataoka, and Naoki Sawada explore the impact digital advertising may be having upon our eyes. As with the care professions and our social status, so in the health sector our choices and consent are fundamental, and the impact of digital transformation a source of many questions and anxieties.

Lastly, in this section, Markus Philipp Zimmer and Jonna Järveläinen introduce the sustainability angle of an ethical approach to digital transformation, suggesting the notion of the triple-bottom-line may help bring a more sustainable digital transformation.

In the second section of the proceedings, Joey Jansen van Vuuren, Louise Leenen, and Anna-Marie Jansen van Vuuren start things off with an increasingly common example of digital law-breaking, presenting a study of ransomware in Africa.

Ayuki Saito, Michele Baccelli, Kazuto Kobayashi, and Mitsuyoshi Hiratsuka then explore issues of patent law and AI, Toru Maruhashi presents a study of how Japanese Law affects automated content moderation, and Mika Nakashima compares the EU, US, and Japanese legal systems' approaches to data portability.

Sticking with international comparisons, Casper Chigwedere, Sam Takavarasha, and Bonface Chisaka present a literature review on regulatory frameworks in developing countries, and Tetsunosuke Jinnai presents a study of international law and cyber-conflicts from a Japanese eye-view.

To conclude the proceedings, Taro Komukai presents a study focusing on privacy issues concerning personal data held by third parties during criminal investigations.

First, however, to begin the proceedings, our two keynote speakers kindly provided summaries of their presentations for us to reproduce in this book. Jiro Kokuryo spoke to us about "Designing Socio-Technical Systems for a Cyber Civilization", and the key element of traceabilty - advances in which "are so fundamental that they may change the shape of our civilization." Hiromi Yokoyama introduced us to her "Octagon Measurements" and "ELSI score" for AI ethics – two key methodologies for advanced science and technology if it is to "be checked for ethical issues from the development stage."

We hope and trust you will enjoy reading the texts within these pages.

x   R. Davison and D. Kreps

References

1. Díaz Andrade, A. and Techatassanasoontorn, A.A. (2021) Digital enforcement: Rethinking the pursuit of a digitally-enabled society, Information Systems Journal 31, 1, 184–197.
2. Gotterbarn, D., and Kreps, D. (2020) Being a Data Professional: Give Voice to Value in a Data Driven Society. AI and Ethics. https://doi.org/10.1007/s43681-020-00027-y

Organization

Conference Chair

Taro Komukai   Chuo University

Conference Co-chair

David Kreps   University of Galway, Ireland

Conference Co-chair

Kaori Ishii   Chuo University, Japan

Program Chairs

Robert M Davison   City University of Hong Kong, Hong Kong
David Kreps   University of Galway, Ireland

Program Committee

Askar Aituov   Kazakh-British Technical University, Kazakhstan
Jawad Hussain Awan   National University of Management and Languages,
                              Pakistan
Kathrin Bednar   Vienna University of Economics and Business, Austria
Petros Chamakiotis   ESCP Business School, Spain
Anna Croon   Umeå University, Sweden
Daniel Curto-Millet   University of Gothenburg
Robert M Davison   City University of Hong Kong, Hong Kong
Richard Dron   Salford Business School
Sisse Finken   IT University of Copenhagen, Denmark
Per Fors   Uppsala University, Sweden
Marthie Grobler   CSIRO's Data61, Australia
Olli Heimo   University of Turku, Finland
Magda Hercheui   University College London, UK
Mitsuyoshi Hiratsuka   Tokyo University of Science, Japan
Jun Iio   Chuo University, Japan
Kai Kimppa   University of Turku, Finland
Jay Kishigami   Keio University, Japan
Jani Koskinen   University of Turku
Mikael Laaksoharju   Uppsala University, Sweden
Chris Leslie   South China University of Technology, China
Takayuki Matsuo   Harvard Law School, USA

Brad McKenna	University of East Anglia, UK
Yosuke Murakami	KDDI Research, Inc., Japan
Kiyoshi Murata	Meiji University
Mika Nakashima	Chuo University, Japan
Trishana Ramluckan	UKZN, South Africa
Minna Rantanen	University of Turku
Deepak Saxena	Indian Institute of Technology Jodhpur, India
Johanna Sefyrin	Linköping University, Sweden
Riana Steyn	University of Pretoria, South Africa
Gopal Tadepalli	Anna University, India
Sam Takavarasha	Women's University in Africa, Zimbabwe
Richard Taylor	International Baccalaureate Organization, UK
Jean-Paul Van Belle	University of Cape Town, South Africa
Will Venters	London School of Economics, UK
Ruth Wario	University of the Free State, South Africa
Martin Warnke	Leuphana University Lüneburg, Germany
Chris Zielinski	University of Winchester, UK
Brett van Niekerk	Durban University of Technology, South Africa

Keynote Talks

Designing Socio-Technical Systems for a Cyber Civilization

Jiro Kokuryo

Keio University, 5322 Endo, Fujisawa-City, Kanagawa 252-0882, Japan
jkokuryo@sfc.keio.ac.jp

As a business scholar, I have long been interested in the interactive evolution of social institutions and technological systems. Recognizing that these are integral parts of larger socio-technical systems [1], I propose that they should be developed concurrently to mutually reinforce each other (Fig. 1). Such an integral approach seems more important than ever, as the social impact of information technology is becoming more profound. In order to realize such an integral design, we need to have bridging concepts that are *meaningful* to the *design* of both technical and social systems.

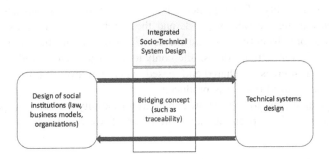

Fig. 1 Socio-technical system design

One such bridging concept that I have been focusing on is traceability, i.e., the ability of shippers to track goods after shipment and of receivers to know the origins of the goods they have at hand. This concept is often discussed in the context of supply chain transparency. Technologies to improve traceability are rapidly developing due to advances in sensors (e.g., QR codes) and network technologies (e.g., wireless). Technologies such as NFT (non-fungible tokens) are expanding the scope of traceability beyond traditional physical goods to people, money, and digital content.

I believe that advances in traceability are so fundamental that they may change the shape of our civilization. To fully understand this, we should start by recognizing that the industrial civilization we live in has been designed assuming a lack of traceability. Factories that emerged following the industrial revolution produced more products than local markets could consume. As a result, the goods had to be sent to distant markets and strangers who could not be trusted. And in the absence of today's sophisticated technologies, the goods were not traceable. In such an environment, the only alternative for businesses was to sell "exclusive rights of disposal (property ownership)" for money as goods were shipped. In other words, a market mechanism needed to be established. One might notice that this mechanism was also about enabling anonymous transactions. In the absence of traceability, businesses had to sell to the anonymous masses. The supermarket, where customers could purchase anonymously without any conversation, was a symbolic manifestation of the system.

One should note that social institutions were developed to support this market mechanism. Constitutional, civil, and commercial laws were established to guarantee ownership as an inviolable human right of individuals. Such institutions were backed by nation-states with the enforcement powers of governments under democracy. Such a combination of basic philosophy, economic institutions, and legal/political systems vastly expanded industrial production.

Once we understand the background of the ownership/exchange model, it becomes easier for us to understand why alternative models such as sharing, as-a-service, and subscription models are emerging as traceability technologies advance. It is no longer necessary to "complete the transaction" each time in the form of an ownership transfer. When both the product and the customer are traceable, it becomes much easier to "license" the accessing of assets.

An additional force driving this shared use of assets is the increasing concern around the sustainability of our planet. The ownership/exchange business model is focused on increasing the sale of goods and the number of transactions. While this system gives strong incentives for businesses, it also burdens the environment by attempting to sell ever more products, often only to be wasted. The world now needs an economy where resources are shared and reused, where the level of utility gained from each good is maximized once it is produced.

Figure 2 is an attempt to depict how enhanced traceability may be incorporated into a "potluck economy" to promote the shared use of various kinds of assets for a

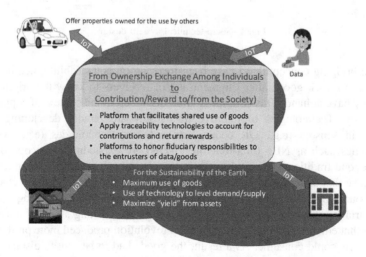

Fig. 2 From exchange economy to Potluck economy

sustainable future [2]. Technologies are developed to allow people to share their assets for use by others while a platform monitors contributions and rewards the contributors for their participation. One might note that the notion of ownership is still alive in this design. The owner of an asset only has to license access to it when they are not using it themselves.

A natural concern when envisioning such a system of sharing is the breach of privacy. Any socio-technical system that promotes the social sharing of goods and data should also incorporate mechanisms to protect the privacy of the people who partici-pate in the system. We already face issues surrounding the governance of the data that is in the hands of major platform providers. We need to address these issues if we want this kind of "potluck economy" to flourish.

While I recognize the presence of technical and legal solutions to this issue, I would like to allude to the benefit of focusing on incentive structures. I say this because I see the current issues surrounding privacy primarily as issues of major platform providers having the incentive to use personal data in the interest of sponsors rather than the individuals who have contributed their data. Figure 3 is a proposal to separate "con-sumer agents" that have no conflict-of-interest issue from the "supplier agents" that work on behalf of the suppliers of goods.

One might note that this arrangement is a departure from the thinking that indi-viduals should have complete control of their data. Instead, the arrangement assumes that consumer agents remain loyal to consumers while consumers are encouraged to contribute to society by allowing others to access and utilize their assets, including data. Consumer agents should be penalized heavily for any breach of the trust placed upon them.

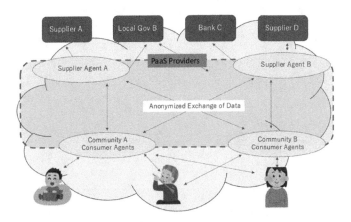

Fig. 3 Resolving the structural conflict of interest

Such design, based on trust and altruism, suggests that perhaps traditional Asian ethics, which are based on trust and loyalty, may be helpful in developing the future ethics of a cyber civilization. The Buddhist tradition of Asia, for example, asks people to free themselves from an obsession with ownership and be altruistic while seeking a society that is mutually protective of others. The Confucian tradition asks people to be loyal to their superiors while giving justification for overturning the rules of those superiors when they lack benevolence to people. These traditions have the potential to provide a philosophical foundation for a "potluck economy" with its strong emphasis on sharing and living in harmony within an ecosystem.

I should add that the notions of trust and loyalty are also present in Western ethics in the form of fiduciary responsibility. There is no conflict with individualistic traditions here, either. The financial industry, for example, has adopted and institutionalized ethics in a practical and sophisticated manner. Perhaps the design of socio-technical systems in a cyber civilization should learn from such examples.

Any new technology is a double-edged sword. We must develop the capability to design socio-technical systems wisely so that powerful technologies may be used to contribute to the greater social good.

References

1. Bostrom, R.P., Heinen, J.S.: MIS Problems and failures: a socio-technical perspective PART I: THE CAUSES. MIS Quarterly **1**(3), 17–32 (1977)
2. Timothy, N.: Blog. https://www.sustainableeconomist.com/the_potluck_economy. Accessed on May 28 2022

"Octagon Measurements" and "ELSI score" for AI ethics

Hiromi Yokoyama

University of Tokyo, Japan
jkokuryo@sfc.keio.ac.jp

Advanced research in science and technology must be checked for ethical issues beginning in the development stage. So far, we have developed two ethics measurements, Octagon Measurements and ELSI. Both may be applied easily by researchers in the field of AI. In this talk, I would like to explain how we developed these two ethics scores and how they can be applied.

Octagon Measures

We focused on eight themes that are common in AI guidelines: privacy, accountability, safety and security, transparency and explainability, fairness and non-discrimination, human control of technology, professional responsibility, and promotion of human values. We also proposed Octagon Measurements, which directly scales these eight

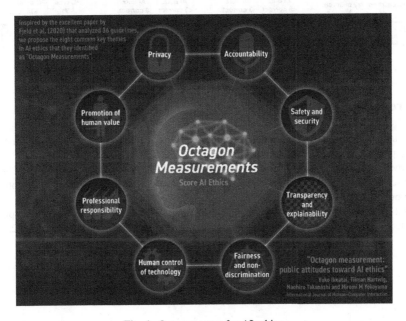

Fig. 1 Octagon score for AI ethics

themes. We prepared four dilemma scenarios (i.e., AI singer, AI shopping, AI drone weapon, and AI criminal tracking) that addressed both positive and negative aspects of new AI technologies, and we checked these to allow for the comparison of overall ethics levels. Our findings showed that older people, women, and those with higher levels of education were more concerned about the social implementation of AI. Figure 1 shows the eight categories, ethics issues, and international differences in the Octagon scores.

ELSI Score for AI

ELSI scores for R&D are emphasized in the social theory of science and technology. We developed the ELSI score using data collected in Japan and the U.S. based on four scenarios. The ELSI score is so simple that it can be used for AI as well as other technologies. It is currently being tested for application to genome editing technologies.

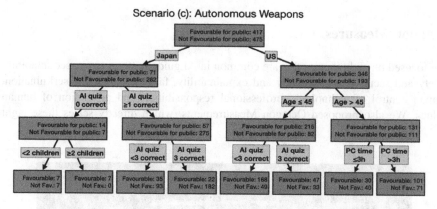

Fig. 2 Decision tree analysis for AI drone weapon using ELSI score

References

1. Ikkatai, Y., Hartwig, T., Takanashi, N., Yokoyama, H.: Segmentation of AI's ELSI concerns in Japan, the US and Germany (submitted)
2. Hartwig, T., Ikkatai, Y., Takanashi, N., Yokoyama, H.M.: Artificial intelligence ELSI score for science and technology: a comparison between Japan and the U. AI Soc. (2022) https://doi.org/10.1007/s00146-021-01323-9
3. Ikkatai, Y., Hartwig, T., Takanashi, N., Yokoyama, H.M.: Octagon measurement: public attitudes toward AI Ethics. International Journal of Human–Computer Interaction (2022)

Contents

Law

Ethics

Promoting Worker Wellbeing in the Era of Data Economy

Salla Ponkala$^{(\boxtimes)}$ (iD), Jani Koskinen (iD), Camilla Lähteenmäki (iD), and Antti Tuomisto (iD)

Information System Sciences, Turku School of Economics,
University of Turku, Turku, Finland
{salla.k.ponkala,jasiko,camilla.k.lahteenmaki,
antti.tuomisto}@utu.fi

Abstract. The data economy is expanding, and SMEs (small- and medium-sized enterprises) have found themselves under increasing pressure to digitalise their processes and to adopt data-based solutions for business development. SMEs act in an ever more networked data economy ecosystems with a great number of information systems, digital technologies, and interfaces to learn to keep up with the competition. Digital transformation has been accelerated by the Covid-19 pandemic, which forced many companies to take immediate digital leaps without proper preparation.

Meanwhile, data economy and digitalisation challenge worker wellbeing in SMEs in an unprecedented way: skills of entrepreneurs and workers related to digitised work seem to lag behind, leaving them with technostress and difficulties with coping and managing one's own work and collaboration. This has potential for serious negative impacts on structural, social and psychological capital, which all affect the overall wellbeing capital in SMEs.

To tackle these issues, Wellbeing at Work from Digitalisation (WWFD) project was established to develop a fair, participatory and sustainable framework for SMEs to build their skills and worker wellbeing in the context of the data economy. It aims at placing the knowledge worker in control of their work by offering tools for building worker wellbeing as wellbeing capital. Based on the initial mapping in Finnish SMEs around Turku region, the toolbox is built around workplace democracy, value alignment, skill development and knowledge sharing to ensure that worker wellbeing is not compromised while encouraging the ever-better acquisition of digital technologies. The toolbox will be piloted in SMEs and refined further, and the final manual for WWFD will be published in Fall 2023.

Keywords: Data economy · Data economy ecosystem · Wellbeing capital · Worker wellbeing · Work engagement · Workplace democracy · Technostress · Digitalisation

Published by Springer Nature Switzerland AG 2022
D. Kreps et al. (Eds.): HCC 2022, IFIP AICT 656, pp. 3–17, 2022.
https://doi.org/10.1007/978-3-031-15688-5_1

1 Introduction

In the last few decades, our world along with the economy has turned online and activities are increasingly done by and with technology. Phenomena such as big data, artificial intelligence (AI), and Internet of Things (IoT) have increasingly steered attention towards ecosystems around data and data usage [13]. Consequently, companies are facing increasing pressure to digitalise their functions and to adopt data-driven technologies for business development to keep up with the competition.

Digitalisation has been ever more highlighted by the Covid-19 pandemic, which has forced many companies to turn their activities online, and the changes were made almost overnight. Knowledge workers had increasing demands in their daily work even prior to the pandemic [16]. Despite of benefits the pandemic may have brought, such as more equal social distribution between remote and on-site workers [56], many have faced unforeseen changes and job demands that are not necessarily compensated with additional job resources.

In the Southwestern Finland, these phenomena overlap with structural changes in regional economy: manufacturing and information technology (IT) industries, among others, have expanded, whereas the number of skilled workers lags behind [2, 37]. Based on preliminary interviews in SMEs, companies seem to struggle with finding skilled workers that understand data economy and are able to cope with new technologies, which can potentially affect the whole ecosystem. The problems seem to be amplified in SMEs that have smaller resources to invest in modern technologies or new employees. Lack of sufficient skills and knowledge is alarming, but recruiting new talent is perceived so risky and time consuming that it does not seem to be a safe option.

These phenomena have raised concerns about knowledge workers' wellbeing at work. Whereas digitalisation that thrives from data-driven systems has great potential to make work in SMEs more efficient, flexible and scalable [55], studies have shown that adopting new digital tools and learning to use them in everyday work can cause significant stress, information overload and interruptions amongst workers, which disrupts workflows and challenges wellbeing [4, 8, 35, 38, 55].

To better understand the relationship between digitalisation and worker wellbeing and to offer tools for the companies to cope with the turbulent environment, the project Wellbeing at Work from Digitalisation (WWFD) was launched in September 2021. The two-year project is conducted by the University of Turku and the Tampere University of Applied Sciences, and it is funded by the European Social Fund as a part of actions in reaction to the Covid-19 pandemic. The project is developing a scalable framework with a set of tools that enables employees in SMEs to better take advantage of the possibilities offered by data economy. In this paper, we present the initial framework built based on a scoping literature review and an initial mapping consisting of seven semi-structural interviews in SMEs.

SMEs were chosen as the object, because of the weaker abilities and need for support in SMEs to address the issues in worker wellbeing [36]. Moreover, their relatively small size and agile structures enable the companies to pilot and implement practices that cover the entire organisation. By doing so, the project aims to develop structures that last from the early stage of development to the time when the companies grow and have ever greater impact on the entire data economy ecosystem. This is achieved by creating a framework around digitalisation that stems from the ecosystem and the individual in the operating environment. The framework thus focuses on worker wellbeing by putting knowledge workers in control of digital transformation: it offers a fairer, more open, sustainable and community-based approach to handling and developing one's work as a part of business development in a networked environment.

In the next Section, we discuss the concept of data economy and its implications for wellbeing in general. In Section three, we focus on how worker wellbeing could be promoted in data-intensive businesses where acquiring sufficient resources and capabilities of knowledge workers are among the core challenges. In Section four, the focus is on workplace democracy and its effect on wellbeing of knowledge workers. In Section five, we introduce the initial WWFD framework that is developed based on a scoping literature review on the effects of digitalisation on worker wellbeing and the initial mapping consisting of semi-structured interviews in Finnish SMEs. The framework describes crucial points of development identified in the Finnish SMEs as a result of data economy and digitalisation and introduces a starting point of a conceptual model for tackling the issues. Finally, in Section six we end up with conclusions.

2 Data Economy Ecosystem as Emerging and Challenging Business Field

Data economy and data ecosystems are new, central terms of digital business today. Yet, they are concepts still under formation and thus they are not established or commonly agreed upon. For example, [24] calls ecosystem a zombie category term, which means that it is a term alive and used but, at the same time, it lacks real content. This underlines the need for proper definition when discussing data economy and data ecosystems. The definition of data economy ecosystems (see Table 1. for key definitions of terms used in this article) calls for data as the main source of business.

Data is ever more important when doing business, and in the future, it will most likely play even bigger role in organisations' business models and competition. This is visible, e.g., in the role of citizen-consumers that have turned from mere buyers into a more integrated in business and have their own channels and networks that may affect the business [30]. If an organisation does not recognise all relevant stakeholders and data that they may provide, it may end up in a situation where competitors possess the data, which can be a crucial advantage in conducting business. Therefore, even if data is not the main source for business today, it may be tomorrow, and this sets new demands for all actors of data economy ecosystems—including companies, employees, customers, citizens, governmental actors, and the third sector.

Data is the key element that has provided new ways of doing business and has created data ecosystems where data is used in different levels of society [39, 58]. Even though data can offer new opportunities, data economy has its dark side as well [54]. Zuboff is describing data economy as *surveillance capitalism,* in which people are a source for information feeding businesses. The logic behind surveillance capitalism is based on the accumulation of data, which is collected from a multitude of sources, then extracted, analysed, commodified, and finally used to make profit [62, 63]. Couldry and Mejias talk about the era of new colonialism, *data colonialism,* which has normalised

Table 1. Definitions for the key concepts used in this article.

Concept	Definition
Data economy	Data economy is a subcategory for the economy, in which data and information are the core assets for business
Data economy ecosystem	"Is a network, that is formed by different actors of ecosystem, that are using data as a main source or instance for business. Different actors and stakeholders are connected directly or indirectly within network and it's value chains. Data economy ecosystem also incorporates the rules (official or unofficial), that direct action allowed in network" [29, p. 2]
Worker wellbeing	Holistic state of experienced wellbeing, strongly linked to and shaped by factors related to work and workload, such as a balance between job resources and job demands
Wellbeing capital	Combination of elements of human capital that contribute to worker wellbeing: social capital, organisation's structural capital and psychological capital [35]
Work engagement	State of feeling vigorous, dedicated and absorbed in work, leading to workers taking initiative, being open for changes and performing well both in terms of formal requirements and voluntary efforts [20, 27, 44]
Technostress	Stress induced by a worker's inability to cope or deal with information technology in a healthy manner [4]
Workplace democracy	A form of corporate governance where all workers regardless of position are seen as stakeholders and thus are included (in varying intensity) in the planning and execution of the company's strategy and actions. No ownership is required
Knowledge worker	A Knowledge worker is a person whose work contains unstructured, intellectual and cognitive tasks to be fulfilled in producing knowledge-based outputs (services or products) [46]

the exploitation of humans through personal data [12]. Like they noted, we should resist building societies based on total algorithmic control, where we are reducing humans to mere resources for economic purposes. This is relevant when thinking about the role of employees in SMEs. This does not mean rejection of data usage and collection, but rejecting current data practises [12] as they do not seem to fit into an idea of fair and ethical data economy [29] and thus an ethical workplace.

One example of a problematic data-based business area is the gig economy. The gig economy refers to a business that is based on short-term, on-demand, occasional, and typically task-based labour [50], such as Uber and DoorDash. The problem is that the gig economy easily lessens the people who provide the service to mere objects that are constantly evaluated and rated by customers and algorithms, have weaker social and legal protection (providers are labour but not employees), are under algorithmic management, and tend to gain lower salaries [50]. As autonomy and respect play an important role in worker wellbeing [18], this can have negative implications for the wellbeing of service providers.

Ever expanding data economy sets new demands for SMEs as it is a demanding area of economy, where specialised skills and knowledge are needed to carry out the business ethically. Problem is that those skills and knowledge may not be at the core of the business itself but are still needed, which creates a conflict concerning the allocation of scarce resources. There are questions of data/knowledge management, strategies, technological competence, data security, privacy, ownership of data, ethics etc. that need to be answered to make ethically and legally sustainable business [52, 59]. There is also a need to focus on the values of employees to ensure that organisations' values and actions do not conflict with them—an issue that may have a critical impact on an organisation but may be forgotten in the context of data economy [42].

Furthermore, studies imply that although digitalisation that thrives from data-driven systems has a great potential to make work in SMEs more efficient, flexible, and scalable [55], adopting new digital tools and learning to use them can induce stress, information overload and interruptions amongst workers, which disrupts workflows and challenges wellbeing [4, 8, 35, 38, 55]. In next Section, we explore in more detail what challenges worker wellbeing in today's data ecosystems and how workplace democracy could be helpful for overcoming the challenges.

3 From Individual Stress Factors to Wellbeing of Ecosystems

In worklife studies, research in the 20th century on worker wellbeing concentrated on analysis of stress factors with negative implications for employees and other aspects that cause unhappiness [10, 26]. Since then, the focus has shifted towards encouraging positive aspects that strengthen wellbeing – a holistic understanding of factors on individual, organisational and environmental level that influence worker wellbeing [20, 35]. In this Section, we explore the key concepts in worker wellbeing studies and their implications for knowledge work in data economy ecosystems in the light of findings from the first round of analysis of the interview data gathered during the initial mapping in Finnish SMEs.

3.1 Key Concepts in Worker Wellbeing Studies

First, the beginning of the 21st century was marked by the raise of positive psychology, which aims at building worker wellbeing and optimising processes around the strengths and job resources of workers, organisations and teams – a model balancing job demands and job resources as an example still relevant today [20, 35, 44, 45]. Today, one of the key concepts in describing and measuring worker wellbeing is work engagement. It is about feeling vigorous, dedicated and absorbed [44], which leads to taking initiative, being open for changes and performing well both in terms of formal demands and requirements but also voluntarily [20, 27]. Work engagement is seen as an ideal, sustainable state that persists over time as a result of worker wellbeing. Although personal attributes and individual wellbeing affects the feeling of work engagement, leadership plays a key role in building and strengthening it [21, 53].

In data ecosystems, worker wellbeing can be experienced collectively. Several studies have found that work engagement is a collective phenomenon that can spread amongst people working together regularly [20]. It has been proposed that worker wellbeing could have positive impact on larger entities than only the organisation itself [43]. Involving the ecosystem – such as customers, partners and academic community – is one of the key factors in successful digitalisation efforts [25]. Our interviews with Finnish SMEs revealed high dependencies among companies and stakeholders, which has relevance on worker wellbeing. This implies that building sustainably better, fairer and happier workplaces could have positive influence over organisational boarders and thus encourage wellbeing in in the ecosystem at large.

In this project, we approach worker wellbeing following a model presented by Manka [35], according to which worker wellbeing as wellbeing capital is a combination of social capital, organisation's structural capital and workers' individual psychological capital. Social capital refers to resources rooted in social aspects of one's work, such as participatory and motivating leadership, communication, and team skills. Structural capital entails organisational structures that enable flexible work and well-functioning environment, clear goals, and opportunities to participation and skill development. Psychological capital consists of workers' physical and mental health. [35] Considering the increasing importance of ecosystems in the context of SMEs, we extend this further to take into consideration elements rooted in the ecosystems as well. It is important to note that a truly holistic perspective on wellbeing includes both wellbeing at work and outside work [36, 43]. Wellbeing cannot be entirely divided into distinct categories – aspects in one's personal life influence the experience of wellbeing at workplace, and *vice versa*. This could be highlighted by the Covid-19 pandemic and the increase of distance work from home. However, in this paper, we will mainly focus on aspects of worker wellbeing that emerge in the interaction between individual workers and workplaces, all by acknowledging this element and potential measures needed to address it later in the project.

3.2 Challenges in Knowledge Workers' Wellbeing in Data Ecosystems

To identify key factors that inhibit and encourage worker wellbeing in the context of knowledge work, a scoping literature review and an initial mapping consisting of seven semi-structured interviews with entrepreneurs and/or management of Finnish SMEs were conducted. The interview data was analysed using qualitative content analysis. Here, the first round of analysis of the interview data is used for constructing the initial framework.

In data ecosystems, companies are ever more dependent on data-driven technologies, regardless of industry. Digitalisation, which has been accelerated by the Covid-19 pandemic [3], has increased pressure to digitalise. However, SMEs might not be prepared for processing big data when it comes to IT infrastructure, analytic tools and ethical aspects of data [59]. Furthermore, even if the management has a strong vision for digitalisation, transformations do not always succeed [25].

One of the consequences for worker wellbeing has been an increase in technostress, referring to "one's inability to cope or deal with ICTs in a healthy manner" [4, p. 832], which can lead to many unwanted consequences, such as health issues and decreasing productivity [3, 4, 34, 35]. Digitalisation can, particularly in the case of experienced workers, weaken the sense of self at work, if the value of pre-existing tacit knowledge is eroded when new tools and technologies are implemented [5]. Hence, digitalisation can be an important contributor to job related stress in today's data economy ecosystems. Technostress is found to be caused by factors related to system performance, such as usability issues and techno-uncertainty, but also ones related to non-system performance, such as techno-complexity, information overload, techno-invasion, and lack of fit between demands and abilities [38]. Correspondingly, technology related aspects that seem to prevent workers from experiencing technostress are rooted in the use of systems, such as reliability, user experience, usefulness, usability, and provision of technical support [38]. This has led to the extension of the concept of work engagement to *techno-work engagement*, which refers to "a positive and fulfilling well-being state or experience that is characterised by vigour, dedication, and absorption with respect to the use of technology at work" [34, p. 2]. Technology can thus be seen as a job resource that has potential to support worker wellbeing. As Mäkiniemi et al. [34] point out, the relationship between technology and worker wellbeing has so far concentrated on negative experiences and technostress, which underlines the need for research on technology's potential for increasing worker wellbeing.

Even if technostress and potential for techno-work engagement were recognised, building a necessary skill set to cope with current technologies is perceived challenging in SMEs [35, 47]. During the interviews, several SMEs hoped for better functioning digital tools. When asked whether the technologies in use support their everyday work, several managers brought up issues in usability, which also led to difficulties in training new employees:

> "The software we have to use was developed in late 70s. [...] It is lagging behind, and I must say that for those born in 2000s, it is really hard to teach a software that was made in the 70s. [...] Learning to use it requires a lot of learning by heart. You just have to remember that this is how it works. The interface is not intuitive."

Yet, threats to worker wellbeing are not limited to the acquisition and use of technology. Data masses enabled by digitalisation appear to complicate information management in individual level [35, 55] but also in organisational level [59], which was brought up by several SME managers in our interviews. In worklife studies, this is conceptualised by the term information ergonomy that has come to accompany the traditional physical ergonomy. Information overflow increases stress levels, decreases productivity and lessens the overall wellbeing at work, including the management of everyday work [35]. Furthermore, digital tools enable and encourage multitasking and create constant interruptions and task fragmentation, which complicates information management [9, 55]. Digital work is easier to take home, making it harder to establish boundaries between work and personal life. Consequently, coping with and internalisation of information becomes harder and endangers worker wellbeing [55].

The interviews also revealed that SMEs hold great amount of tacit knowledge, which further challenges both workers' and entrepreneurs' information management and skill development. To encourage diffusion of tacit knowledge, SMEs can utilise both formal and informal organisational structures. First, enabling informal structures and organisational culture for storytelling and information circulation is vital to take use of tacit knowledge and to support problem solving, adaptation of new technologies and skill development [7, 51]. Second, establishing formal documentation and feedback loops as well as collecting best practices to be explicitly shared [51] further enhances capturing tacit knowledge.

Coping with new technologies and enabling techno-work engagement thus requires more attention to skill development, effective and well-working digital tools that enable uninterrupted workflows, and ways to make tacit knowledge visible. Entrepreneurs and managers in SMEs seemed to be aware of most of the issues in their organisations but did not know how their employees or business partners experienced worker wellbeing and impacts of digitalisation. The work will thus continue by mapping the perspectives of employees in these companies. In the next Section, we explore adopting participatory processes to address these issues.

4 Workplace Democracy in Strengthening Knowledge Workers' Wellbeing

We argue that introducing aspects of workplace democracy in a company has potential to support the construction of a communicative and interactive workplace where the values of employees and organisation are aligned and where successful digitalisation reduces friction in workers' everyday tasks.

Several studies suggest that adopting participatory practices and leadership yields better results in digitalisation efforts, including acquisition of new technologies, information systems and software [1, 25, 32]. For example, whereas problems in information systems implementation are often related to user resistance, lack of understanding the systems and poor compatibility of a system with organisation's tasks [11], it seems that including all stakeholders in planning, developing, and implementing new technologies can mitigate resistance and lead to better understanding of the systems. Truly including workers who know their tasks could enhance the results of digitalisation efforts. Furthermore, workplace democracy is rooted in values, such as individual freedom, equality and justice, which are all aspects that play a role in worker wellbeing [35], having thus potential in creating healthier, happier and fairer workplaces in the data ecosystems.

Workplace democracy is subject to active debate [17–19, 22, 31, 57]. Democracy itself is a complex concept without uniform definition. However, there is a shared idea that the power over workplaces should be shared to a certain extent between all stakeholders – workers included. Arguments that support workplace democracy are constructed around themes such as firm-state analogy [14, 31], meaningfulness of work [61], justice [23, 40], whereas the critical arguments contest its efficiency, implementation potential and its role in liberal economy [18].

The relevance of democratic practices is ever highlighted in data economy: As defined by Koskinen et al. [29], data ecosystem consists of actors and stakeholders that are connected within the network and its value chains. Anyone whose data is involved in data economy should thus be considered a stakeholder and should have agency in decision-making that concerns the data ecosystem. In Europe, people strive for control over data and data sharing, fairness and transparency of data processing, and usage and being informed on how personal data is used in the data economy ecosystems [42], which reflects democratic values. Similar values have also been connected to stronger worker wellbeing, when adopted at workplace [33, 41, 48, 49, 60].

At first glance, this seems to be in line with propositions of democratic theorists who argue for the workplace democracy for its own sake instead of its instrumental benefits. According to Dahl [14], the strong principle of equality – one of the corner stones of democracy according to which each citizen is equal and should thus be entitled to participate in decision-making that considers oneself – applies to workplaces as institutions just as well as to nation states. Dahl thus draws a direct analogy between a state and a workplace and places equality in the centre of human agency as universal principle that should not be tied to a specific institutional setting.

The state-firm analogy is, however, among the most debated arguments for workplace democracy. Frega [17] contests Dahl's analogy by arguing that the state and the firm are not in a horizontal but a hierarchical relationship, due to which the analogy leads to a category mistake. Furthermore, he argues that rooting workplace democracy on open lists of values is not justifying workplace democracy, and that these analogies shift the focus away from defining what the workplace democracy actually looks like [17]. On the other hand, Landemore and Ferreras [31] and Ferreras [15] argue that firms are political entities acting in a democratic society, and thus, firms should be subject to democratic principles. Hence, the debate around the analogy remains active.

Several instrumental arguments for workplace democracy bring up factors that have been identified to encourage worker wellbeing. A study conducted in Danish companies found a positive impact of workplace democracy on worker wellbeing [28]. Moreover, arguments that highlight the potential of workplace democracy to strengthen autonomy and practices for recognition [18] are highly relevant for worker wellbeing. Hirvonen and Breen [22] argue that for the workplace to fulfil the workers' basic need for recognition by respect and by esteem, each worker should be treated equally and given an opportunity to participate in decision-making. According to them, any other situation would be unequal [22]. These elements matter, because research indicates a connection between job meaningfulness and worker wellbeing, comprising the need for recognition and autonomy [20, 35]. Furthermore, several studies have shown that participatory practices and inclusion of workers in decision-making have positive impact on worker wellbeing, either by increasing the success of digitalisation and adoption of new technologies [11, 32] or directly by strengthening different aspects identified to contribute to worker wellbeing [6, 20, 35].

Yet, the potential positive impact of workplace democracy on worker wellbeing is not certain. For example, high involvement management, which includes aspects common with workplace democracy, usually increases job demands. If not balanced with appropriate job resources, such as enhanced autonomy, it can weaken worker wellbeing [6]. Democratic workplace does not offer solutions to all challenges brought by digitalisation in data ecosystems. To build a framework that addresses the issues introduced above as extensively as possible, it is necessary to develop tools that extend further than only democratic practices. For example, although workplace democracy can foster culture that supports organisational learning and workers' skill development, it is not alone sufficient to train workers on data economy and digitalisation. Nevertheless, workplace democracy seems to have strong potential to enable structures that lead to more efficient, fairer and happier workplaces by establishing sustainable values and participatory structures. In this project, we aim to put this hypothesis to test and put workplace democracy in the very centre of the WWFD model which we present in the following Section.

5 WWFD - Framework for Wellbeing at Work from Digitalisation in Data Economy Ecosystems

Based on the scoping literature review and semi-structured interviews described above, to support SMEs in their digitalisation efforts in a way that sustains and builds worker wellbeing, we introduce a framework for SMEs to train their employees to better understand data economy and digitalisation, all by establishing democratic practices and further supporting worker wellbeing (Fig. 1.).

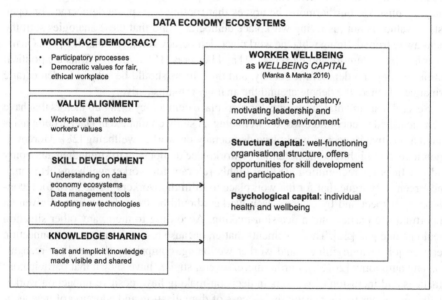

Fig. 1. WWFD framework

The framework aims at offering tools for building wellbeing capital in data ecosystems. First, workplace democracy aims at building social and structural capital via participatory processes and psychological capital via value alignment. WWFD framework draws from both instrumentalist statements and arguments on democracy's value per se (see Fig. 2.) We explore the potential of workplace democracy as an instrument for increasing worker wellbeing, while simultaneously considering democracy as a goal per se to ensure fair, ethical workplaces and value alignment. We expect fairness and worker wellbeing to be interlinked, forming sustainably better workplaces as part of data ecosystems.

Secondly, promoting value alignment aims at building psychological capital by supporting workers' mental wellbeing as well as social capital by easing communication.

Third, skill development contributes to structural capital by developing skills to cope with the changing environment and to enhance organisational learning, and to psychological capital by strengthening the feeling of coping in one's work by reducing techno-stress and strengthening techno-work engagement. Finally, knowledge sharing reaches all three dimensions by strengthening community (social capital), enables skill development (structural capital) and helps to cope and manage one's workload (psychological capital).

Based on this framework, the project has begun the development of a set of tools for SMEs. They will be piloted in three rounds, between which they will be evaluated and refined. In the first piloting round, SMEs will be offered tools such as methods for dialogue to find a shared understanding of their initial situation, recommendations on building transparent and communicative platforms for everyday interaction, participatory processes for successful digitalisation initiatives, and feedback models for efficient and interactive organisational learning. They will be guided on how to choose the most acute point of development in collaborative processes and how to pursue the process in a way that fits the organisation's needs and resources.

The number of interviews included in the initial mapping is expected to grow as the project advances, and several rounds of further analyses will be conducted – the framework is built iteratively. Thus, to proceed with the first pilots, this is the first understanding of the framework to be brought into academic discussion.

Finally, based on the WWFD framework and the fine-tuned toolbox, a guidebook will be drafted and published around August 2023. The guidebook will be freely available online for all.

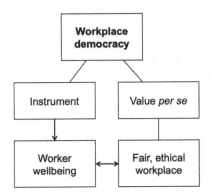

Fig. 2. Role of workplace democracy in WWFD framework

6 Conclusions

In this paper, we introduce a Wellbeing at Work from Digitalisation (WWFD) framework for increasing worker wellbeing in SMEs in data economy ecosystems. The study is conducted as a part of a research project that aims to help SMEs with developing their skills to match the requirements and aspirations arising from the data economy, all by strengthening worker wellbeing.

In the course of the project, we have examined the effects of data economy and digitalisation on worker wellbeing. SMEs act in an ever more networked data economy ecosystems with a great number of information systems, digital technologies, and interfaces needed to keep up with the competitive environment. Working with data raises questions on ethics and how the organisation's values are aligned with those of the workers when collecting and processing data. It was recognised that these aspects might have severe negative impacts on knowledge workers' wellbeing at work.

The initial mapping conducted by WWFD project in form of first round of semi-structured interviews with entrepreneurs and managers of seven Finnish SMEs in Turku region supported the existing literature in implying an increase in technostress and difficulties with managing the vast amount of information and digital tools in everyday work, which was due to pressure to go digital and use data-based technologies for business development. The interviews suggested that many companies would like to take existing data-based technologies in use, but knowledge and skills were missing, and recruitment was considered risky for small businesses. The interviews are still ongoing as new companies join the project, and further rounds of analyses are conducted using methods of qualitative content analysis.

To address these issues, we introduce the initial WWFD framework in Section five. The model aims at strengthening worker wellbeing as wellbeing capital by offering tools around workplace democracy, value alignment, skill development and knowledge sharing. These elements are expected to positively affect a) social capital by strengthening participation, motivation and communication, b) structural capital by reducing friction in organisation's daily functions, supporting skill development and participation, and c) psychological capital by contributing to the feeling of coping and managing one's work with a sense of agency and sufficient recognition. Based on this model, we will provide SMEs with practical tools that will be piloted in three rounds during 2022 and 2023. Between the rounds, the toolset and the framework are iteratively developed further based on interview analyses and piloting experiences.

We hope this model inspires others working on building better workplaces to address issues caused by digitalisation and spark discussion on other viable tools and aspects found elsewhere. This project is focusing on SMEs in Turku region, because of a recognised need for skilled workers in expanding fields, such as manufacturing industries, technology, and all supporting actions.

References

1. Abelein, U., Paech, B.: Understanding the influence of user participation and involvement on system success–a systematic mapping study. Empir. Softw. Eng. **20**(1), 28–81 (2015)
2. Aho, E.: Kasvun mahdollisuus–positiivisen rakennemuutoksen hyödyntäminen lounais-suomessa (2017)
3. Amankwah-Amoah, J., Khan, Z., Wood, G., Knight, G.: Covid-19 and digitalization: the great acceleration. J. Bus. Res. **136**, 602–611 (2021)
4. Ayyagari, R., Grover, V., Purvis, R.: Technostress: technological antecedents and implications. MIS Q. **35**, 831–858 (2011)

5. Billett, S.: Mediating worklife learning and the digitalisation of work. Br. J. Educ. Tech. **52**(4), 1580–1593 (2021)
6. Böckerman, P., Bryson, A., Ilmakunnas, P.: Does high involvement management improve worker wellbeing? J. Econ. Behav. Organ. **84**(2), 660–680 (2012)
7. Brown, J.S., Duguid, P.: organizational learning and communities-of-practice: toward a unified view of working, learning, and innovation. Organ. Sci. **2**(1), 40–57 (1991)
8. Califf, C.B., Sarker, S., Sarker, S.: The bright and dark sides of technostress: A mixed-methods study involving healthcare it. MIS Q. **44**(2) 809–856 (2020)
9. Chen, A., Karahanna, E.: Life interrupted: the effects of technology-mediated work interruptions on work and nonwork outcomes. MIS Q. **42**(4), 1023–1042 (2018)
10. Cooper, C.L., Cartwright, S.: Healthy mind; healthy organization—a proactive approach to occupational stress. Hum. Relat. **47**(4), 455–471 (1994)
11. Cooper, R.B., Zmud, R.W.: Information technology implementation research: a technological diffusion approach. Manage. Sci. **36**(2), 123–139 (1990)
12. Couldry, N., Mejias, U.A.: Data colonialism: rethinking big data's relation to the contemporary subject. Telev. New Media **20**(4), 336–349 (2019)
13. Curry, E., Sheth, A.: Next-generation smart environments: from system of systems to data ecosystems. IEEE Intell. Syst. **33**(03), 69–76 (2018). https://doi.org/10.1109/MIS.2018.033 001418
14. Dahl, R.A.: Democracy and its Critics. Yale University Press, London (2008)
15. Ferreras, I.: Firms as Political Entities : Saving Democracy through Economic Bicameralism. Cambridge University Press, Cambridge (2017)
16. Field, J.C., Chan, X.W.: Contemporary knowledge workers and the boundaryless work–life interface: Implications for the human resource management of the knowledge workforce. Front. Psychol. **9**, 2414 (2018)
17. Frega, R.: Against analogy: why analogical arguments in support of workplace democracy must necessarily fail. Democratic Theor. **7**(1), 1–26 (2020)
18. Frega, R., Herzog, L., Neuhäuser, C.: Workplace democracy—the recent debate. Philos Compass **14**(4), e12574 (2019)
19. Gerlsbeck, F., Herzog, L.: The epistemic potentials of workplace democracy. Rev. Soc. Econ. **78**(3), 307–330 (2020)
20. Hakanen, J.: Työn imua, tuottavuutta ja kukoistavia työpaikkoja? – kohti laadukasta työelämää. Työsuojelurahasto, Helsinki (2009)
21. Hesketh, I., Cooper, C.: Wellbeing at Work: how to Design, Implement and Evaluate an Effective Strategy. Kogan Page Publishers, London (2019)
22. Hirvonen, O., Breen, K.: Recognitive arguments for workplace democracy. Constellations Int. J. Crit. Democratic Theor. **27**(4) (2020)
23. Hsieh, N.H.: workplace democracy, workplace republicanism, and economic democracy workplace democracy: why not? Revue de philosophie économique **9**(1), 57–78 (2008)
24. Hyrynsalmi, S., Hyrynsalmi, S.M.: Ecosystem: a zombie category? In: 2019 IEEE International Conference on Engineering, Technology and Innovation (ICE/ITMC), pp. 1–8 (2019). https://doi.org/10.1109/ICE.2019.8792658
25. Ivančić, L., Vukšić, V.B., Spremić, M.: Mastering the digital transformation process: business practices and lessons learned. Technol. Innov. Manag. Rev. **9**(2), 36–50 (2019)
26. Karasek Jr, R.A.: Job demands, job decision latitude, and mental strain: Implications for job redesign. Adm. Sci. Q. **24**(2), 285–308 (1979)
27. Knight, C., Patterson, M., Dawson, J.: Building work engagement: a systematic review and meta-analysis investigating the effectiveness of work engagement interventions. J. Organ. Behav. **38**(6), 792–812 (2017)
28. Knudsen, H., Busck, O., Lind, J.: Work environment quality: the role of workplace participation and democracy. Work Employ Soc. **25**(3), 379–396 (2011)

29. Koskinen, J., Knaapi-Junnila, S., Rantanen, M.M.: What if we had fair, people-centred data economy ecosystems? In: Proceedings - 2019 IEEE SmartWorld, Ubiquitous Intelligence and Computing, Advanced and Trusted Computing, Scalable Computing and Communications, Internet of People and Smart City Innovation, SmartWorld/UIC/ATC/SCALCOM/IOP/SCI 2019, pp. 329–334 (2019). https://doi.org/10.1109/SmartWorld-UIC-ATC-SCALCOM-IOP-SCI.2019.00100

30. Lammi, M., Pantzar, M.: The data economy: How technological change has altered the role of the citizen-consumer. Technol. Soc. **59** (2019). https://doi.org/10.1016/j.techsoc.2019.101157

31. Landemore, H., Ferreras, I.: In defense of workplace democracy: towards a justification of the firm–state analogy. Polit. Theor. **44**(1), 53–81 (2016)

32. Larjovuori, R.L., Ligthart, R., Heikkilä-Tammi, K., Keränen, K., Bordi, L., Laakkonen, T., Mäkiniemi, J.P.: Digimuutos tehdään yhdessä (2020)

33. Lawson, K.J., Noblet, A.J., Rodwell, J.J.: Promoting employee wellbeing: the relevance of work characteristics and organizational justice. Health Promot. Int. **24**(3), 223–233 (2009)

34. Mäkiniemi, J.P., Ahola, S., Joensuu, J.: A novel construct to measure employees' technology-related experiences of well-being: empirical validation of the technowork engagement scale (technowes) (2020)

35. Manka, M.L., Manka, M.: Työhyvinvointi (2016)

36. Martel, J.P., Dupuis, G.: Quality of work life: theoretical and methodological problems, and presentation of a new model and measuring instrument. Soc. Indic. Res. **77**(2), 333–368 (2006)

37. Nieminen, J.: Alueelliset kehitysnäkymät–kevät 2018 (2018)

38. Nisafani, A.S., Kiely, G., Mahony, C.: Workers' technostress: a review of its causes, strains, inhibitors, and impacts. J. Dec. Syst. **29**, 1–16 (2020)

39. Oliveira, M.I.S., Lima, G.D.F.B., Lóscio, B.F.: Investigations into data ecosystems: a systematic mapping study. Knowl. Inf. Syst. **61**(2), 589–630 (2019)

40. O'Neill, M.: Three Rawlsian routes towards economic democracy. Revue de philosophie économique **9**(1), 29–55 (2008)

41. Prilleltensky, I.: Wellness as fairness. Am. J. Community Psychol. **49**(1–2), 1–21 (2012)

42. Rantanen, M.M., Koskinen, J.: Humans of the European data economy ecosystem - what do they demand from a fair data economy? In: Kreps, D., Komukai, T., Gopal, T.V., Ishii, K. (eds.) HCC 2020. IAICT, vol. 590, pp. 327–339. Springer, Cham (2020). https://doi.org/10.1007/978-3-030-62803-1_26

43. Reiman, A., Väyrynen, S.: Holistic well-being and sustainable organisations–a review and argumentative propositions. Int. J. Sustain. Eng. **11**(5), 321–329 (2018)

44. Schaufeli, W.B., Bakker, A.B.: Job demands, job resources, and their relationship with burnout and engagement: a multi-sample study. J. Organ. Behav. Int. J. Ind. Occup. Organ. Psychol. Behav. **25**(3), 293–315 (2004)

45. Seligman, M.E., Csikszentmihalyi, M.: Positive psychology: an introduction. In: Flow and the Foundations of Positive Psychology, pp. 279–298. Springer (2000)

46. Shujahat, M., Sousa, M.J., Hussain, S., Nawaz, F., Wang, M., Umer, M.: Translating the impact of knowledge management processes into knowledge-based innovation: the neglected and mediating role of knowledge-worker productivity. J. Bus. Res. **94**, 442–450 (2019). https://doi.org/10.1016/j.jbusres.2017.11.001, https://www.sciencedirect.com/science/article/pii/S014829631730440X

47. Sorger, M., Ralph, B.J., Hartl, K., Woschank, M., Stockinger, M.: Big data in the metal processing value chain: a systematic digitalization approach under special consideration of standardization and SMEs. Appl. Sci. **11**(19), 9021 (2021)

48. Soto, W.C., DiDona, T., Aguililla, A.L.G., Ramirez, R., Marrero, P.: Wellbeing, fairness, and supervisor's ability and support. Int. J. Sci. Res. Pub. **8**(5), 90–100 (2018)

49. Sparr, J.L., Sonnentag, S.: Fairness perceptions of supervisor feedback, LMX, and employee well-being at work. Eur. J. Work Organ. Psy. **17**(2), 198–225 (2008)
50. Tan, Z.M., Aggarwal, N., Cowls, J., Morley, J., Taddeo, M., Floridi, L.: The ethical debate about the gig economy: a review and critical analysis. Technol. Soc. **65**, 101594 (2021). https://doi.org/10.1016/j.techsoc.2021.101594, https://www.sciencedirect.com/science/article/pii/S0160791X21000695
51. Taylor, H.: Tacit knowledge: conceptualizations and operationalizations. Int. J. Knowl. Manag. (IJKM) **3**(3), 60–73 (2007)
52. Timan, T., van Oirsouw, C., Hoekstra, M.: The role of data regulation in shaping AI: an overview of challenges and recommendations for SMEs. In: Curry, E., Metzger, A., Zillner, S., Pazzaglia, J.-C., García Robles, A. (eds.) The Elements of Big Data Value, pp. 355–376. Springer, Cham (2021). https://doi.org/10.1007/978-3-030-68176-0_15
53. Van Dierendonck, D., Haynes, C., Borrill, C., Stride, C.: Leadership behavior and subordinate well-being. J. Occup. Health Psychol. **9**(2), 165 (2004)
54. Van Doorn, N., Badger, A.: Platform capitalism's hidden abode: producing data assets in the gig economy. Antipode **52**(5), 1475–1495 (2020)
55. Vuori, V., Helander, N., Okkonen, J.: Digitalization in knowledge work: the dream of enhanced performance. Cogn. Technol. Work **21**(2), 237–252 (2019)
56. Waizenegger, L., McKenna, B., Cai, W., Bendz, T.: An affordance perspective of team collaboration and enforced working from home during covid-19. Eur. J. Inf. Syst. **29**(4), 429–442 (2020)
57. Walters, J.D.T.: On the efficiency objection to workplace democracy. Ethical Theor. Moral Pract. **24**, 803–815 (2021). https://doi.org/10.1007/s10677-021-10192-6
58. Wamba, S.F., Akter, S., Trinchera, L., De Bourmont, M.: Turning information quality into firm performance in the big data economy. Manag. Decis. **57**(8), 1756–1783 (2019)
59. Wang, S., Wang, H.: Big data for small and medium-sized enterprises (SME): acknowledge management model. J. Knowl. Manag. **24**, 881–897 (2020)
60. Yean, T.F., et al.: Organizational justice: a conceptual discussion. Procedia Soc. Behav. Sci. **219**, 798–803 (2016)
61. Yeoman, R.: Meaningful Work and Workplace Democracy: A Philosophy of Work and a Politics of Meaningfulness. Springer, London (2014). https://doi.org/10.1057/9781137370587
62. Zuboff, S.: Big other: surveillance capitalism and the prospects of an information civilization. J. Inf. Technol. **30**(1), 75–89 (2015). https://doi.org/10.1057/jit.2015.5, https://doi.org/10.1057/jit.2015.5
63. Zuboff, S.: Surveillance capitalism and the challenge of collective action. New Labor Forum **28**(1), 10–29 (2019). https://doi.org/10.1177/1095796018819461

Privacy in Internet of Things Ecosystems – Prerequisite for the Ethical Data Collection and Use by Companies

Mikko Vermanen$^{(\boxtimes)}$ ⓘ, Minna M. Rantanen ⓘ, and Jani Koskinen ⓘ

Information System Sciences, Turku School of Economics,
University of Turku, Turku, Finland
mjverm@utu.fi

Abstract. The abstract should summarize the contents of the paper in short terms, i.e. 150–250 words. The expansion of IoT implementations in organisations has resulted in more and more people getting involved in technical ecosystems not only as users but also as data sources. While the surveillance capabilities of IoT solutions grow in terms of scale and accuracy, it is inevitable that individuals end up in a position where information involving them is collected, either directly or indirectly. While the motives behind data collection and distribution may not be malicious, the availability of personal information always produces an opportunity for intentional or unintentional misuse. However, ensuring complete privacy in highly surveilled environments is practically impossible to achieve. While legislation appears to provide a comparatively safe environment for employees, regulations alone do not guarantee that sufficient focus is directed towards ethics. Rather, we focus on proposing constructive approaches to ensure ethicality by deliberative and transparent cooperation between customers and companies likewise between employees and employers.

Keywords: Customers · Employees · Employers · Ethics · Internet of Things (IoT) · Privacy · Surveillance

1 Introduction

Internet of Things (IoT) is a term originally introduced by Kevin Ashton in 1999 [14]. IoT can be described as a network binding together the end-users and different monitorable or measurable entities or targets ranging from physical objects, such as buildings and vehicles [16], to immaterial interests, for instance, collective traffic and consumer behaviour [6]. The added value achieved from the data produced by IoT solutions can appear in many forms, including personal, professional, and economical. Data gathered through IoT can be used by various groups or actors, including academia, industry, and government. [11] As an example from the business perspective, companies can aim for higher performance and reduced manual labour through more efficient and accurate data collection capabilities by utilising modern IoT solutions [26].

However, the consequences towards employees or customers – from whom the data is collected directly or indirectly – may not be unambiguously positive. This is partly due to the observation that the developed monitoring capabilities and the possession of personally identifiable data can provide opportunities for both intentional and unintentional misuse [26]. In addition to the human element, technological issues have a significant role in IoT privacy and security. The safety of every IoT device, sensor, and unit of information can become increasingly compromised, partly due to the vulnerabilities resulting from the rapid development of IoT as the security measures may not keep up with the risks. [5] Thus, a large variety of privacy-threatening factors need to be acknowledged and addressed when implementing these solutions - not only related to the current practices but also in terms of potential long-term risks resulting from gathering, storing, and distributing identifiable data.

To tackle this conflict between benefits and negative consequences of data collection [4, 20], we need new kinds of procedures how to control data collection and use to achieve privacy that e.g. the General Data Protection Regulation act (GDPR) demands [22]. Koskinen et al. [12] proposed an ethical governance model for data economy ecosystems where all stakeholders are creating the rules for the data ecosystem by rational discourse to ensure fair, ethical data use and supervision over the ecosystem [12]. This kind of approach for data use helps to see the different viewpoints and demands for data use practices in a networked environment where a wide perspective is essential, instead of focusing on single views or merely fulfilling the demands of regulations.

This paper focuses on examining the potential issues related to the privacy of individuals involved in IoT ecosystems as directly or indirectly identifiable information sources the from the perspective of employees and employers. On a practical level, the ethical sustainability of IoT implementations is supported by introducing guidelines aiming to help companies to retain the benefits of IoT while protecting the privacy of their employees, customers or other individuals.

The paper is structured as follows. In Chapter Two, we introduce the concepts of surveillance and privacy in the context of IoT. Chapter Three provides further insight into the connection between surveillance and privacy, and what are the actions required to ensure privacy. In Chapter Four, we introduce topics for further investigation. Finally, conclusions are provided in Chapter Five.

2 IoT, Surveillance and Privacy

We have entered into an information society where mass surveillance has been realised through the possibilities offered by modern information technology [7]. For example, AI that uses the data collected via IoT offers new kinds of monitoring possibilities for companies but with the cost of the privacy of the people connected with IoT devices if data is retrieved from them or traceable to them. Thus, implementing IoT devices in a working environment in an ethical manner is a matter of balancing needed surveillance and privacy demands.

2.1 Surveillance

IoT solutions provide companies with a diversity of surveillance tools enabling them to inspect factors such as efficiency and performance of employees [24] or customer behaviour. While this kind of surveillance can be targeted towards material objects, individuals, environment, or a combination of those [25], we focus on settings where individuals are in some way connected to the data collection either directly or indirectly.

For instance, industrial companies can monitor machinery usage by tracking specific attributes, such as their movement, with a simple sensor-based IoT device. In this example, personal information is easily available if the monitored machine does not function fully automatically but is operated by employees. At least, it can be derived by linking IoT-based information to other sources. As another example, a delivery company can track their vehicles with location and movement sensors. In these cases, employees practically always contribute to the created data while the vehicle is moving. What makes these surveillance solutions especially vulnerable in terms of privacy is that individuals can be tracked at any time while operating the vehicle, regardless of whether they are on duty or not.

However, the availability of personal information does not mean that personal information is stored, processed or distributed in an identifiable form, as the party behind the data collection is in many cases capable of determining the level of retaining privacy. For example, an IoT device can be configured so that attributes involving human contribution are not collected. Similarly, timestamps can be either removed, or their sample cycle lengthened, in which cases the data considers aggregate users instead of separate individuals [2]. Additionally, methods such as pseudonymisation [17] can be leveraged to add a privacy layer to the collected information.

Whether the actions and attributes of physical objects, environment or individual users are being surveilled affects how privacy-related matters should be considered [26]. Naturally, information from different sources will be involved in most cases, as it is often possible to track who was using a particular de vice at the given time and given environment. Notable is that surveillance tends to change the behaviour of the person who is under surveillance [7]. Changing the behaviour may be one of the aims that some organisations have in using surveillance technology—to affect e.g. employees or even customers to act efficiently, coherently, and predictable. However, this kind of constant monitoring and emphasise on efficiency is problematic at least from three points.

First, it has a similar problem to Taylorism. Humans are not technical systems that can be boosted by forcing them to be more and more efficient like machinery. This phenomenon was noted, for example, in coal mine studies by Trist and Bamford [23], which led to the realisation of the socio-technical nature of systems [8] where individuals are not seen as a mere technical resource. Secondly, we do not know clearly the effects of surveillance on individual's behaviour or attitude [29]. However, people who are monitored can alter their behaviour that can be judged as suspicious—phenomenon known as chilling effect [7, 19]. However, the question is whether people act differently or just reveal the desired side of their actions, which affects the quality of the collected data and, therefore, reduces its usability. Thirdly, the constant monitoring of people itself is ethically, and legally problematic [1, 18, 21, 27].

2.2 Privacy

Discussion of privacy is old as mankind and it has roots in protection of ones body and home [10]. The problem is, that privacy is a concept that is not self-evident even if it may look alike in first sight. Brandeis and Warren described privacy The right to the privacy —in their influential article—as a right to be let alone, although not without exceptions [3].

Another well-known article is Alan Westin's Privacy and freedom [28], which describes privacy as self-determination, where individuals, groups, or institutions determine how information about them is revealed [10]. Privacy as a right to be left alone, or self-determination of what information is revealed from one, is an understandable and even justified claim if those are not conflicting with the justified rights of others. However, the nowadays society, which is more and more "online", challenges these views of privacy.

In the context of IoT, the boundaries of what is private and what is not are bending. Especially when technology —here IoT— is pervasive and ubiquitous in our society, via exploding number of artifacts that can monitor us and collect an enormous amount of data, we face the illusion of privacy. It seems that we can be physically alone, but we may be under constant surveillance by the surrounding IoT-artifacts—worn or even implemented in the near future. Once again, this should remind us to consider our privacy from the perspective of the information society era. Therefore frameworks like PAPA [15] are more fruitful as those are created to describe the ethical issues of the information age that we are living in today. We narrow our focus on the Internet of Things (IoT), a topic that represents technology in the sense of how hidden it may be, and usually is, for people.

In this chapter, we introduce central privacy-related implications and questions from the perspective of an individual employee, general management, and data management.

Combining the variety of technical pitfalls with the potential risks resulting from the actions and decisions of human actors, we are facing a highly complicated ensemble of threats towards the privacy of individuals involved in these ecosystems, difficult to comprehend even by the large companies and dedicated experts. Regardless of the potentially catastrophic consequences towards individuals' privacy, little research has been conducted related to the nature and magnitude of human factors, especially from the ethical perspective. Thus, our contribution is to investigate the potential risks and causes thereof by examining the role of ethical factors and the related managerial decisions. However, we must acknowledge that building an all-encompassing, yet not exhaustive or unusable, ethical framework is not a realistic expectation. Rather, our goal is to provide understandable guidelines on an abstraction level that fits the purpose of remaining practical.

3 Securing Privacy in IoT Surveillance Implementations

Finding the balance between maintaining personal privacy and enabling companies to benefit from IoT is crucial when pursuing practical value, compared to conducting a one-sided analysis. In this chapter, we introduce potential advantages and disadvantages related to different approaches to IoT data collection and distribution from the standpoint of employees and management involved in IoT ecosystems.

Considering the position of employees, we should clarify whether they are given an ability to control what, how, when, and why data is collected and/or distributed [26]. Autonomy is seen as one of the key issues in ethics. Without autonomy, actors do not have the possibility to choose and thus make ethical decisions. When employees are the sources of information, it would be questionable that they do not possess any control over information that might compromise their privacy.

Another relevant question is, can the gathered data be combined and attributed to a specific person within the organisation. In general, the employees involved in IoT ecosystems should be able to approve, prohibit, or control [2] the collection and distribution of any identifiable data which may potentially cause personal harm. We find this important not only from the perspective of ethics but also as a factor affecting the employees' acceptance towards the change.

As a whole, the justification for surveillance must be based on the interest of both parties, the employer and the employee. If the gathered data remains anonymous throughout its life-cycle or can be guaranteed not to cause negative effects on an individual, significant ethical violations are less likely to occur. Even then, we propose that data collection should be kept to a bare minimum in terms of scale, time and location. This is emphasized in settings where individuals can be monitored continuously, for example, when sensors are attached to vehicles or devices that employees carry with them—sometimes on and off duty. This reduces the number of potential ethical pitfalls caused by unnecessary surveillance. Similar issues should be considered between the customer or companies if customers are monitored in similar manners.

From the perspective of general management, conducting ethical IoT implementations requires collecting informed consent from the employees from whom data is collected and distributed. To fulfill this criterion, management should define equitable and documented conditions that employees can voluntarily comply with. For this purpose, the employees should be thoroughly educated about what, how, when, and why data is collected and/or distributed, to whom the data is distributed, and how the privacy and security of the employees are guaranteed. A transparent and well-documented approach will not only provide fair, practical foundations but can also positively affect the employees' voluntary contribution and the aforementioned level of acceptance, which has been questionable in the context of IoT, both technologically and socially [2].

In terms of data management, it is critical for the management, employees and even customers to be aware of what information is revealed to external parties, how the data is protected, and who is responsible for the protection. When sharing data with external parties, the default approach should be to minimize the volume of individuals' information or avoid it altogether. However, to actually reach the benefits of collaboration with partners and other related parties, companies are forced to distribute information. If and when data sharing cannot be avoided, it should be carefully considered what is truly necessary to distribute and whether it could violate the position of the related individuals.

4 Discussion

While aiming to build socially just implementations and ecosystems, we must acknowledge that technologies such as IoT rely on the collected data. If we were to focus solely on the position of individuals, we would likely end up discouraging data collection and distribution altogether. Hence, the consequences of heightened privacy protection may not be solely positive [13]. In fact, ending up under surveillance is practically inevitable in any area or environment where a sensor network is deployed [2], and as the number of IoT implementations keeps growing, it becomes clear that complete privacy cannot be achieved. This leads us to an intersection where a satisfactory balance between the individuals' and organisations' benefits and needs has to be achieved in order to support technical development.

From a legislative perspective, the challenge is how ethical factors can be regulated in the first place, partly due to the subjectivity in defining what is ethical. While regulations do contribute significantly to enhancing the privacy of individuals, following proper practices from both legislative and ethical standpoint is eventually dependent on the behaviour of the people in control—in this case, the management. As long as no formal ethical regulations exist, it is not possible to force employers to change their approach in terms of respecting individual privacy to a further degree than what is required by law. Hence, we are only able to offer general recommendations and guidelines that eventually require voluntary compliance from the companies. Thus, we see motivation as the strongest utility for driving development towards an ethically sustainable direction.

Therefore we propose using the concept of fair governance model for data economy ecosystem, where the rules are commonly agreed on between all relevant stakeholders [12]. There the rules and procedures—how information is collected, used, and distributed—are decided by the rational discourse that is open and emancipatory by the nature [9]. This kind of discourse is based on respect of people as equal participants; pays attention to peoples' needs, preferences, and socio-cultural circumstances; adopts the individuals' and communities' perspectives; enables people the education and support they need and acts fairly for the common good [12].

This kind of deliberative way of defining the rules of how collected data is used is suitable for all stakeholders (here employees and employers) and thus more likely ethically justified. Ideally the situation is like Koskinen et al. [12] state:

> *"fair data economy ecosystem governance model is model that includes the rules, technical and non-technical requirements for actors, controlling bodies and representation of all stakeholders(board) to ensure legal, ethical, transparent, trustworthy, secure and fair data use and supervision of it — in defined data economy ecosystem."*

This approach is applicable in the IoT context, where we are currently building foundations for ethical implementations rather than proposing strict and exact requirements for the ethical use of IoT. In conclusion, we aim to contribute to creating a culture that takes into account the whole IoT ecosystem (here, especially employees and employers) and encourages participating in ethically sustainable development through the common adoption of ethically sustainable practices by the deliberative approach.

A complex dimension besides data distribution itself is the related responsibility. In this paper, we mainly challenge the organisation's responsibilities within a controlled and limited ecosystem, as potential parties forming privacy threats do not end there. While internal data collection and distribution restrictions are crucial, IoT ecosystems can involve a variety of external actors, such as service providers and partners with whom data may be shared. Additionally, phenomena such as rising cybercrime form significant risks, further underlining that gathering and storing personal data comes with high responsibility for the organisations. Be it a result of negligence or becoming a victim of an attack, the outcome for the compromised personal data remains as severe. The responsibility of organisations should cover the use of IoT even when some risks are from outside.

5　Conclusions

Leveraging the surveillance capabilities of IoT solutions while protecting employees' privacy forms a challenging combination because IoT is dependent on collecting data, which in many cases is inevitably linked to individuals either directly or indirectly. Hence, to provide applicable practical recommendations aiming for implementing ethics as an integral part of doing business, it is necessary to build balanced IoT deployment approaches that aim to protect the position of individuals and support the technical development and financial competitiveness of companies. Even as compromises cannot be avoided from the standpoint of either party, foundational ethical principles can be applied without losing the majority of the available benefits. We claim that companies are, in most cases, able to configure the deployed IoT solutions in a manner that respects the privacy of their employees and customers, as a variety of different data collection and distribution approaches are available. Organisation can, for example, limit data gathering to anonymous targets, use aggregated data instead of small sample sizes that allow identification, and utilize pseudonymisation in cases where identification cannot otherwise be avoided. Similarly, we see that majority of privacy risks related to data distribution can be avoided by carefully limiting the group of receivers and defining what specific information is necessary to be shared with each party.

In current circumstances, where the deployment rate of IoT keeps rising rapidly, the collection and distribution of data connectable to specific individuals cannot be entirely eliminated. Rather, we encourage focusing on minimizing redundant surveillance, which could either significantly endanger privacy or does not provide meaningful value to the company. Hence, moderation must be applied when proposing reformed procedures, which the companies are in many cases not formally obligated to follow, as the coverage of ethical regulations is reasonably limited. We claim that enhancing the companies' motivation to respect the privacy of their employees and customers through motivation and collective contribution to the fairness of the economy is one of the most efficient methods to support ethically sustainable development.

Modern legislation appears to provide a comparatively safe environment for individuals. However, regulations alone cannot be assumed to result in a holistically ethical mindset. Financial motives may overshadow ethical principles, especially if specific surveillance methods are not prohibited from a legal perspective. From a long-term perspective, we should aim for building practises that prevent misuse and negligence. However, in current reality, the implementation of ethics as an axiomatic feature of doing business is in its infancy.

References

1. Regulation (EU) 2016/679 of the European parliament and of the council of 27 April 2016 on the protection of natural persons with regard to the processing of personal data and on the free movement of such data, and repealing directive 95/46/ec (general data protection regulation). Official Journal of the European Union (2016)
2. Atzori, L., Iera, A., Morabito, G.: The internet of things: a survey. Comput. Netw. **54**(15), 2787–2805 (2010)
3. Brandeis, L., Warren, S.: The right to privacy. Harv. Law Rev. **4**(5), 193–220 (1890). https://doi.org/10.2307/1341305
4. Celik, Z.B., Fernandes, E., Pauley, E., Tan, G., McDaniel, P.: Program analysis of commodity IoT applications for security and privacy: challenges and opportunities. ACM Comput. Surv. (CSUR) **52**(4), 1–30 (2019)
5. Conti, M., Dehghantanha, A., Franke, K., Watson, S.: Internet of things security and forensics: challenges and opportunities. Futur. Gener. Comput. Syst. **78**, 544–546 (2018)
6. Gubbi, J., Buyya, R., Marusic, S., Palaniswami, M.: Internet of things (IoT): a vision, architectural elements, and future directions. Futur. Gener. Comput. Syst. **29**(7), 1645–1660 (2013)
7. Hakkala, A., Koskinen, J.: Personal data protection in the age of mass surveillance. J. Comput. Secur. 1–25 (2022)
8. Herbst, P.G.: Socio-Technical Design: Strategies in Multidisciplinary Research. Tavistock, London (1974)
9. Hirschheim, R., Klein, H.K.: Realizing emancipatory principles in information systems development: the case for ethics. MIS Q. **18**(1), 83–109 (1994). https://doi.org/10.2307/249611
10. Holvast, J.: History of privacy. In: The History of Information Security, pp. 737–769. Elsevier (2007)
11. Khan, R., Khan, S.U., Zaheer, R., Khan, S.: Future internet: the internet of things architecture, possible applications and key challenges. In: 2012 10th International Conference on Frontiers of Information Technology, pp. 257–260. IEEE (2012)
12. Koskinen, J., Knaapi-Junnila, S., Rantanen, M.M.: What if we had fair, people centred data economy ecosystems? In: 2019 IEEE SmartWorld, UbiquIntelligenceigence & Computing, Advanced & Trusted Computing, Scalable Computing & Communications, Cloud & Big Data Computing, Internet of People and Smart City Innovation (Smart-World/SCALCOM/UIC/ATC/CBDCom/IOP/SCI), pp. 329–334. IEEE (2019)
13. Lee, I., Lee, K.: The internet of things (IoT): applications, investments, and challenges for enterprises. Bus. Horiz. **58**(4), 431–440 (2015)
14. Madakam, S., Lake, V., Lake, V., Lake, V., et al.: Internet of things (IoT): a literature review. J. Comput. Commun. **3**(05), 164–173 (2015). https://doi.org/10.4236/jcc.2015.35021
15. Mason, R.O.: Four ethical issues of the information age. MIS Q. 5–12 (1986). https://doi.org/10.2307/248873
16. Miorandi, D., Sicari, S., De Pellegrini, F., Chlamtac, I.: Internet of things: vision, applications and research challenges. Ad Hoc Netw. **10**(7), 1497–1516 (2012)
17. Riedl, B., Grascher, V., Fenz, S., Neubauer, T.: Pseudonymization for improving the privacy in e-health applications. In: Proceedings of the 41st Annual Hawaii International Conference on System Sciences (HICSS 2008), p. 255. IEEE (2008)

18. Royakkers, L., Timmer, J., Kool, L., van Est, R.: Societal and ethical issues of digitization. Ethics Inf. Technol. **20**(2), 127–142 (2018)
19. Schauer, F.: Fear, risk and the first amendment: unraveling the chilling effect. BUL Rev. **58**, 685 (1978)
20. Sollins, K.R.: IoT big data security and privacy versus innovation. IEEE Internet Things J. **6**(2), 1628–1635 (2019)
21. Taylor, L.: What is data justice? The case for connecting digital rights and freedoms globally. Big Data Soc. **4**(2), 2053951717736335 (2017)
22. Tikkinen-Piri, C., Rohunen, A., Markkula, J.: EU general data protection regulation: changes and implications for personal data collecting companies. Comput. Law Secur. Rev. **34**(1), 134– 153 (2018). https://doi.org/10.1016/j.clsr.2017.05.015, https://www.sciencedirect.com/science/article/pii/S0267364917301966
23. Trist, E.L., Bamforth, K.W.: Some social and psychological consequences of the longwall method of coal-getting: an examination of the psychological situation and defences of a work group in relation to the social structure and technological content of the work system. Hum. Relat. **4**(1), 3–38 (1951). https://doi.org/10.1177/001872675100400101
24. Vermanen, M., Harkke, V.: Findings from multipurpose IoT solution experimentations in Finnish SMEs: common expectations and challenges. In: Proceedings of the 52nd Hawaii International Conference on System Sciences, pp. 5246–5255 (2019). https://doi.org/10.24251/HICSS.2019.631
25. Vermanen, M., Koskinen, J., Harkke, V.: Internet of things (IoT) data accessibility: ethical considerations. In: Cacace, M., et al. (eds.) Well-Being in the Information Society. Fruits of Respect, pp. 197–208. Springer, Cham (2020). https://doi.org/10.1007/978-3-030-57847-3_14
26. Vermanen, M., Rantanen, M.M., Harkke, V.: Ethical framework for IoT deployment in SMEs: individual perspective. Internet Res. https://doi.org/10.1108/INTR-08-2019-0361
27. Wachter, S.: Normative challenges of identification in the internet of things: Privacy, profiling, discrimination, and the GDPR. Comput. Law Secur. Rev. **34**(3), 436–449 (2018). https://doi.org/10.1016/j.clsr.2018.02.002, https://www.sciencedirect.com/science/article/pii/S0267364917303904
28. Westin, A.F.: Privacy and freedom. Washington Lee Law Rev. **25**(1), 166 (1968)
29. Yost, A.B., Behrend, T.S., Howardson, G., Darrow, J.B., Jensen, J.M.: Reactance to electronic surveillance: a test of antecedents and outcomes. J. Bus. Psychol. **34**(1), 71–86 (2019)

The Use of Live Facial Recognition Technology by Private Entities in Public Places: A Study of Recent Case in Japan

Aimi Ozaki[(⊠)] [iD]

Faculty of Social Sciences, Kyorin University, Tokyo, Japan
ai-ozaki@ks.kyorin-u.ac.jp

Abstract. In July 2021, East Japan Railway Company introduced a face recognition function to some of its security cameras. However, the company was criticized by society for not fully disclosing its detailed operation policy, and later withdrew some of its operations. Recently, Japan has seen an increase in the number of indiscriminate killings and injuries on trains, and there are growing calls for the need for AI-based countermeasures against suspicious persons. Therefore, why did East Japan Railway Company receive social criticism? In this paper, I would like to clarify the reasons and explore the ideal form of legal regulation for facial recognition systems used by private entities.

Keywords: Live facial recognition · Privacy · Personal data · Fairness

1 Current Situation in Japan

1.1 Use of Facial Recognition Automated Gates and Its Guidebook

As it stands in 2022, guidelines for face recognition technology have been established in Japan for some use cases. For example, in March 2020, the Ministry of Land, Infrastructure, Transport and Tourism (MLIT) published a guideline on the handling of personal data such as passenger facial images, passport information, and boarding information. (This guideline is called the "Guidebook on the Handling of Personal Data in One ID Services Using Face Recognition Technology at Airports [1].) Narita Airport and Haneda Airport are currently preparing to introduce the "One ID Service," a boarding process that uses facial recognition technology. However, there has been strong social criticism of the acquisition of facial image information. This is because facial image information is an identifier that is highly immutable and can be easily acquired without the person's will, and thus has a strong tracking function. Therefore, this guidebook outlines three matters that should be considered when handling personal information at the time of introducing the "One ID Service". The first is prior notification and public announcement, the second is obtaining passenger consent, and the third is establishing a mechanism for receiving complaints and consultations regarding personal information from passengers. The following three points should be considered in the operation of the

D. Kreps et al. (Eds.): HCC 2022, IFIP AICT 656, pp. 27–35, 2022.
https://doi.org/10.1007/978-3-031-15688-5_3

One ID service. First, the use of personal data should be limited to the boarding process; second, facial recognition should be used only for passengers who wish to use it, and the existing procedures should remain in place; and third, in principle, personal data should be deleted within 24 h, and audits should be conducted periodically.

1.2 Facial Recognition System Provided by East Japan Railway Company

In Japan, there are various examples of the use of face recognition technology, including in fields other than airports. In July 2021, East Japan Railway Company announced that it would introduce a new security method using security cameras at some stations in the Tokyo metropolitan area during the Tokyo Olympics and Paralympics [2].

The security cameras are equipped with behavior analysis technology and face recognition technology to detect suspicious persons and objects. When the camera detects a suspicious person or object, the security center will report the incident to the security guards, who will respond promptly. Furthermore, in the event of an emergency situation such as a terrorist attack, East Japan Railway Company will transmit the images from the security cameras to the police through the emergency image transmission system [3], and will work with the police to deal with the situation.

The emergency image transmission system consists of a 3D face shape database conversion system and an automatic matching system. The 3D face shape database conversion system (1) estimates 3D face shape data from photographic images, (2) creates 2D face image data from various angles from 3D face shape data, and (3) registers the created face image data to the MPD server. The automatic matching system (1) transmits the face image data extracted from the security camera images to the MPD server, (2) matches the transmitted face image data with the data registered in the MPD server, and (3) stores the transmitted face image data in the MPD server. (3) If the transmitted face image data and the data registered in the MPD server match, the police station is notified. (4) If the transmitted face image data and the data registered in the MPD server do not match, the transmitted face image data will be automatically deleted.

1.3 Press Reports

In August 2021, through press reports, it became clear that East Japan Railway Company was targeting not only (1) suspicious persons, but also (2) persons who had been released or paroled after serving time in prison for major crimes related to the company, and (3) persons wanted by the police [4]. According to subsequent media reports, East Japan Railway Company was planning to receive information on people released from prison from the standpoint of victims, based on the "Victim Notification System," which informs victims of incidents of their release or parole [5]. In addition, stickers stating "face recognition camera in operation" were placed near some ticket gates, although East Japan Railway Company replied to the newspaper that it could not reveal the detailed location and number of security cameras installed.

This report caused many opinions to be sent to East Japan Railway Company. Some of them were rather criticized. According to the report, some people were worried that the symptoms of their chronic illnesses might make them look suspicious. East Japan Railway Company's press release stated that the system would be implemented "during the Tokyo 2020 Games," so some people thought it was understandable if the system was implemented during the Olympics, although they did not expect it to continue after the Games closed. Later, investigative reports revealed that "serious incidents" were assumed to be terrorist incidents in which passengers were targeted, and not sex crimes or theft. Furthermore, East Japan Railway Company did not disclose how users could request for disclosure or deletion, and did not disclose the retention period of the video images taken of passengers. In September 2021, East Japan Railway Company suspended the detection of people released from prisons because "social consensus has not yet been reached. However, East Japan Railway Company appears to have continued to detect (1) suspicious persons and (2) persons wanted by the police.

An East Japan Railway executive commented in an interview that the measures were taken out of a single-minded desire to protect the safety of passengers. In Japan, there have been many sex crimes committed on trains, and recently, there has been an increase in indiscriminate killings on trains. Against this situation, there are increasing calls for the need for AI-based countermeasures against suspicious persons. Therefore, why has East Japan Railway Company been socially criticized? In this paper, I would like to clarify the reasons and explore the appropriate form of legal regulation for face recognition systems used by private entities.

2 Guidelines of the Personal Information Protection Commission and East Japan Railway COMpany's Measures

East Japan Railway Company explained that they had consulted with the Personal Information Protection Commission and had taken measures in compliance with the law. The Personal Information Protection Commission also commented, "Act on the Protection of Personal Information strikes a balance between protection and use, and East Japan Railway Company's case is not out of balance if the use is limited to the purpose of crime prevention". However, in September 2021, the Personal Information Protection Commission revised the " QUESTIONS AND ANSWERS on the "Guidelines for the Act on the Protection of Personal Information" and the "Handling of Personal Data Leaks and Other Incidents" [6]. In the following, after examining the contents of the revised QUESTIONS AND ANSWERS on the Act on the Protection of Personal Information, it will be discussed whether East Japan Railway Company's measures can be considered to be in line with this QUESTIONS AND ANSWERS.

2.1 Questions and Answers on Act on the Protection of Personal Information

Under the Act on the Protection of Personal Information, the taking and recording of camera images that can be used to identify individuals constitutes the acquisition of personal information. Therefore, it is necessary for the business operator to disclose the purpose of use of personal information to the user in advance, or to notify or disclose the purpose of use of personal information promptly after the acquisition of personal information. Previously, the Personal Information Protection Commission explained that when a business operator takes a picture using a security camera only for the purpose of crime prevention, the business operator does not need to notify users of the purpose of use of personal information or make it public because the purpose of use is clear. (Article 18, Paragraph 4, Item 4 of the Act on the Protection of Personal Information).

However, in September 2021, the Personal Information Protection Commission changed its previous interpretation. The following is the new interpretation of the Personal Information Protection Commission.

The Personal Information Protection Commission answers the assumed question, "What precautions should be taken when a business operator intends to introduce a facial recognition system for crime prevention purposes, limiting the target to criminal acts such as theft?" The following is an answer to the question. "If a business operator builds a personal information database by systematically composing camera images and face recognition data that can be used to identify a user, the information including individual camera images and face recognition data will fall under the category of personal data. Therefore, in this case, the business operator needs to handle the information appropriately in accordance with the Personal Information Protection Law. In addition, when a business operator intends to use personal data including face recognition data by installing a face recognition system for the purpose of crime prevention, limiting the target to criminal acts such as theft, the business operator must register the data with the face recognition system to the minimum extent necessary to achieve the specified purpose of use, and must keep the personal data It is necessary to maintain accurate and up-to-date content. Specifically, business operators should set up internal rules on what criteria should be used for registration in the database. In addition, service providers should establish a system whereby registration to the facial recognition system is made only when a crime is objectively confirmed, and the necessity and accuracy of the registration is confirmed by a responsible person within the service provider. Furthermore, when businesses use security cameras to acquire camera images and extract face recognition data from them for use, the users themselves cannot reasonably predict or assume that such handling will take place. In addition, facial recognition data is personal information that can also be used for marketing purposes. Therefore, businesses shall specify the purpose of use so that users can predict and assume that camera images and face recognition data using face recognition technology will be handled for security purposes. In addition, the business operator must notify the user of the purpose of use of the acquired data, either publicly in advance or promptly after acquiring the data. Business operators are required to post at the entrance or at the installation site, etc., that the security cameras are in operation, and to take measures to make it easily recognizable to users that their personal information is being obtained by the security cameras. In addition, the entity that acquires the camera images, the contents of the camera images, the purpose of use of the camera images and face recognition data, and the contact information for inquiries must be clearly indicated at the entrance of the store or at the installation site, or the URL or QR code of a website containing such information must be shown so that the user himself/herself can check it."

2.2 Measures Taken by East Japan Railway Company

East Japan Railway Company's measures in this case appear to be inadequate. According to media reports, East Japan Railway Company only placed a sticker (3.5 cm in length and 27 cm in width) near some ticket gates that read "Face Recognition Camera in

Operation. This is not a sufficient measure to make it easy for users to recognize that their personal information is being obtained.

In addition, East Japan Railway Company's website states in its "Basic Policy on the Handling of Personal Information" that "Images obtained from security cameras installed in stations will be registered in a face recognition database created by the Company, to the minimum extent necessary, only when necessary to ensure security in stations and trains. It will be used for crime prevention and security in stations and trains. This was the only wording in the document. Therefore, it cannot be concluded that the purpose of use of the facial recognition data was clearly stated.

2.3 Special Care-required Personal Information

Information that a person has served time in prison is considered "Special care-required personal information" under the Act on the Protection of Personal Information. "Special care-required personal information" in Act on the Protection of Personal Information means personal information comprising a principal's race, creed, social status, medical history, criminal record, fact of having suffered damage by a crime, or other descriptions etc. prescribed by cabinet order as those of which the handling requires special care so as not to cause unfair discrimination, prejudice or other disadvantages to the principal. (Article 2, Paragraph 3 of the Act on the Protection of Personal Information.)

3 Discussion in Japan

The cause of this issue is that East Japan Railway Company started the system without disclosing the details of the system, even though a "social consensus" on the use of the facial recognition system in public spaces had not been formed.

For example, Prof. Makoto Ibusuki of Seijo University, an expert in criminal procedure law pointed out that detecting facial information of released prisoners and parolees is inconsistent with the direction of Act for the Prevention of Recidivism, which encourages the prevention of recidivism and rehabilitation of those who have committed crimes [7]. Furthermore, Professor Ibusuki suggests that we must thoroughly debate whether we really need such a discriminatory surveillance system, because identifying people with criminal records in public spaces could become a modern version of "digital tattooing.

In response to such criticism, East Japan Railway Company has stopped detecting people released from prisons. However, this does not mean that there are no problems with East Japan Railway Company's ongoing methods of detecting suspicious persons and those wanted by the police. For example, in the United States, it has been suggested that whether stored, real-time, or through third-party image searches, building a system with the potential to arbitrarily scan and identify individuals without individualized suspicion and to discover personal information about their location, interests, or activities should simply be banned by law [8]. In the following, I will introduce the discussion in Japan and suggest what the legal regulations for facial recognition systems used by private entities ought to be.

3.1 Requirements for Private Entities to Use Facial Recognition Systems in Public Spaces

Professor Ibusuki states that there are three requirements for businesses to use facial recognition systems in public spaces.

The first is the consent and approval process at the facial information collection stage. Contrary to fingerprints and DNA, facial information can be easily collected without the user's consent. Consent and approval processes are necessary not only for identifying facial images in public spaces, but also for collecting facial information in the original data. Second, the purpose and use of facial recognition technology should be made public and evaluated by a third party. As long as businesses are not accountable, the use of such technologies will not be allowed. The third is to establish an independent, neutral, and technologically savvy nationwide review body that will check the use of facial recognition technology in advance and verify the actual operation.

3.2 Opinion by Japan Federation of Bar Association

The Japan Federation of Bar Associations ("JFBA") compiled an opinion paper, "Opinion on Statutory Regulations on the Use of Facial Recognition Systems by Public and Private Sector Organizations and Incorporated Administrative Agencies," dated September 16, 2021, and submitted it on September 21, 2021 to the Commissioner General of the National Police Agency; the Superintendent General of the Metropolitan Police Department; the Chiefs of Prefectural Police Headquarters; the Minister of Internal Affairs and Communications; the Minister of Health, Labour and Welfare; the Chairperson of the Personal Information Protection Commission; prefectural governors; and mayors of the cities designated by Cabinet Order [9].

The Government should exercise strict control as listed below over the use of facial recognition systems aimed at the general public, regardless of being used by public or private sector organizations or by incorporated administrative agencies, to ensure that their use of the systems will not violate the right to privacy and associated rights of citizens unjustifiably:

(i)   Prohibit, in principle, creating facial recognition databases and other data sources, and using the facial recognition system without the data subject's explicit consent.
(ii) Set strict criteria for exceptional cases where public administrative agencies, private businesses, and incorporated administrative agencies may create facial recognition databases and other data sources, and use the facial recognition system.
(iii) Provide effectual oversight by the Personal Information Protection Commission.
(iv) Publicize basic information about facial recognition systems
(v)   Enact legislation embracing the protection of rights of data subjects who are likely to have been entered into the database by mistake

Subsequently, the Japan Federation of Bar Associations issued a Chairman's Statement requiring the suspension of the use of facial recognition systems by railroad operators. The contents of the Chairman's Statement are as follows [10].

The inside of a station is a space managed by a railroad operator. Nevertheless, station premises are extremely public spaces that are used by an unspecified number of people on a daily basis and can be considered essential to everyone's life. If it is a store, users can choose another store that does not introduce the facial recognition system. However, in the case of public transportation, it is not necessarily possible for users to make other choices. The introduction of a face recognition system by a railroad operator may become a de facto compulsion for users, which would seriously infringe on their right to privacy.

The detection of a wanted suspect by a railroad operator is not the same as a station attendant who happens to find a wanted criminal, even if it is for the purpose of cooperation in an investigation by the private sector. It is a surveillance of all people in many stations. In a sense, it is as if the railroad operators are systematically and continuously operating a wanted criminal detection device 24 h a day. In effect, this is equivalent to the police setting up a facial recognition system and using it without any legal basis or court warrant, and it is a violation of the statutory principle of compulsory punishment. (Proviso of Article 197, Paragraph 1, of the Code of Criminal Procedure).

Furthermore, since the definition of "suspicious person" is ambiguous, there is a risk that private businesses will operate arbitrarily based on subjective judgment criteria. In other words, there is a risk that people will be regarded as suspicious without their knowledge, and their baggage will be searched or the police will be called. This is a threat to a free civil society.

Currently, it is possible to search, match, and utilize facial image data in real time. Once the facial image data is registered in a database, the person's behavior can be accurately tracked back to the past and then continuously monitored. In the European Union, the use of facial recognition systems for unspecified persons in public places is prohibited in principle. In the United States, state laws and regulations are in progress. These are based on the same awareness of the problem.

In Japan as well, the use of facial recognition systems should be based on strict legal provisions with careful consideration of necessity and reasonableness. In addition, it is difficult to easily justify the use of facial recognition systems in highly public spaces, even by legislation, if the users do not give their consent. Therefore, the use of facial recognition systems by railroad operators should be stopped immediately.

3.3 Conclusion

Professor Ibusuki's view is based on movements in developed countries that have already adopted face recognition systems, and extracts the requirements for businesses to use facial recognition technology in public spaces in Japan. Therefore, the three requirements are at a level of detail comparable to recommendations in other countries. However, as pointed out by Professor Ibusuki, obtaining consent as a legal measure does not work well because of the ease with which biometric information can be collected. When businesses use facial recognition technology, it will be necessary to discuss among stakeholders whether the consent model should be maintained or whether an alternative to the consent model should be designed.

The views of the Japan Federation of Bar Associations are more stringent. They have issued a chairman's statement stating that railroad operators should immediately stop using facial recognition systems because they do not comply with the above conditions. However, with the increasing number of indiscriminate killings on trains in Japan, there are growing calls for the need for AI-based measures against suspicious persons. In such a situation, abolishing suspicious person detection systems may go against social demands.

In December 2021, the Personal Information Protection Commission established a study group to discuss the appropriate use of camera images for crime prevention in public spaces. It is anticipated that legal regulations for facial recognition systems will be advanced in Japan in the future. In this situation, legal regulations or guidelines should be formulated for each type and use case of facial recognition technology after establishing a basic framework.

In the first place, the reason behind the social criticism of East Japan Railway Company is that there are deep-rooted concerns that the facial recognition system will infringe on the privacy of users, and furthermore, that it will lead to a surveillance society and infringe on freedom of expression. In addition to these concerns, it has been pointed out that the facial recognition system has the potential to promote prejudice and discrimination. Actually, in this case of East Japan Railway Company, the initial target of detection was persons who had been released or paroled from prison, which could have resulted in social exclusion for persons who had completed atoning for their crimes. This kind of discriminatory operation must be prevented.

In addition, East Japan Railway Company's ongoing method of detecting suspicious persons and those wanted by the police is not without its problems. The face recognition system introduced by East Japan Railway Company in this case is live facial recognition. The Information Commissioner's. Office(ICO)provides the following description of live facial recognition. "It is directed towards everyone in a particular area rather than specific individuals. It has the ability to capture the biometric data of all individuals passing within range of the camera automatically and indiscriminately. Their data is collected in real-time and potentially on a mass scale. There is often a lack of awareness, choice or control for the individual in this process" [11].

For this reason, the EU has proposed a draft regulation that would, in principle, prohibit live facial recognition in public spaces for law enforcement purposes, except in exceptional cases. The exceptional cases are the search for missing children, the prevention of imminent terrorist threats, and the arrest of suspects of serious crimes. The exceptional use of live facial recognition would require authorization by a judicial or other independent body. Restrictions are also placed on the databases to be used and the time and place coverage.

East Japan Railway Company states that the emergency image transmission system will only be activated in the event of an emergency situation such as terrorism, but the conditions for its activation are unclear. In addition, in order to implement the emergency image transmission system, cooperation with investigative agencies is essential. However, it is also unclear how information is shared between railroad operators and investigative agencies. This is because the Act on the Protection of Personal Information considers that the consent of the user himself/herself is not required when an investigative agency requests a business operator to provide information about the user for the purpose of investigation [12].

In the U.K., where live facial recognition is increasingly regulated, The ICO have published a Commissioner's Opinion on the use of LFR in public places by private companies. The ICO requires controllers that they must be transparent with the public about who is processing their personal data and for what purpose and they must be communicated clearly, including through any signage, other communications and associated privacy information.

In Japan as well, when operators share information with investigative agencies, they will need to maintain the transparency described above. This is the first step for businesses to obtain a "social consensus" to use facial recognition systems in public spaces. In designing future legal regulations for facial recognition systems in public spaces for the purpose of crime prevention, it is essential to provide guidelines on how information should be shared with investigative agencies.

References

1. Ministry of land, infrastructure, transport and tourism (MLIT), guidebook on the handling of personal data in one id service using face recognition technology at airports. https://www.mlit.go.jp/report/press/content/001332966.pdf
2. East Japan railway company, efforts to improve railway security for the Tokyo 2020 olympic and paralympic games. https://www.EastJapanRailwayCompany.co.jp/press/2021/20210706_ho02.pdf
3. Tokyo metropolitan government, "A New Tokyo" created by citizens first: an action plan for 2020. https://www.kantei.go.jp/jp/singi/tokyo2020_suishin_honbu/kanjikai/dai7/sankou.pdf
4. Masako WAKAE, more transparency needed with facial recognition technology, The Japan News, Sep 1, 2021 at 3
5. East Japan railway company's facial recognition watch list attracts scrutiny / Targeted individuals set to include ex-prisoners, The Japan News, 22 Sep 2021 at 1
6. The personal information protection commission, QUESTIONS AND ANSWERS on the "Guidelines for the act on the protection of personal information" and the "Handling of personal data leaks and other incidents. https://www.ppc.go.jp/personalinfo/faq/2009_APPI_QA/
7. Makoto IBUSUKI, "Identifying the faces of all passengers with surveillance cameras," What was wrong with East Japan railway company's system for detecting people leaving prison?, President Online, 29 Oct 2021. https://president.jp/articles/-/51210?page=1
8. Ferguson, A.G.: Facial recognition and the fourth amendment. Minn. L. Rev. 1105, 197-1198 (2021)
9. Japan federation of bar associations, opinion on statutory regulations on the use of facial recognition systems by public and private sector organizations and incorporated administrative agencies. https://www.nichibenren.or.jp/en/document/opinionpapers/210916.html
10. Japan federation of bar associations, chairman's statement calling for the discontinuation of the use of facial recognition systems by railroad operators. https://www.nichibenren.or.jp/document/statement/year/2021/211125.html
11. The information commissioner's. office, information commissioner's opinion: the use of live facial recognition technology in public places. https://ico.org.uk/media/2619985/ico-opinion-the-use-of-lfr-in-public-places-20210618.pdf
12. Komukai, T.: Privacy protection in the criminal investigations on the personal data held by third parties. J. Inf. Commun. Policy 4(1), 63-80 (2020). https://www.soumu.go.jp/main_content/000719095.pdf

Repair of Unstable Sociomaterial Relations: A Study on Librarians' and Social Workers' Practices in Addressing the Needs of Their Clients

Johanna Sefyrin(✉) [ID] and Mariana S. Gustafsson [ID]

Linköping University, 581 83 Linköping, Sweden
{johanna.sefyrin,mariana.s.gustafsson}@liu.se

Abstract. In this paper we address the increased digitalization of the fabric of modern welfare societies, and the expectations on individuals to be independent and digitally capable that follows from this. We focus on enactments of repair aimed at maintaining the lives of individuals situated in unstable sociomaterial relations in the context of social care and a public library in Sweden. The purpose was to explore enactments of repair in two Swedish empirical contexts: one in a social service setting, and one in a municipal library setting. The analysis was conducted with the help of the concept of repair, understood as maintenance or transformation. We conducted interviews and observations in these two settings and analyzed these with the help of the concept of repair. The analysis shows that in the context of social service, repair was enacted differently in relation to different interpretations of existing legislation concerning minimal livelihoods, and that in the context of the public library repair was enacted in relation to expectations of the library visitors to become digitally independent. The analysis showed that in both of these contexts repair was enacted as maintenance rather than as transformation.

Keywords: Repair · Life sustaining web · Social services · Libraries · Digitalization

1 Introduction

Digitalization of welfare services and public administrations increases the demands on citizens and other members in society to be enough digitally capable to be able to find the information they need, to navigate in the ecosystems of digital services provided by various public and private organizations and to maintain the complex sociomaterial relations they are immersed in [1–4]. In digitalized societies digital technologies are essential in the thick sociomaterial fabric in which humans are situated, and increasingly difficult to disentangle from other relations. The term sociomaterial, based on Suchman [5], is used to indicate how the material and the social are closely entangled, and that the boundaries between them are enacted in practices, rather than given. Barad [6] instead uses the term material-discursive, and Haraway [7] material-semiotic. In this paper we

© IFIP International Federation for Information Processing 2022
Published by Springer Nature Switzerland AG 2022
D. Kreps et al. (Eds.): HCC 2022, IFIP AICT 656, pp. 36–46, 2022.
https://doi.org/10.1007/978-3-031-15688-5_4

focus on repair, defined by Jackson [8] as "the subtle acts of care by which order and meaning in complex sociotechnical systems are maintained and transformed". In this short formulation Jackson includes in repair both maintenance – the practice of maintaining existing orders and relations – and transformation, those practices which serve to change the existing, as a point of departure for innovation and change of the status quo. Also Henke [9] distinguish between repair as maintenance and repair as transformation. Here we focus on repair since humans, things, systems and relations break down, they grow old, sick, are worn out or are damaged. That is part of the cycle of life and death in naturecultures [10, 11], including partly digitalized systems and environments constituted by technologies and humans. Repair in terms of and "infrastructural maintenance… contribute to stability and order (or the appearance of order) through regular processes of engagement and tinkering with things" [12]. Jackson [8] includes care in his definition of repair, and also Buser and Boyer [12] understand repair as a form of care. Joan Tronto writes about care as: "everything we do to maintain, continue, and repair our world so that we can live in it as well as possible. That world includes our bodies, ourselves, and our environment, all that we seek to interweave in a complex, life sustaining web" [13: 103]. Our point of departure is that humans are situated in and constituted by unstable sociomaterial relations – a "life sustaining web", relations which are in need of more or less constant care and repair [4, 8, 9, 14]. This life sustaining web increasingly include digital technologies, services and systems (together with access to clean water, electricity, sanitation, housing, hospital care, medicine and schools and many other things). In this paper we focus on human vulnerability and the repair work that is required when the life sustaining web threatens to rupture, so that it can continue working, or be transformed when there is need for that, in order to continue being life sustaining.

Based on this our purpose is to explore enactments of repair in two Swedish empirical contexts: one in a social service setting, and one in a municipal library setting. In the social service context, we studied how social workers worked to repair the life sustaining webs of their clients; individuals situated in life sustaining webs threatening to rupture since they did not have a paid job and depended on financial aid. Some of the clients were coping with psychosocial problems, had been out of the labor market for a long time due to different illnesses or addictions and had lost their entitlements to the general insurance allowances. In the library context, we studied how library employees worked to repair some of the digital issues in the life sustaining webs of their visitors, who needed access to digital welfare services provides by for instance the Swedish Social Insurance Agency, the Swedish Public Employment Service, the social services or the unemployment fund, private banking, as well as maintaining relations to friends and families through digital channels. These can be understood as two different cases in which repair was enacted in different ways.

2 Previous Research and Analytical Framework

Jackson [8: 223] (2014, p. 223) underscores that "the world is always breaking, it's in its nature to break. That breaking is generative and productive". He asks who "fixes the devices and systems we "seamlessly" use?" and argues for the need for articulation work (with reference to [15] Star and Strauss 1999), "the myriad (often invisible) activities that enable and sustain even the most seemingly natural or automatic forms of order in the world". A central argument which he brings forward is that repair of that which is breaking down is a prerequisite for innovation and transformation of the existing, and he thus situates repair as an ongoing practice necessary to maintain some sort of stability in life, as well as for change. Repair is especially central in a world in which resources are scarce and it is necessary to reuse and recycle [8] (Jackson 2014). Jackson [8] emphasizes that even though repair is a necessary practice in ongoing efforts to care for and sustain human life, it is often placed in the background in favor of design and innovation of the new, also when repair practices are part of processes which result in something new. This relates to the difference between repair as maintenance and repair as transformation mentioned above. This difference is also underscored by Henke [9] (2007) who argues that "[r]epair as maintenance is an attempt to solve problems by 'tweaking' elements within the structure of a system, keeping much of the system intact while remedying the trouble. Buser and Boyer [12] distinguish between preventive maintenance and repair as something which is done when infrastructures fail or are break down. Repair as transformation is a more radical set of changes to the actual ecology, in which the very relationships between culture, practice, and environment are substantially reordered" [9: 138] (Henke 2007, p. 138). Henke also underscores that when repair concerns maintenance practices these generally serve to repair existing power relations, that is, to maintain these, while transformation serves to challenge and reconfigure these relations, and hence give way for other power relations. Houston et al. [16] (2016) place the concept of repair in a human computer interaction (HCI) context, and underscore "the contingent nature of repair work" and how technologies routinely break downs and hence require repair of relations between humans and computers to be maintained. These authors relate repair to infrastructures which, as underscored by Star and Ruhleder [17] (1996), tend to fall into the background and become invisible, when they do not break down, that is, when they are not repaired. Jackson [8: 231] (2014, p. 231) relates repair to ethics of care, "routinely forgotten relations of humans to things in the world … an ethics of mutual care and responsibility". Care can be understood as a notion which includes practices and doings aimed at taking care of human and non-human bodies, and the preconditions for life, and indicates the necessity and embeddedness of such practices in everyday life [13, 18] (de la Bellacasa 2011, Haraway 2016). The concept of care [11, 14, 18] focus on the intimate, fragile and entangled relations between humans and non-humans [5, 6, 18] (e.g. Haraway 2016, Barad 2007, Suchman 2007), and involve concerns for gendered hierarchies and excluded actors, positions and identities. While care includes not only practices and doings, but also the often complex and sometimes painful affections involved in this work [11], the concept of repair as we understand this, relates more to the material aspects and activities involved in caring [8, 12]. These activities involve maintenance and transformation of the complex entanglements of humans with non-humans, the infrastructural and biological, natural-cultural webs of relations that make it possible for humans to co-habitate this world with nonhumans or other-than-humans, that make up "the fabric of biological and social existence" [19] (Martin et al. 2015). This "fabric of biological and social existence" includes human relations to technologies and infrastructures that enable everyday life in a digitalized world [2, 16, 17] (Houston et al. 2016, Star and Ruhleder 1996, Karasti and Blomberg 2018).

3   The Method

Our analysis is based on two case studies [20] on public servants' work to support individuals' access and use of welfare services. Both the municipal libraries and the social services are financed and run by the municipalities in Sweden, making them part of the same organization and political governance. The library case is based on empirical material consisting of a series of 29 observations, seven semistructured interviews with library staff and managers, two focus groups with asylum seekers taking introduction to society course run by the library and several feed-back meetings with library personnel and visitors in two Swedish municipalities (Linköping and Norrköping) (see table with an overview of the empirical material below). The material was collected during the years 2018–2019. The Income support case is based on empirical material consisting of seven observations, a total of 25 interviews, workshops and meetings with social workers and their management in three Swedish municipalities (Motala, Norrtälje and Nacka). In addition documentary material supporting library work and income support services was consulted. This material was collected during 2020 (Table 1).

Table 1. Collected data in two case studies/welfare services.

Method	Municipal libraries	Income support
Interviews	7 (library staff and managers)	20 (social workers, management)
Meetings	1 (Library management, librarians)	6 (social workers, management)
Focus-groups/workshops	2 (asylum seekers)	2 (social workers and the manager)
Observations	29 (during 2018–2019)	7 (2020)

The material from the library case has previously been analyzed in terms of care [4], and when we found research about repair, we were interested in exploring what this would add to an analysis. Thus, in terms of analysis, we have operationalized the concept of repair to make it work in the empirical context of the paper – the social work and library case. These are somewhat different cases, with different focus, and while digital technologies are central in the library case, other issues are in focus in the social work case. Hence repair in the library case concerned digital issues which were often related to relations with public organizations and authorities, while in the social service case repair concerned social problems and relations, and problems with economy, work, and health. We understand repair as something which is enacted to maintain or transform those life sustaining webs of relations which humans are situated in and constituted by, and which include human and other-than-human bodies, such as digital technologies.

We make each case in part to illustrate and reflect upon how public servants from different professions (in a social work and library context), based on different professional norms, legislation, and organizational practices, worked to, in different ways repair the life sustaining webs of their clients and visitors. We do not make comparisons within the cases or among municipalities, instead we discuss the two cases on public servants' work and relate them to the concept of repair.

4   Enactments of Repair in the Social Services

Based on the Swedish Social Services Act [21] (SFS 2001:453), income support services are designed for the people whose life sustaining webs for some reason does not work as such and aim to support and coach them towards sustainable livelihoods. Managed by the municipality administrations, the services are based on principles of equality of living conditions, economic and social security and active participation in society [22] (Gustafsson and Wihlborg 2019). Individuals' responsibility for their own lives is a main principle in the Social Services Act [21] (SFS 2001:453), upon which the front-line public officials, in this case most often social workers (but also increasingly other professions), base their decisions for support and coaching. In addition, like all public services they follow the Local Government Act [23] (SFS 2017:725) and the Administrative Procedure Act [24] (SFS 2017:900). The social workers rely on the mentioned legislation which define when someone is entitled to a specific kind of support. This legislation specifies what, up to a minimum standard, is included in the life sustaining web: food, clothes and shoes, leisure and play, hygiene articles, children's insurance, consumables, daily newspaper and telephone, and internet connection [25] (the National Board of Health and Welfare, 2021). Also digitalization is included in this legislation, and understood as part of the life sustaining web, but the support is not sufficient for expensive telephones, computers or internet connections. In practice, front-line public officials' repair practices aim at maintaining the life sustaining webs of the clients by providing economic support and advice on how to meet daily needs. Some of the clients need not only economic support but have problems with physical or psychical health or social problems which make it harder for them to find and hold a job, and thus need repair also of social relations, such as help in order to be able to find and hold a position as an employed. In this context we understand the clients as situated in sociomaterial webs which are on the verge of rupturing – or have already done so – and are in need of repair.

The Swedish Social Services Act is a national legislation, but the social services are administrated by municipalities, which have a certain amount of freedom in their enactment of the legislation. Based on our study in two municipalities, we found two different approaches in social work: one with a focus on employment and integration in the labor market, and another, more 'traditional' approach, focusing not only on employment, but also on psycho-social aspects of life – a more encompassing part of the life sustaining web. The former seems to be a limited version of the second, broader and traditional approach which takes into consideration the full life situation and relations of the client, not only the economic aspects thereof. These two approaches can be understood as different enactments of repair, one limited to the economic dimensions of the entangled sociomaterial relations that the clients are situated in, and one which concerns a larger amount of these relations. One of the interviewed social workers described her work in terms of social problems and economic problems as being related:

"... people come to us with social problems, where the economy is perhaps a consequence of their social problems. And then I think you should meet someone who works with social services and who has the relevant education. You should not meet... a labor market coordinator. I do not think it is right for those we meet. Because even if it's work for many ... many times, like I said, I think, the economy is a consequence of you having social problems....We work on the basis of the Social Services Act. We will not become job brokers, or like case workers at the Swedish Social Insurance Agency with templates, and things. Without us having to make individual needs assessments, no matter what you apply for, you have the right to have the matter tried" (Interview, Senior Social worker)

We also studied digitalization in the social services, and the municipalities in our study are either preparing or have already automatized entire or parts of the case management in income support. In the Swedish Income support services, the most known model, applied in Trelleborg municipality, made possible reallocation of time and personnel resources to coaching the clients towards reintegration on labor market [26], but automation is currently implemented in more than 24 Swedish municipalities. Such changes bring with them new questions and challenges for the public servants' work. Standardization of processes is a pre-requisite for automatization, but there was a tension between those who understood social work as rule compliance, and those who understood it as something far more complex. This tension showed up when IT-developers demonstrated new functionalities for case management, while the social workers interrupted to ask myriads of questions relating to a diversity of dimensions of their cases. Tensions raised from a partial, black-or-white perception of what decision making on the cases involved on behalf of the IT-developers, and the social workers' difficulties to see what parts of the process could be standardized. Here it became obvious that the IT developers saw only a rather simplified part of the complex reality of the clients which the social workers saw, and that this affected how they viewed repair in this context.

Based on this material we could see three different enactments of repair; one related to traditional social work which encompassed the economic situations of the clients as well as the psycho-social aspects of their lives, one which was limited to only the economic aspects of the clients' lives in terms of work integration and employment, and one in which IT developers working with automatization of the legislation and organizational practices in social work understood this rather simplistic, as they attempted to reduce an entangled reality into something that could be standardized. For the clients these repair practices resulted in different decisions with regards to their entitlement to support. In those practices which were based on the more narrow, economic, view of the clients lives the clients received economic support but no help with finding a job or nurturing social relations, while in those practices which were based on a more encompassing view of the clients' situation, the client received help with such issues too. These two different practices were involved in the digitalization process too, and if the IT developers had their way, it seems as though the narrower view of the clients would be built into their design. In Henke's [9] (2007) terms, these repair practices can be understood as closer to maintenance than to transformation, since transformational repair would require changes on a system level. However, for an individual client help with issues such as nurturing social relations and finding a job might be a form of help to self-help, which for the individual could be transformational, if this leads to a strengthened capability to individually repair the life sustaining web which one is situated in.

5 Enactments of Repair in a Library Context

Public libraries act in accordance with their mission of folk education in the spirit of Democracy and work to ensure individuals' access and use of information [27] (SFS 2013:801). The Library Act establishes the role of public libraries in promoting transfer of knowledge, free opinion building and universal participation as key values in the life sustaining web of a democratic society [27] (SFS 2013:801). In the context of advancing digitalisation and the diversification of digital needs, libraries are to support digital literacy as a democratic value [28] (Swedish Library Association, 2015) and work for digital inclusion, which in the Swedish context is obviously understood as an important ingredient in the life sustaining web. The mission is also meant to address the diverse needs of those who lack the capacity to acquire the information needed in their livelihoods, due to economic, social, technical or other reasons [28] (Swedish Library Association, 2015). The law is clearly specific about libraries' mission of paying particular attention to persons with disabilities and national minorities in their access to information. The public library mission also includes increasing knowledge on 'how digital technologies can be used' in order to access and use information.

Libraries are open to everyone, but among those who are most frequently asking for help concerning e-services or other IT-related needs we found partly the same individuals who apply for income support [4, 29] (Gustafsson et al. 2020; Sefyrin et al. 2019). Their questions often concerned the need to print something, for instance a withdrawal of their bank account in order to ensure that they were entitled to economic support from the social services, or to ensure that they had applied for the required number of jobs and were entitled to unemployment insurance fund. Their errands were sometimes private, but often related to other public agencies and digitalized welfare services, webs of relations which needed to be maintained in order to keep being life sustaining. Their questions and needs showed that seemingly simple digital issues such as log-in passwords and electronic identification use, were central in their life sustaining webs, and were complex issues which they needed help with. One of the librarians told us about the kind of questions that library visitors might ask, a seemingly simple question which turned out to be rather complex after all:

> "Mm. And there it gets, if it's somewhat more advanced stuff, then, if often turns out that the other staff refers to some of us who work with [IT] guidance, who are somewhat more used to these things. But if it's things that we see that "Yes, but this, this takes time" then, then we use to say that "Yes but then you will have to book an IT guidance session in that case, because we cannot solve this immediately" kind of. But one, kind of one might, be such a simple thing as a print out, like, one

comes with a phone "Here, I want to have this" and then... yes but one, doesn't have the password to the mail, so one cannot log in to the mail and print out from our computers. Then one has to download an app... to be able to print out, then perhaps one cannot download the app because one doesn't have... one isn't logged in to a Google account on the phone, for example perhaps one had it [the phone] from a friend and it's not fixed. And then it might become a whole... very much ado about something that simple, so. (Librarian 2)

Most of the visitors came to the library for help because neither friends or family, nor the other involved organizations would or could provide the kind of help they needed. The library employees believed that some visitors came to the library also because they were lonely. These visitors' questions to the library employees made visible how entangled they were in digitalized relations both to friends and family, but also with other public and private organizations, contacts which were often digitalized. The library employees made their best to repair these visitors' partly broken sociomaterial entanglements [4] (Sefyrin et al. 2021). Helping visitors with digital issues has become an increasing part of the library employees' work since at least the beginning of the 2000s, and the library employees understood this as part of their democratic assignment in relation to the Library Act [27].

The library employees offered repair of some of the digitalized relations which were part of the life sustaining webs which their clients were situated in. The main aim was to help the visitors become more informed and capable of solving digital issues on their own, but many of the visitors, we were told, came back for help with the same or similar problems. In this context repair practices were enacted in relation to more or less explicit expectations of the visitors to being informed and capable citizens in a democratic society in which the exercising of rights (such as accessing the benefits of public welfare services) and obligations are increasingly entangled with access to and knowledge of digital services, technologies and infrastructures. Repair in this sense was related to maintenance of relations which were partly or fully digitalized, rather than to more transformational repair practices which in Henke's [9] (2007) terms would require change on a system level. However, as in the case of the social services, for an individual, help provided by the library employees could, when this work as the intended help to more individual capability to solve upcoming digitally related problems, be a form of repair as transformation on an individual level.

During the pandemic many municipal libraries closed down in order to decrease the risk for infection, and the librarians we talked to did not know where their regular visitors went during the pandemic, or where they turn for help with repair of their digital problems. Since these (former) library visitors were situated in rather vulnerable positions, there is a risk that their vulnerability was further reinforced by the pandemic.

6   Discussion and Conclusions

Seen through the lens of repair, the enactments of the social workers as well as the librarians can be understood as repair of the complex, life sustaining web which Tronto [13] writes about. In the context of the social services repair was enacted in relation to expectations concerning agency and independence, to the capability of independently becoming financially and socially self-sustainable. In this sense, the repair enacted by the social workers can be understood as repair in terms of maintenance, that is, in order for the life sustaining web to keep working as such, even though this might be on what in a Swedish context is understood as a minimum level. It became clear though that these expectations were enacted differently in different municipalities, also when the decisions made in the social services were being developed and translated into automated digital systems. In the context of the library, repair was enacted in relation to expectations of being, or becoming, an independent, informed and capable citizen, who is capable of navigating in a digitalized society in which exercising rights and obligations is entangled with digital technologies. In a highly digitalized society, the capability to manage digitalized relations with various public and private agencies, as well as private relations (friends and family) is understood as central aspects of the life sustaining web. Also in the library context the repair practices we learned about can be understood as closer to repair as maintenance than to repair as transformation. However, on an individual level, repair in the form of help from the social services as well as from the library can be transformational, as long as this repair helps the individual to more independently managing the relations s/he is situated in. A central observation from this study is that since the life sustaining web is unstable and fluid, it requires recurrent attention of skilled maintenance workers, and through the lens of repair also social workers and librarians can be understood as such maintenance workers. Researchers who study infrastructures [e.g. 15, 17] often underscore how those who work with the maintenance and repair of these are often invisible and undervalued, as infrastructures are invisible until the break down. Therefore, we underscore the importance of making visible and acknowledging the repair work enacted by the social workers and the librarians.

Acknowledgments. This research was made possible due to the publicly funded projects 'A digital Norrköping for everyone. The library's mission to work for digital inclusion in a society with new challenges', funded by Norrköping's research fund, and 'Automated decision making in social services: a study of institutional, organizational and professional tensions in the introduction of robotic process automation in the Swedish Income Support', financed by the Swedish Research Council for Health, Working Life and Welfare.

References

1. Bernhard, I., Gustafsson, M., Hedström, K., Sefyrin, J., Whilborg, E: A digital society for all? meanings, practices and policies for digital diversity. In: 52nd Hawaii International Conference on System Sciences (HICSS-52), pp. 3067–3076. Grand Wailea, Maui (2019)
2. Karasti, H., Blomberg, J.: Studying infrastructuring ethnographically. Comput. Support. Coop. Work (CSCW) **27**(2), 233–265 (2018)
3. Pipek, V., Karasti, H., Bowker, G.C.: A Preface to 'Infrastructuring and Collaborative Design.' Comput. Support. Coop. Work (CSCW) **26**(1–2), 1–5 (2017). https://doi.org/10.1007/s10606-017-9271-3
4. Sefyrin, J., Gustafsson, M., Wihlborg, E.: Addressing digital diversity: care matters in vulnerable digital relations in a Swedish library context. Sci. Pub. Policy **48**(6), 841–848 (2021)

5. Suchman, L.: Human-Machine Reconfigurations: Plans and Situated Actions, 2nd edn. Cambridge University Press, Cambridge (2007)
6. Barad, K.: Meeting the Universe Halfway: Quantum Physics and the Entanglement of Matter and Meaning. Duke University Press, Durham (2007)
7. Haraway, D.: Modest_Witness@Second_Millennium. FemaleMan©_Meets_OncoMouse™. Feminism and Technoscience. Routledge, New York, London (1997)
8. Jackson, S.: Rethinking repair. In: Gillespie, T., Boczkowski, P., Foot, K. (eds.). Media Technologies: Essays on Communication, Materiality and Society. MIT Press, Cambridge (2014)
9. Henke, C.R.: Situation normal? Repairing a risky ecology. Soc. Stud. Sci. **37**(1), 135–142 (2007)
10. Haraway, D.: The companion species manifesto: Dogs, people, and significant otherness. Prickly Paradigm Press, Chicago (2003)
11. de la Bellacasa, M.P.: Matters of Care: Speculative Ethics in more than Human worlds. University of Minnesota Press, Minneapolis (2017)
12. Buser, M., Boyer, K.: Care goes underground: thinking through relationsof care in the maintenance and repair of urban water infrastructures. Cult. Geogr. **28**(1), 73–90 (2020)
13. Tronto, J.: Moral Boundaries: A Political Argument for an Ethic of Care. Routledge, New York (1993)
14. de La Bellacasa, M.P.: Matters of care in Technoscience: Assembling Neglected Things. Soc. Stud. Sci. **41**(1), 85–106 (2011)
15. Star, S.L., Strauss, A.: Layers of silence, arenas of voice: the ecology of visible and invisible work. Comput. Support. Coop. Work (CSCW) **8**(1), 9–30 (1999)
16. Houston, L., Jackson, S.J., Rosner, D.K., Ahmed, S.I., Young, M., Kang, L.: Values in repair. In: Proceedings of the 2016 CHI Conference on Human Factors in Computing Systems, pp. 1403–1414. San José, CA (2016)
17. Star, S.L., Ruhleder, K.: Steps toward an ecology of infrastructure: design and access for large information spaces. Inf. Syst. Res. **7**(1), 111–134 (1996)
18. Haraway, D.: Staying with the Trouble. Making Kin in the Chthulucene. Duke University Press, Durham and London (2016)
19. Martin, A., Myers, N., Viseu, A.: The politics of care in technoscience. Soc. Stud. Sci. **45**(5), 625–641 (2015)
20. Myers, M.D.: Qualitative Research in Business & Management. SAGE, London (2013)
21. SFS 2001:453. Socialtjänstlag [Social Services Act]
22. Gustafsson, M.S., Wihlborg, E.: 'It Is always an individual assessment': a case study on challenges of automation of income support services. In: Lindgren, I., et al. (eds.) EGOV 2019. LNCS, vol. 11685, pp. 45–56. Springer, Cham (2019). https://doi.org/10.1007/978-3-030-27325-5_4
23. SFS 2017:725. Kommunallag [Local Government Act]
24. SFS 2017:900. Förvaltningslag [Administrative Procedure Act]
25. National Board of Health and Welfare (2021). Riksnormen för försörjningsstöd 2021. See https://www.socialstyrelsen.se/stod-i-arbetet/ekonomiskt-bistand/riksnormen/
26. Valcon (Producer). Process automation in Trelleborg municipality, 2017, 04 Mar 2019. Accessed. https://vimeo.com/212078783
27. SFS 2013:801. Bibliotekslag [The Library Act]. Retrieved from Sveriges Riksdag. http://www.riksdagen.se/sv/dokument-lagar/dokument/svenskforfattningssamling/bibliotekslag-2013801_sfs-2013-801
28. Swedish Library Association. Promoting the development of a democratic society: The Swedish Librarians' Association. Professionalism and Professional Ethics (2015). Accessed https://www.ifla.org/files/assets/faife/codesofethics/sweden.pdf

29. Gustafsson, M.S., Wihlborg, E., Sefyrin, J.: Technology mediated citizenship: what can we learn from library practices. In: Hofmann, S., et al. (eds.) ePart 2020. LNCS, vol. 12220, pp. 109–120. Springer, Cham (2020). https://doi.org/10.1007/978-3-030-58141-1_9

Autonomy Alliances and Data Care Practices

Barbara Nino Carreras[⊠] [iD] and Sisse Finken [iD]

IT University of Copenhagen, Rued Langgaards Vej 7, Copenhagen, Denmark
{barb,sisf}@itu.dk

Abstract. Recent studies focusing on the digitalization of welfare provision draw attention to digital infrastructures that produce new forms of social inequality and disempowerment due to inaccessibility. Against this backdrop, we study the practices of a Danish public library in supporting citizens with digital applications for welfare benefits. Through a grounded theory approach to data collection and analysis, we draw on ethnographic materials and Catriona Mackenzie's multidimensional analysis of autonomy to conceptualize *autonomy alliances* and *data care practices*. These are collective efforts that attempt to subvert inaccessible and autonomy-undermining public digital infrastructures. Drawing on a relational view of autonomy, we examine how certain design choices can constrain citizens' personal autonomy and equal access to welfare services. For this reason, we discuss the importance of studying political decisions affecting the design and organization of digital welfare services, as well as the local practices that compensate for discriminatory design choices through social inclusion and a commitment to equity.

Keywords: Relational autonomy · Digital welfare · Public library · Equity · Digital inclusion · Inaccessibility

1 Introduction

Across science and technology studies, human-computer interaction, and related fields, a growing body of literature is tracing and critically attending to how governments digitalize the provision of welfare services. These studies indicate that public digital infrastructures can create new citizen responsibilities [1], render citizens' needs and affective interactions invisible to the state [2], fail to comply with web accessibility guidelines [3], demand new skills [4, 5], reinforce or produce exclusion [6], or undermine citizen's personal autonomy and data rights [7, 8]. Also, a crucial concern in these studies, is how digital infrastructures used in welfare provision can constrain the citizen's capacity to enact personal autonomy and have control over data collection, and decisions taken in relation to such datasets [7–9]. In this vein, Velden et al. explore a relational [10] and socio-material understanding of autonomy that articulates how different actors enact, negotiate, and constrain citizens' personal autonomy [11]. As the authors argue, a relational understanding of autonomy can be generative to trace how technological actors, such as information and communication technologies, promote or hamper citizens' personal autonomy and rights.

D. Kreps et al. (Eds.): HCC 2022, IFIP AICT 656, pp. 47–57, 2022.
https://doi.org/10.1007/978-3-031-15688-5_5

Against this backdrop, we draw on an ethnographic study conducted at a Danish public library to explore how library employees support citizens with digital applications for welfare benefits. Through this study, we reflect on wider national concerns voiced by civil society organizations in Denmark regarding present social inequalities produced by inaccessible mandatory digital infrastructures [12, 13]. When unfolding the work of the library, we conceptualize *autonomy alliances* and *data care practices* as collective efforts performed by frontline workers and community members to promote citizens' self-governing agency when navigating autonomy-undermining digital infrastructures. Bridging our analysis to design justice [14] and critical disability literature [15], we reflect on the value of studying grassroots projects, that compensate for exclusionary design choices in digital welfare provision.

In what follows, we first provide a brief overview of Catriona Mackenzie's multidimensional analysis of autonomy to study socio-material relations promoting or undermining autonomy. We outline the value of exploring personal autonomy in digitalized versions of welfare provision as a collective responsibility, rather than solely as a matter of individual traits, resources, or skills. Second, we contextualize mandatory digital self-service in Denmark and outline our grounded and ethnographic approach to data collection and analysis, including our ethical and data protection considerations. Third, we analyze ethnographic materials collected at a Danish public library. Throughout our analysis we develop *autonomy alliances* and *data care practices* as concepts to think with when exploring exclusionary digital infrastructures. Lastly, we conclude our paper by discussing how choices in the organization and design of public digital infrastructures are political and have both enabling and disabling effects. In conceptualizing *autonomy alliances* and *data care practices,* our paper draws attention to a local initiative that subverts and reimagines more equitable and accessible versions of digital welfare.

2   Theorizing Relational Autonomy

Drawing on the work of feminist philosopher Catriona Mackenzie [9], a relational understanding of autonomy can be generative to recognize people's different positionalities, interdependence, and liberties in the study of welfare provision. When reflecting on individualistic notions of autonomy, found within neoliberal political discourse [1, 10], Mackenzie argues that only paying attention to individual behaviors and traits, is insufficient to account for how social inequalities and systems of power influence a person's opportunity to live a self-determining life. For this reason, she draws on feminist relational autonomy theory, committed to social justice, to unpack how social discrimination and inequalities influence a person's opportunity to enact autonomy. Drawing on her multidimensional analysis of autonomy we focus on Mackenzie's three conceptual and interdependent dimensions: self-determination, self-governance, and self-authorization [10, 16] that we find helpful as sensitizing concepts [17] and starting points in our analysis.

First, Mackenzie outlines self-determination, explored as a status, in which she draws attention to external structural conditions, often regulated by the state, namely freedom and equal opportunity. For example, anti-discrimination laws or political and personal liberties are important structural factors influencing the status of a person in being a self-determining agent. Equal access to goods and opportunities, and freedom from domination and discrimination are therefore paramount [10]. Second, Mackenzie outlines self-governance, explored as a capacity, in which she identifies internal agential conditions for autonomy such as the capacity to enact choices that cohere with one's own values, commitments and identity [10]. Importantly, rather than conceiving self-governance as an isolated capacity of individuals, she considers the interdependencies between interpersonal and social relations and how these constrain and enable people's self-governing agency. With the example of projects helping women in abusive relations or drug rehabilitation programs, Mackenzie argues that social scaffolding efforts must respect people's agency and facilitate participation and dialogue. In this vein, the third conceptual layer is self-authorization. Through this notion, Mackenzie draws our attention to social relations of recognition and oppression that produce self-evaluative attitudes, e.g., self-respect and self-esteem, that influence how people enact personal autonomy.

Through Mackenzie's multidimensional analysis of autonomy, we have briefly outlined the social and interpersonal factors we are interested in analyzing and unpacking empirically in the study of a Danish public library supporting citizens with digital applications for welfare benefits. In what follows, we first contextualize current concerns on digital inequalities in Denmark and why a public library is an insightful space to study digitalized versions of welfare provision. Second, we delineate the methodological orientation and ethical concerns of the study.

3   Empirical Setting's Background

In the context of Denmark, and since the early 2010s, applications for welfare benefits have been transformed into mandatory online forms as "self-service" digital infrastructures [18]. Due to the increasing lack of in-person support and the inaccessibility of websites and mobile applications provided by the authorities, civil society organizations and the Danish Institute for Human Rights have raised concerns regarding discrimination and digital inequality affecting diverse groups [13, 19, 20]. Whilst disability rights organizations have been vocal about the lack of web accessibility compliance across public sector websites and mobile applications [19, 20], organizations representing minority communities have raised concerns regarding the lack of in-person services and accessible communication [13, 19].

What these concerns illustrate is that increasingly, more welfare benefits are delivered via digital self-service infrastructures that fail to meet citizens' diversity. In this regard, recent statistics indicate that approximately 20 percent of the population is "digitally challenged" [12]. As we are interested in the tension between inaccessible digital infrastructures and the authorities' categorization of some citizens as digitally challenged, we use ethnographic methods [21, 22] to explore the work of a Danish public library financing and developing learning and support activities for diverse citizens who encounter accessibility barriers. Due to the diverse ways in which public libraries support citizens across Denmark, our empirical materials are specific to the library and municipality of study and cannot be generalized. As other researchers indicate, policymakers have tasked public libraries with the responsibility to support citizens in using and adopting public digital infrastructures, yet not all libraries have accepted this responsibility, and support varies across Denmark's 98 municipalities [18].

4 Methodological Orientation and Research Ethics

In the summer of 2021, the first author conducted fieldwork at a Danish public library in Copenhagen as a part of her PhD study mapping formal and informal work supporting citizens who encounter inaccessible public digital services in Denmark. The use of ethnographic methods in this study allows us to map and analyze situated practices and social relations [22, 23] involving citizens, digital infrastructures, and library employees. Over the course of three weeks, the first author spent 34 hours conducting observations and writing detailed fieldnotes on a physical notebook. Further, she conducted 6 semi-structured interviews on-site with library employees and volunteers. To include citizen perspectives and remain mindful of their time and privacy, she took notes of what citizens wished to share with her through informed consent. Information that directly identifies citizens has been modified or pseudo anonymized (e.g., name, age, nationality). Our approach to data analysis and collection draws on feminist grounded theory [24]. This involved a series of situated and ongoing coding exercises through the software NVivo in combination with monthly discussions reflecting on the main themes emerging from the data. While analyzing data, the first author was in dialogue with research participants through follow-up emails or via short additional interviews.

The first author designed her study according to the General Data Protection Regulation and created consent forms that clearly explained the purpose of the study and provided relevant legal and contact information to research participants. Furthermore, she followed government guidelines during fieldwork to maintain adequate physical distance with citizens to prevent the spread of Covid-19.

5 Digital Inclusion at a Danish Public Library

Since 2013, employees and volunteers with diverse educational backgrounds (public administration, library science, digital project management) organize myriad activities dedicated to digital inclusion for teenagers, adults, and seniors, with diverse ethnic backgrounds and citizenships. Library employees explained that their approach to digital inclusion is influenced by their own interpretation of the Danish tradition of *Folkeoplysning* (public education) that dates to N. F. S. Grundtvig, a pastor and an important figure in modern Danish national identity [25]. As the Head of Section for Service and Materials explained:

> "The *Folkeoplysning* tradition is the DNA of public libraries. And the library's approach to citizen service and digitalization is thus to use the tradition of *Folkeoplysning* as a supportive method. We contact and support citizens who have had a hard time in the new digital reality. There are many who feel they are left behind at the gate and cannot hop on the train. We have learned that there are many more who are digitally challenged than we anticipated. There were also digitally well-functioning citizens who had problems because the digital solutions were so

difficult to understand at first. This applies, for example, to the online application for housing benefits (boligstøtte), which was virtually impossible to figure out. Therefore, in 2013 it made sense to take on functions such as NemID[1], Digital Post[2], and online banking. But for the library, it was also important to offer help beyond citizen service tasks. Here I am thinking of digital everyday challenges that you as a citizen must master to function in a society. So, when we said yes to taking on the tasks, it was important for the library to help set a new inclusive agenda." (Own translation, July 2021)

Through *Folkeoplysning*, across interviews, library employees described digital inclusion as an integral activity of the library committed to helping citizens participate equally in all aspects of a digitalized society. This responsibility was apparent in practice through different activities, in which citizens were taught how to use digital infrastructures and were helped to apply for welfare benefits step-by-step. Public organizations such as the Agency for Digitization or the national network of public libraries had previously showcased their activities as exemplary to other libraries across Denmark. This meant the library's work had been recognized on a national level. However, library employees voiced concerns regarding the difficulties they experienced in providing feedback when digital infrastructures were inaccessible or lacked key functionalities. As one library employee explained:

"Giving feedback is a very opaque process. Especially when it comes to who to contact, you can feel like a drop in the ocean. For example, at a public digitalization conference I approached an IT consulting firm that designed a digital solution for immigrants. I asked them: 'may I give you some feedback on your solution because it works really poorly'. And of course, they said 'yes!' and they seemed interested. I told them that the solution was only available in Danish, but users of this service speak many other languages. I also told them that it was impossible to log out. When I helped different citizens, it was difficult to help more than one person on the same computer [..] And then I wrote a private message to one of them again on LinkedIn a year later, but I have not heard back from them." (Own translation, June 2021).

During observations it was apparent that public digital infrastructures, useful to immigrants who recently arrived in Denmark, were in Danish by default. Furthermore, many application forms required that citizens used a computer, while most citizens requesting assistance at the library could only afford a mobile device. Library employees also admitted that some websites were not intuitive or lacked functionalities, as the example above illustrates. Difficulties in providing feedback meant that even though the library was recognized for its work on a national level, it was difficult for the library to influence the improvement of digital services. Considering these challenges, library employees found other ways to help citizens, namely through collaborations across the municipality.

---

[1] NemID is a personal log-in solution necessary to access public digital services in Denmark and online banking.
[2] Digital Post is a mandatory digital mailbox to communicate with the authorities and banks.

This was the case of an activity called *Hverdagsrådgivning* (*Everyday Counseling*). This weekly "digital guidance project", as library employees called it, lasted 2 h and was visited on average by 13 to 16 citizens each week. *Everyday Counseling* was financed and organized in collaboration with an organization offering counseling and learning activities to families with an ethnic-minority background or refugee status. To advertise *Everyday Counseling*, library employees explained they had joined many local events organized by representatives of minority communities and offered digital assistance outside the library: at the local health center, in social housing areas and at local schools. A manager at the library also explained the importance of hiring employees who had similar backgrounds and mother tongues to underrepresented citizens needing help. In addition, the library offered the services of interpreters in e.g., Urdu, Tigrinya, and Arabic. Interpreters were physically present at the library and, in exceptional circumstances, library employees could be supported by an interpreter speaking other languages on the phone. This option, however, was limited due to budget constraints.

6 Autonomy Alliances and Data Care Practices at Everyday Counseling

The atmosphere at *Everyday Counseling* was friendly and the architecture of the building provided different common areas, where citizens could sit at their computers. The library had 10 laptops that citizens could borrow if they did not own a computer. Many citizens spoke more than two languages and had various levels of digital and Danish language skills. In what follows, we bring to the forefront one ethnographic fieldnote where we meet Ana, who recently arrived in Denmark and urgently needs assistance to apply for housing benefits (*boligstøtte* in Danish).

Ana's Application for Housing Benefits. A library employee [a man in his 30s], carrying a Lenovo laptop, introduces me to a citizen who like me, speaks Spanish as her mother tongue. I say hello in Spanish. Ana smiles and tells me where she is from, she has been living in Denmark for just a few months. I inform Ana about my research, and she agrees to participate in my observations. The library employee takes us to a quiet area, in an open space, close to the music and films section. We sit at a free desk. Luckily, this area of the library is not in use while we are here. I sit opposite Ana and the library employee because they are going to interact with different digital interfaces and Ana will type various usernames and passwords. Now, the library employee positions his laptop in front of Ana, and then proceeds to make a phone call. Meanwhile, Ana explains to me that her job counselor referred her to the library because she needs to apply for housing benefits, but she has not yet completed her Danish language course. She voices embarrassment for not being fluent in Danish. I quickly tell her it took me more than a year to learn Danish, and I admit feeling insecure about my Danish sometimes. We smile at each other and then the library employee addresses Ana in Danish. I try to translate: "he says that he is calling an interpreter who speaks Spanish." The library employee turns on the speaker function and the interpreter addresses Ana in Spanish. The interpreter kindly explains to Ana that information shared on the phone is confidential, and that the sole purpose of the translation is to help her with the application. Ana nods and while looking at the library employee, she communicates with the interpreter she understands.

First, Ana is asked to log into her Gmail, Digital Post, and an online application for housing benefits through the website borger.dk (citizen.dk). The library employee guides Ana through the process. Ana is told that she is responsible for typing her information correctly, and logging into different systems with her username and passwords. The library employee reads aloud information on the screen step by step, and the interpreter translates carefully, finding the correct terms, so that Ana understands what she needs to type on different interfaces. While Ana logs into the online form, the library employee explains that her income is automatically shown on the screen, and that she needs to verify if the data are correct. Ana must also disclose the square meters of her home and other information such as the names and personal identification numbers of her children who live with her. The library employee reassures Ana by saying, "great, let's take a look at the next question!" […]. During the application, Ana needs to attach her rental contract. She then opens her Gmail on the library's laptop. When Ana finds her contract, the librarian asks for permission to download the document to the library's laptop. He promises to delete it later. He then quickly helps her attach the file to the online application. Each step of the way, the library employee describes what he is doing, and the interpreter translates accordingly. Ana also asks questions when she is in doubt. In the process of applying for housing subsidies and going through the form, the system asks for her son's online signature and the disclosure of his income. Ana explains her son is over 18 years old. The library employee explains to Ana, through the interpreter, that her son must sign the application and disclose his income for Ana to be able to complete the application. As Ana's son is not present at the library, Ana gets nervous and decides to call her son. He does not reply. Ana tries to text him while the library employee and interpreter wait patiently in silence. In the meantime, the library employee reviews the application. After a couple of minutes, Ana receives a message from her son. Ana explains that her son has logged into the application, disclosed his income, and signed the application digitally with his NemID. After some minutes, Ana and the library employee browse through the application and the library employee asks her to press send. Then he explains to Ana she will be notified via Digital Post once the application is reviewed. The interpreter on the phone says goodbye to the library employee and wishes Ana good luck. We spent approx. 40 min together. (Fieldnote, June 2021).

Through this ethnographic fieldnote, we follow a situation in which design decisions materialize as constraints and collective resistance. Ana, her son, the library employee, and the interpreter, support each other to complete the application. Within the space of *Everyday Counseling*, we observe different examples of *autonomy alliances* that promote Ana's self-determination, self-governance, and self-authorization, despite the limitations of the online form that does not meet her needs and automatically collects data about her. Ana and her helpers collectively reconfigure the application from being intended as a screen-based service, to being a service based on social relations of recognition. Instead of problematizing Ana's language skills, *Everyday Counseling* problematizes the online form as insufficient to meet Ana's communication needs. In this way, promoting Ana's self-governance, to take decisions that are her own, in her language, and through informed consent.

Ana, the library employee, and the interpreter exemplify different care relations. These are noticeable through small gestures, such as waiting patiently while Ana tries to communicate with her son on the phone or by anticipating what the online form will ask her. Care is enacted when the library employee articulates aloud what he is doing, while asking for consent and having the interpreter translate what he is saying. Through these collaborative practices, Ana and her helpers enact subtle *digital care practices* in which Ana is supported in providing consent and modifying data that are collected about her within the possibilities of different digital interfaces.

When reflecting on the online form's default language, small design decisions can ration who benefits and who is constrained by an online application that is necessary to access welfare services. As Sasha Costanza-Chock notes [14], default language settings are important design choices that privilege certain groups over others. Non-native speakers, of different backgrounds, continue to be problematized in Denmark as "digitally challenged" by virtue of not speaking Danish well enough [12]. However, we argue, the work of the library reformulates "being digitally challenged" as a result of digital infrastructures that fail to meet citizens' diverse needs.

7 Subverting Individualistic Ideals of Citizens and Fostering Equity

As Hjelholt and Schou unfold in the Danish context [26], policy discourses influenced by neoliberal values in recent digital reforms have constructed ideas of citizenship based on self-responsibility, individual autonomy, and citizen homogeneity. As we have learned through the work of one Danish public library, these dominant discourses have materialized in digital infrastructures that erase citizens' diversity and do not meet the needs of citizens visiting the library. Furthermore, design decisions in digitalized versions of welfare provision enable and constrain citizens' data rights and access to welfare benefits. When digital inclusion solely focuses on honing people's skills, and the authorities and companies making digital infrastructures are not held accountable for their design choices, citizens can experience rights violations, and dire financial and emotional consequences. As critical disability scholars continue to voice, discriminatory values and attitudes in technology development reproduce social inequalities and stigma [27]. For this reason, it is increasingly important to trace how digital inequalities and social inequalities configure each other [28] and impact people's self-determination, self-governance and self-authorization.

The library, as a site to explore these dimensions of autonomy, unveils different ways in which digital welfare services can be repurposed and supplemented in meaningful ways. However, our study indicates library employees are not powerful enough to finance their activities in isolation or influence the design of mandatory digital infrastructures on a national scale. For this reason, it is important to reflect on wider systemic inequalities and political decisions that govern how citizens can exercise their rights and easily claim welfare benefits.

8 Conclusion

Through Catriona Mackenzie's multidimensional analysis of autonomy and ethnographic materials generated at a Danish public library, we have described how citizens and library employees attempt to subvert autonomy-undermining online applications through *autonomy alliances* and *data care practices*. These grounded concepts help us make sense of collective efforts tackling inaccessible and mandatory digital infrastructures. In providing qualitative detail to situated practices at one Danish public library, we draw attention to local initiatives that can help us reformulate the questions we ask and the values we embed in the digitalization of welfare provision and digital inclusion projects. Importantly, whilst local efforts can compensate for discriminatory design, future research should explore more directly how public authorities can be held accountable for political and design choices gatekeeping universal welfare benefits. Drawing on social justice orientations to design [14, 15, 29], we believe it is increasingly important to ask: What organizational and design choices constrain certain people from experiencing the benefits that digitalization promises? And how might we repair such choices collectively so that digitalization fosters equitable relations and addresses people's differences, interdependence, and liberties?

Acknowledgements. We are grateful to the citizens, library employees, and their collaborators who participated in the study and welcomed the first author to the library. We are thankful to Cæcilie Sloth Laursen who participated in a study group concerned with public sector digitalization, care, and data practices. We thank members of the Technologies in Practice group and the first author's main supervisor, Brit Ross Winthereik, for conversations about the library's work. We also thank our anonymous HCC reviewers for their generous feedback. Finally, we thank Nordforsk for funding the first author's PhD project, as part of the Nordic collaboration Infrastructures for Partially Digital Citizens: Supporting Informal Welfare Work in the Digitized State (nr. 100742).

References

1. Schou, J., Hjelholt, M.: Digital citizenship and neoliberalization: governing digital citizens in Denmark. Citizsh. Stud. **22**, 507–522 (2018). https://doi.org/10.1080/13621025.2018.147 7920
2. Morris, A., Coles-Kemp, L., Jones, W.: Digitalized welfare: systems for both seeing and working with mess. In: 12th ACM Conference on Web Science Companion, pp. 26–31. Association for Computing Machinery, NY (2020). https://doi.org/10.1145/3394332.3402825
3. Lewthwaite, S., James, A.: Accessible at last? What do new European digital accessibility laws mean for disabled people in the UK? Disabil. Soc. **35**, 1360–1365 (2020). https://doi.org/10.1080/09687599.2020.1717446
4. Pors, A.S.: Becoming digital – passages to service in the digitized bureaucracy. J. Organ. Ethnogr. **4**, 177–192 (2015). https://doi.org/10.1108/JOE-08-2014-0031
5. Skaarup, S.: The role of domain-skills in bureaucratic service encounters. In: Viale Pereira, G., et al. (eds.) EGOV 2020. LNCS, vol. 12219, pp. 179–196. Springer, Cham (2020). https://doi.org/10.1007/978-3-030-57599-1_14
6. Schou, J., Pors, A.S.: Digital by default? A qualitative study of exclusion in digitalized welfare. Soc. Policy Adm. **53**, 464–477 (2018). https://doi.org/10.1111/spol.12470

7. Holten Møller, N.L., Fitzpatrick, G., Le Dantec, C.A.: Assembling the case: citizens' strategies for exercising authority and personal autonomy in social welfare. Proc. ACM Hum. Comput. Interact. **3**, 1–21 (2019). https://doi.org/10.1145/3361125

8. Jørgensen, R.F.: Data and rights in the digital welfare state: the case of Denmark. Inf. Commun. Soc. **0**, 1–16 (2021). https://doi.org/10.1080/1369118X.2021.1934069

9. Ruppert, E., Scheel, S. (eds.): Data Practices: Making Up a European People. Goldsmiths Press, S.l. (2021)

10. Mackenzie, C.: Feminist innovation in philosophy: relational autonomy and social justice. Womens Stud. Int. Forum **72**, 144–151 (2019). https://doi.org/10.1016/j.wsif.2018.05.003

11. van der Velden, M., Bratteteig, T., Finken, S., Mörtberg, C.: Autonomy and automation in an information society for all. In: Information Research in Scandinavia (IRIS), vol. 32, pp. 9–12. Molde, Norway (2009)

12. Agency for Digitization, Local Government Denmark: Digital inklusion i det digitaliserede samfund (2021)

13. Struve Nielsen, P.: Alle skal have ret og adgang til egne penge. https://www.borgerforslag.dk/se-og-stoet-forslag/?Id=FT-07624. Accessed 11 Aug 2021

14. Costanza-Chock, S.: Design Justice: Community-Led Practices to Build the Worlds We Need. The MIT Press, Cambridge (2020)

15. Hamraie, A.: Designing collective access: a feminist disability theory of universal design. Disabil. Stud. Q. **33** (2013). https://doi.org/10.18061/dsq.v33i4.3871

16. Mackenzie, C.: Three dimensions of autonomy: a relational analysis. In: Autonomy, Oppression, and Gender. Oxford University Press, New York (2014). https://doi.org/10.1093/acprof:oso/9780199969104.003.0002

17. Bowen, G.A.: Grounded theory and sensitizing concepts. Int. J. Qual. Methods **5**, 12–23 (2006). https://doi.org/10.1177/160940690600500304

18. Gottrup, R., Møller, M.H.: Borgerservice og offentlige digitale løsninger på bibliotekerne: Retlige og biblioteksfaglige udfordringer i vejledningen. Nordisk Tidsskrift for Informationsvidenskab og Kulturformidling **5**, 21–38 (2016). https://doi.org/10.7146/ntik.v5i3.25787

19. Faye Jacobsen, A.: Digital Kommunikation i kommunerne. The Danish Institute for Human Rights (2017)

20. Stentoft, D.: Det er de digitale løsninger, der er inkompetente – ikke borgeren. https://pro.ing.dk/digitech/holdning/det-er-de-digitale-loesninger-der-er-inkompetente-ikke-borgeren. Accessed 31 Mar 2022

21. Blomberg, J., Karasti, H.: Reflections on 25 years of ethnography in CSCW. Comput. Support. Coop. Work **22**(4–6), 373–423 (2013). https://doi.org/10.1007/s10606-012-9183-1

22. Hammersley, M., Atkinson, P.: Ethnography: Principles in Practice. Routledge, London (2007)

23. Emerson, R.M.: Writing Ethnographic Fieldnotes. University of Chicago Press, Chicago (2011)

24. Morse, J.M., Stern, P.N., Corbin, J., Bowers, B., Clarke, A.E., Charmaz, K.: Developing Grounded Theory: The Second Generation. Routledge, Walnut Creek (2009)

25. Hall, J.A., Korsgaard, O., Pedersen, O.K.: Building the Nation: N.F.S. Grundtvig and Danish National Identity. Kingston, Montreal, Ithaca (2015)

26. Schou, J., Hjelholt, M.: Digitalizing the welfare state: citizenship discourses in Danish digitalization strategies from 2002 to 2015. Crit. Policy Stud. **13**, 3–22 (2019). https://doi.org/10.1080/19460171.2017.1333441

27. Shew, A.: Ableism, technoableism, and future AI. IEEE Technol. Soc. Mag. **39**, 40–85 (2020). https://doi.org/10.1109/MTS.2020.2967492

28. Zheng, Y., Walsham, G.: Inequality of what? An intersectional approach to digital inequality under Covid-19. Inf. Organ. **31**, 100341 (2021). https://doi.org/10.1016/j.infoandorg.2021.100341

29. Dombrowski, L., Harmon, E., Fox, S.: Social justice-oriented interaction design: outlining key design strategies and commitments. In: Proceedings of the 2016 ACM Conference on Designing Interactive Systems, pp. 656–671. Association for Computing Machinery, NY (2016). https://doi.org/10.1145/2901790.2901861

An Analysis Between SNS and Social Capital Types in Japan

Jay Kishigami[1]([⊠]), Shigenori Ohashi[2], Noritaka Maeda[1], Shigeru Fujimura[2], and Atsushi Nakadaira[2]

[1] Keio University, Tokyo, Japan
jay@kishigami.net, katarino@gj9.so-net.ne.jp
[2] NTT Social Informatics Laboratories, Tokyo, Japan
{shigenori.ohashi.ur,shigeru.fujimura.wg,
atsushi.nakadaira.hy}@hco.ntt.co.jp

Abstract. Social capital is expected as a concept to evaluate the potential of autonomous cooperative behavior of a person in a group. We aim to analyze the relationship between individuals and group and their conditions from the viewpoint of social capital and establish an intervention method that leads to well-being in a group of various sizes. We assume that individual's type of social capital can appear in the behavior on Twitter. We report the results of a questionnaire survey. The questionnaire survey suggested that the types of social capital that are bonding and bridging may cause differences in behavior on Twitter, especially in the types of tweets that respond.

Keywords: Social capital · SNS · Bonding · Bridging

1 Introduction

In the short period of time since the start of mobile communication services, the means of interaction between people via networks has been changing rapidly. What started as pager-centered one-way communication has now evolved into SNS-centered communication with the spread of smartphones [1]. Changes in the means of communication have enabled not only the communication of "business" with distant parties, but also the communication of emotions such as enjoyment and empathy. Recently, the use of virtual spaces has been attracting attention, and the evolution of means of interaction is expected to continue in the future. In addition, the use of virtual space is also attracting attention, and it is expected that the means of exchange will continue to evolve in the future.

Although the term "social capital" itself has been used by various people since the beginning of the 19th century, in 1993, Putnam wrote in "making democracy work" [2] that "social capital is the ability to increase social efficiency by stimulating cooperative behavior. Since then, the concept has been widely used. It is often replaced by the

D. Kreps et al. (Eds.): HCC 2022, IFIP AICT 656, pp. 58–66, 2022.
https://doi.org/10.1007/978-3-031-15688-5_6

proposition of how each person should relate to other people and society in order to enhance social life.

Social capital, which is explained as a way to avoid the "tragedy of the commons," in which the efficiency of land use is reduced when many people act selfishly on the land they share, is a concept that should be reevaluated in the unprecedented situation brought about by COVID-19. We have analyzed the current situation and how information can contribute to the situation brought about by COVID-19 and the future. In Japan, in particular, we have been experiencing major environmentally critical situations due to disasters, but the critical difference between this situation and the past is that we are dealing with a situation in which the Internet has ensured the acceptability of information.

The results of examining the degree of prosperity of each country from 12 perspectives: safety and security, individual freedom, governance of power, social capital, investment environment, corporate environment, market access and infrastructure, quality of economic system, living environment, health, education, and natural environment have been investigated [3]. This report indicated that Japan is ranked 19th in the world, but only social capital belongs to the lowest group, 143rd in the world. This must be a shocking result. This is what prompted us to start this research.

Social networks, which are generated from connections between people, are thought to bring benefits to individuals and groups as well as physical and human capital. They have been conceptualized as social capital and have attracted attention in various fields such as sociology, economics, and welfare [4–7]. The definition has been proposed variously. For example, Coleman (1988) [8] proposed that social capital is defined by its function, and that there are two common elements. One is that all social capital has an aspect of social structure. The other is that all social capital promotes some actions of the actors within the structure. In other words, it is contained within the structure of relationships between actors, and is included in the purpose and purpose of the actors Putnam (2000) [9] defines social capital as "social networks and their associated. Although there are various definitions of social capital, social networks of people and people share some value and function in common.

Putnam (2000) also took up the concepts of bonding and bridging as the most important distinction between social capital. Bonding social capital has an inward orientation, stabilizes specific reciprocity, and strengthens solidarity. In contrast, bridging social capital has an outward orientation and strengthens connections and communication with external resources. Most groups and the individuals who make up them have two aspects of these social capital.

The development of various means of interaction through networks, described above, can be incorporated into people's daily lives, facilitating interaction with friends, family, and colleagues, and increasing these social capital [10]. On the other hand, it is also necessary to understand that there are people who do not benefit from the development of means of exchange. In Japan, following the United Kingdom, the Minister for Solitude has been established, and efforts are being made to eliminate social loneliness and isolation [11]. Even if means of exchange increase, if connections cannot be formed, maintained, and utilized using those means, they may not lead to connections, but to divisions and isolation. It will be necessary to find an appropriate balance between groups of people while taking into consideration the characteristics of bonding and bridging social capital, and to consider intervention methods as necessary.

Our goal is to assess the state of people in groups of various sizes and to establish interventions that lead to wellbeing. The enhancement of the means of interaction through the Internet will continue to support the change from traditional communities based on locality to those centered on networked individuals [10].

In this paper, we report the results of a basic survey on the relationship between cognitive social capital and information sources, and the relationship between cognitive social capital and behavior on Twitter.

The structure of this paper is as follows: Sect. 2 introduces existing research on measuring online social capital; Sect. 3 introduces the methods and results of a basic survey on the relationship between cognitive social capital and behavior on Twitter; Sect. 4 discusses the results of the survey; and Sect. 5 provides future plans and summaries.

2 Internet Social Capital Scales

Social-related capital is a multifaceted concept, and various measures have been devised to measure it. Focusing on the social-related capital of a group, there are measures that use indicators obtained by processing statistical data on various community activities [9, 12], measures that create and analyze indicators through questionnaire surveys [13], and measures that focus on the social-related capital of an individual and analyze the social networks of each individual, such as neighbors, friends, and relatives, from the viewpoints of closeness of relationships, social standpoints, and support that can be obtained [14–16]. Methods have also been devised to estimate social-related capital by distinguishing it into bonding and bridging types.

In recent years, SNS and online information dissemination have become widely used, and the resources available to each individual are no longer limited to direct acquaintances. To investigate the impact of the Internet on social capital, Williams (2006) [17] created the Internet Social Capital Scales (ISCS), which measures bonding and bridging social capital in both online and offline contexts. ISCS measures each individual's cognitive social capital by a group of similarly worded questions online and offline. Ellison et al. (2007) [19], referring to Williams (2006), proposed social capital of the relationship maintenance type in addition to the bonding type and the bridging type, focusing on the extent to which old acquaintances and friendships can be maintained. (2007) conducted a survey using ISCS, including the relationship maintenance type, and pointed out the strong relationship between Facebook use and social capital. In particular, it was pointed out that individuals with low life satisfaction and low self-esteem may have higher social capital as a bridge by using Facebook than individuals with high life satisfaction and self-esteem. Hofer and Aubert (2013) [20] investigated the relationship between Twitter use and social capital as an online bonding type and a bridging type. We examined the relationship between the number of followers and social capital as well as the number of followers and the bridging type company.

Studies using ISCS have shown that there are different characteristics of social capital between bridging and bonding types, and that there are different relationships between SNS usage attitudes.

Some argue that the bonding and bridging type social capital measures derived from Williams (2006) do not reflect actual social capital [18], but there are many reports that measure different aspects of bonding and bridging type social capital measures derived from Williams (2006). This paper also uses the measures derived from Williams (2006).

In the next section, we will explain our basic research on the types of social capital and the differences in trust in information sources, including SNS, and responses to information on Twitter.

3 Research on the Relationship Between Social Capital and Twitter Behavior

3.1 Details of the Investigation

In order to investigate the relationship between social capital, trust in information sources including SNS, and behavior on Twitter, a questionnaire was used. For the recognition of bonding and bridging social capital, the top three items with the highest factor loadings corresponding to the online bonding and bridging types which were developed by Williams (2006) were translated into Japanese and used as a scale. The questions were answered on a 5-point scale from "Not at all agree" to "Strongly agree." In response to the question, "How much do you trust information from the following channels in order to know the general information that you are talking about?" four routes were used: newspapers, television, social networking services "From a friend I know first-hand (Whether by face-to-face, telephone, SNS, etc.)", and social networking services (except for information from direct friends). The response items were classified into four categories, ranging from "not at all" to "fully trust."

In regard to Twitter's actions, we asked for the possibility of each action, along with approval or disapproval, for seven examples of fictitious tweets, as six types: likes, positive replies, negative replies, retweets, quoted retweets with positive comments, and quoted retweets with negative comments. We also asked for the possibility of each action if the attribute of the person who posted the tweets was added to the conditions of "if he/she met someone on the Internet" and "if he/she knew someone in real life." We created seven examples of fictitious tweets based on actual tweets and made them fictitious in addition to the contents of tweets such as account names and icons.

Fictional Tweet Example 1 is a tweet from a mother who has a child, in which she expresses her joy at the consideration of the other person when she talks with her friend in the park. Fictional Tweet Example 2 is a tweet from a healthcare worker who is busy with the coronavirus and asks for a relaxing stay at home to reduce the number of infected people. Fictional Tweet Example 3 is a tweet criticizing a person who links GoTo's policies to the spread of the coronavirus. Fictional Tweet Example 4 is a tweet criticizing people who say "corona is just a cold" as being treated as a cult. Example 5 is a tweet criticizing people who say there is no safety problem because many people die from vaccination overseas. Example 6 is a tweet stating the safety of mRNA vaccines and stating that smoking is riskier. Example 6 is a tweet containing a link (fictitious) to an underlying Web page. Example 7 is a tweet appealing for the right to choose a vaccine. The tweet is coming from the fact that there are differences inside reactions depending on the type of vaccine.

3.2 Survey Method

A total of 1369 responses were received over a 3-day period from March 2, 2021. Of the 1369 responses, 758 were males and 611 were females. In the age group, 182 were males in their 20s and younger, 254 were females in their 30s, 332 were males in their 40s, 333 were males in their 50s, and 268 were females in their 60s.

The primary objective of this survey was to determine the subjective meanings that users ascribe to the information they receive and act upon on social networking sites. For this reason, we intentionally asked about subjective awareness. After confirming certain trends through this process, we believe it is possible to argue the significance of examining the relationship with composite data, such as actual behavior on SNSs.

The survey was conducted by screening about 1,400 respondents from a panel of 120,000 people, equalizing age, gender, and other factors, and then asking them questions. Since the survey is conducted via the Internet with incentives, the response rate is extremely high, and responses can usually be obtained in one or two days.

The analysis was performed using jamovi [21], and the correlation calculation was performed by calculating the partial correlation [22] as well as the normal correlation.

3.3 Survey Results

Table 1 shows the results of factor analysis of the Social Relational Capital Scale, the coefficients of each factor, and the correlation coefficients between the factors. We used the ordinary least squares (unweighted least squares) to extract the factors from the Oblimin rotated factor pattern matrix. The two factors were interpreted as the online bridging factor and the online binding factor, respectively, following previous studies. The three questions of the online bridging factor and the online binding factor were used as the measures of each social relationship capital. When the scale scores were calculated, the results were M = 2.71, SD = 1.00 for the online bridging factor, and M = 2.35, SD = 0.93 for the online binding factor.

Table 2 shows the results of the analysis of the correlation between the trust in information sources and the type of social capital. Although the correlation coefficient data obtained were relatively small, the analysis focused on significance levels of 1%. The responses for SNS (except for information from friends with direct knowledge) showed a significant correlation with both the online bridging type and the online bonding type, while the responses for newspaper and TV showed no significant correlation with both the online bridging type and the online bonding type. The responses for "From a friend I know firsthand (Whether by face-to-face, telephone, SNS, etc.)" showed different results for the online bridging type and the online bonding type, with a significant correlation only with the online bridging type.

This paper presents the results of analyzing the correlation between actions and social capital types for the seven examples of tweets.

The behaviors of "likes" were analyzed. The results are shown in Table 3. When analyzed at a significance level of 1%, the online bonding type showed a correlation with tweets 3, 4 and 5. On the other hand, the correlation of the online bridging type shows relatively high values for Tweet Examples 1, 2, 6, and 7, but not for Tweet Examples 3, 4, and 5. Furthermore, the correlation tended to be higher when conditions for online and real acquaintance were established.

Table 1. Factor analysis of social capital scale. Factor analysis results (least squares method, Oblimin rotation, N = 1369)

Questionnaire	1st factor	2nd factor	Commonality
Socializing on the Internet makes me want to try new things	**0.68**	0.19	0.68
Socializing on the Internet has made me curious about the rest of the world	**1.00**	−0.07	0.90
Socializing on the Internet makes me feel more connected to the larger world	**0.77**	0.11	0.72
There are people on the Internet that I can trust to help me with my problem	0.19	**0.67**	0.67
There are people on the Internet that you can ask for advice when making important decisions	−0.09	**0.90**	0.70
Those who associate with me on the Internet will enhance my reputation	0.13	**0.71**	0.65

Table 2. Correlation between trust in information sources and social capital type. Partial correlations (using Spearman's correlation coefficient) of each social capital excluding each other's influence are described. (correlation coefficient/significant probability)

Information source	Bridging	Bonding
Newspaper	0.04/0.105	−0.01/0.600
TV	0.05/0.91	−0.01/0.663
From a friend who knows firsthand	**0.13/<0.001**	0.02/0.369
SNS, exclude the above friend	**0.14/<0.001**	**0.14/<0.001**

4 Discussion

According to the results of factor analysis (Table 1), there is a high correlation between bridging and bonding social capital, and both are strongly related. The results shown in Table 2 indicate that the accumulation of online social capital, regardless of whether it is a bonding or a bridging type, is related to a sense of trust in information on SNS. Similarly, in Table 2, the relationship between trust in information from "friends with direct knowledge" differs between the bonding social capital and the bridging social capital. Existing research [23], which has analyzed the differences between the bonding and the bridging type, uses an index for ties with family and relatives for the bonding social capital, and an index for ties with friends for the bridging social capital, which is consistent with existing research.

The results of the analysis in Table 3 indicate that there is a difference between the online bridging type and the online bonding type in the number of tweets that respond.

Table 3. Correlation between "likes" and social capital type for seven fictional tweet examples. Correlation coefficient and significant probability are described according to the order of "normal/online acquaintances/real friend"

Tweet example	Online bridging correlation coeff	Online bridging significant probability *np: <0.001	Online bonding correlation coeff	Online bonding significant probability *np: <0.001
1	**.11/.20/.22**	np/np/np	.12/.03/−.01	np/.287/.800
2	**.15/.18/.20**	np/np/np	.08/.07/.01	.003/.015/.808
3	.02/.05/.06	.402/.095/.019	**.19/.17/.15**	np/np/np
4	−.03/−.00/−.01	.293/.991/.833	**.21/.20/.19**	np/np/np
5	−.04/−.03/−.03	.109/.260/.277	**.21/.21/.20**	np/np/np
6	**.09/.08/.09**	np/.002/.001	**.13/.14/.12**	np/np/np
7	**.12/.13/.13**	np/np/np	**.13/.11/.10**	np/np/np

The online bonding type seems to tend to "like" without distinguishing the target, compared to the online bridging type. The bonding type is considered to understand and respond to the content of tweets that contain criticism, because it creates a clear boundary between us and them and has a mechanism that encourages commitment to us while generating a certain degree of exclusivity [7]. The bridging type breaks down the boundary between the inside and outside, and connects other groups to each other, which are relatively highly correlated with those of the bridging type, request the sharing of happy feelings and the cooperation of each person to reduce the number of infected people, making it difficult to imagine groups that would be directly disadvantaged. By extracting differences in responses to tweets, it is possible to estimate cognitive social capital.

Conversely, tweets that respond to the online bonding type, tweets that respond to the online bridging type, and both types of social capital might be able to estimate the influence and quality of information from different trends in information propagation.

By further testing these hypotheses, we believe that cognitive social capital can be estimated from social networking services and other activities, leading to time-series changes in the group and assessment of its status. In the case of actual Twitter analysis, liking is a behavior that is likely to be controversial. We believe that a method of analysis focusing on liking is necessary.

5 Summary

To estimate the type of cognitive social capital of everyone from observable data, we conducted a basic study using a questionnaire on the relationship between cognitive social capital and behavior on Twitter. The results of the basic study suggested that differences in cognitive social capital might cause differences in behavior on Twitter. Bonding social capital tends to "like" without distinguishing between subjects, or to respond to content of tweets that include criticism. On the other hand, bridging social capital tends to be unresponsive to content of tweets that include criticism. Social relations capital tended to respond to tweets that did not disadvantage a particular population.

In the future, it will be necessary to verify whether it is possible to estimate social capital using data on actual SNS.

References

1. The Ministry of Internal Affairs and Communications: A Study on the Impact of Digitization on Lifestyle and Workstyles. https://www.soumu.go.jp/johotsusintokei/linkdata/r01_02_hou koku.pdf. Accessed 06 Jan 2022
2. Putnum, R.D.: Making Democracy Work: Civic Traditions in Modern Italy. Princeton University Press, Princeton (1993)
3. https://www.prosperity.com/. Accessed 29 Jan 2022
4. Scrivens, K., Smith, C.: Four interpretations of social capital: an agenda for measurement. OECD Statistics Working Papers, OECD Publishing (2013)
5. Konno, N.: Wisdom of a small, happy country The Netherlands: an innovation society unmatched by disaster, PHP Shinsho (2012). (in Japanese)
6. Ito, M.: Social Capital's Economic Analysis 1: Will "Connections" Revitalize Communities? Keio University Press (2018). (in Japanese)
7. Misumi, K.: Social Relations Capital Theory Integration Challenge Minerva Shobo (2013). (in Japanese)
8. Coleman, J.S.: Social capital in the creation of human capital. Am. J. Sociol. **94**, S95–S120 (1988)
9. Putnam, R.D.: Boling Alone - The Collapse and Revitalization of the American Community. Kashiwa Shobo (2006). (in Japanese translated by Y. Shibauchi)
10. Chambers, D., Tsuji, D., Kubota, H., (translation), Sonoko, T., (translation), Fujita, T., (translation): A society of friendship without a new connection in Katanization, Iwanami Shoten (2015). (in Japanese)
11. Cabinet Secretariat: Priority Policy Program on Solitude and Isolation. https://www.cas.go. jp/jp/seisaku/jutenkeikaku/jutenkeikaku.htm. Accessed 11 Jan 2022 (in Japanese)
12. Yamauchi, N.: A trial of measuring regional differences using the citizen activity index "ESP" economic planning association, pp. 40–44 (2003). (in Japanese)
13. Cabinet Office: Social capital: rich relationships and the city for a virtuous cycle of civil activities. https://www.npo-homepage.go.jp/toukei/2009izen-chousa/2002social-capital. Accessed 14 Jan 2022 (in Japanese)
14. Burt, R.S.: Network items and the general social survey. Soc. Netw. **6**(4), 293–339 (1984)
15. Lin, N., Dumin, M.: Access to occupations through social ties. Soc. Netw. **8**(4), 365–385 (1986)
16. Van Der Gaag, M., Snijders, T.A.: The Resource Generator: social capital quantification with concrete items. Soc. Netw. **27**(1), 1–29 (2005)
17. Williams, D.: On and off the 'Net: scales for social capital in an online era. J. Comput.-Mediat. Commun. **11**(2), 593–628 (2006)
18. Ryan, S., Junker, B.W.: The development and testing of an instrument to measure youth social capital in the domain of postsecondary transitions. Youth Soc. **51**(2), 170–192 (2019)
19. Ellison, N.B., Steinfield, C., Lampe, C.: The benefits of Facebook "friends:" social capital and college students' use of online social network sites. J. Comput.-Mediat. Commun. **12**(4), 1143–1168 (2007)
20. Hofer, M., Aubert, V.: Perceived bridging and bonding social capital on Twitter: differentiating between followers and followees. Comput. Hum. Behav. **29**(6), 2134–2142 (2013)

21. The jamovi project: jamovi (Version 2.2) [Computer Software]. https://www.jamovi.org. Accessed 12 Jan 2022
22. Kim, S.: ppcor: Partial and Semi-Partial (Part) Correlation [R package]. https://cran.r-project.org/package=ppcor. Accessed 12 Jan 2022
23. JRI: Social Capital and Policy in Japan - JRI 2007 National Survey Results Report, JRI (2008). (in Japanese)

Possible Utilization of Personal Data and Medical Care in Japan, Focusing on Japan's Act on Anonymously Processed Medical Information to Contribute to Medical Research and Development

Mayu Terada[1,2](✉)

[1] International Christian University, 3-10-2 Osawa Mitaka, Tokyo 181-0015, Japan
tmayu@icu.ac.jp
[2] RIKEN AIP, Nihonbashi 1-Chome Mitsui Building, 15th Floor, 1-4-1 Nihonbashi, Chuo-ku, Tokyo 103-0027, Japan

Abstract. In Japan, there is no special law for the comprehensive utilization of personal data in the medical field, and a comprehensive legal system has been lacking for decades. This paper examines the background and issues of the cancer registration law specific to cancer and the legal structure of medical information in Japan and points out that one of the problems that has become clear in dealing with COVID-19 is the difficulty of handling the complicated system of anonymously processed information and the difficulty of using it for the purpose. The report also points out that the Medical Big Data Law, which is also based on the premise of anonymous use, has a complex mechanism in addition to that of the Personal Information Protection Law. A system to certify certification bodies and other protection measures will be introduced yesterday, but before examining the specifics of anonymization, it is necessary to establish a fundamental system that enables the use of more basic information in a way that can be easily understood by healthcare professionals. In conclusion, this paper points out that in the future, while protecting personal information, it will be useful to reorganize it into a special law that is easier to understand from a comprehensive point of view, and to construct a law that makes medical information available to contribute to medical research and development, to reduce the increase in medical costs.

Keywords: Utilization of personal data · Medical information · Medical big data

Published by Springer Nature Switzerland AG 2022
D. Kreps et al. (Eds.): HCC 2022, IFIP AICT 656, pp. 67–85, 2022.
https://doi.org/10.1007/978-3-031-15688-5_7

1 Introduction

Until now, a comprehensive legal system on the utilization of personal information in the medical field is lacking in Japan[1]. And it is heavily discussed as a problem to hinder the utilization and development of various knowledge of the medical field[2].

In response to COVID-19 (new coronavirus infection), these problems have become apparent because the Japanese medical system and the protection of personal information are insufficient[3]. As will be seen later, Japan is currently collecting various medical information on a request basis, and many points have been raised from the viewpoint of the effectiveness of regulations and the future use of information.

For example, it has been pointed out that there is not enough data to determine the cost of medical care in our country.

Therefore, in this paper, current situation of Japanese law on medical big data including the handling of medical data in an emergency such as COVID-19 is reviewed[4]. Specifically, the current situation in Japan where there have been no regulations on personal information in the medical field is introduced, and the so-called "accreditation body" enacted under the Act on Anonymously Processed Medical Information[5] to contribute to research and development in the medical field is considered. Then, issues related to the development of regulations on the handling of personal information in the medical field in Japan is discussed, while referring to the regulations in Europe and other countries to the extent possible.

2 Current Situation on Privacy Law and Medical Care in Japan

2.1 Personal Data Protection Law

In recent years in Japan, various regulations have been put in place regarding personal information in general, including reorganization into the Personal Information Protection Commission[6]. The Act on the Protection of Personal Information revised in 2015[7], the Act on the Protection of Personal Information Held by Administrative Organs was revised

---

[1] Japan's Kantei (the prime minister's official residence) website, The Healthcare Policy and The New System of Medical R&D, https://www.kantei.go.jp/jp/singi/kenkouiryou/en/pdf/doc1.pdf.

[2] Fumio Shimpo, The revised Japanese Personal Information Protection Act and the utilization of Big Data from Medical Records, Igaku no Ayumi, vol. 259, No. 7, at 787–791. See also, George Shishido, 'Personal Information Protection Law and Privacy: For the Cross-linking of Medical Affairs Law and Information Law (Records of the 48 Annual Meeting of the Medical Affairs Law Society) – (Symposium Frontier of Medical Information), Medical Law (34), at 87–96, (2019).

[3] Shimpo, above note 2, at 790–791.

[4] Shimpo, above note 2, at 789–791.

[5] It is also described a Next Generation Medical Infrastructure Bill.

[6] Kaori Ishii, Present and Future of Personal Data Protection Law, Keiso Shobo Publishing, 2017, pp. 443–452.

[7] Ishii, above note 6, pp. 443–452. See also, Kaori Ishii, Masahiro Sogabe, Ryoji Mori ed., Commentar for Personal Information Protection Law, Keiso Shobo publishing, 2021, pp. 654–705.

in 2016[8], and the Act on the Protection of Personal Information Held by Incorporated Administrative Agencies came into full force on May 30, 2017[9]. Plus, major revisions were made in 2019 and 2020, and the 2020 revision is expected to be a major reform of the personal information protection system[10].

In particular, the 2015 revised Personal Information Protection Law in Japan created a new "anonymously processed information" framework. The idea of anonymously processed information is that after personal data is processed to become "anonymously processed information", it can be used with flexibility[11]. However, in the first place, the Act on the Protection of Personal Information requires the handling of medical records (history of illness), results of medical and genetic examinations as equivalent to medical records, health guidance, medical examination and prescription information, etc. in a particularly careful manner, stating that "Special care-required personal information"[12]. Therefore, in the medical field, it has been pointed out that it may not be possible to utilize personal information in the fields of community comprehensive care and home care[13].

The status of anonymous processing has been integrated into pseudonym processing information. However, as will be looked at later, there is no comprehensive legal system regarding how to handle medical information in a special manner, and the handling of medical data is left to the interpretation.

Thus, at Sect. 2.2 and below, a specific example of the Cancer Registration Act, which only specifies data for specific diseases, will be examined as an example for processing medical data.

2.2 Cancer Registration Act

Regarding "cancer" as a specific disease, the "Act on Promotion of Cancer Registration"[14] has been established. Based on this law, the government is aiming to record and maintain databases on cancer and other diseases nationwide.

However, there was a problem that this cancer registration method was for the specific disease of "cancer". In fact, with the law, only information related to "cancer" is recorded and stored in databases for the utilization of personal information to provide medical care by integrating information. As a result, this law only has a database for specific

---

[8] Ishii, above note 6, pp. 443–452.

[9] Ishii, above note 6, pp. 443–452.

[10] Shizuo Fujiwara, George Shishido, Background and Future of the 2020 Revision of the Personal Information Protection Law, Jurist 1551, Nov 2020, pp. 14–29., Personal Information Protection Commission website,The revised Personal Information Protection Act of 2021.(Review of the Personal Information Protection System through the Public and Private Sectors) (https://www.ppc.go.jp/personalinfo/minaoshi/).

[11] Tomomi Hioki, Yoichiro Itakura, 'Structure of the Personal Information Protection Law' Shoji Homu Publishing, 2017, p. 104.

[12] Article 2, sentence 3 of Act on Protection of Personal Data, and Article 2 of the Order for the Act on Protection of Personal Data.

[13] Above note 2, Shishido, 'Future and Present of Information Law' at 175.

[14] Act No. 111 of 2013, hereinafter referred to as "Cancer Registration Act.

diseases such as cancer, and it does not contribute to the overall utilization of medical information.

Plus, there was a problem that this cancer registration method was for the specific disease of "cancer". In fact, only information related to "cancer" is recorded and stored in databases for the utilization of personal information to provide medical care by integrating information. After all, this law only has a database for specific diseases such as cancer, and it is not in a situation that contributes to the utilization of overall medical information[15].

3 Background History and Issues of the Cancer Registration Law in Japan

The background and issues of the Cancer Registration Act are discussed below.

The "Cancer Registration Act" was enacted through coordination with various related organizations in order to collect information on the specific disease of cancer, which is the leading cause of death in Japan, and thereby contribute to the improvement of cancer medical care[16].

3.1 Brief Background to the Establishment of the Cancer Registration Law

In Japan, the regional cancer registration as an exception of the personal information protection ordinance was made in each region. In many countries, especially in Europe and the United States, this has created a situation in which regional differences exist in that regional cancer registries are not based on a nationwide legal system, compared with the fact that regional cancer registries were legally established as a basic measure of cancer countermeasures.

As background to the Cancer Registration Act, for example, from around 2005, the "A Study on the Development of a Legal Ethical Environment for Local Cancer Registration" was conducted as part of the Ministry of Health, Labour and Welfare's Third

---

[15] The number one death rate in Japan is "cancer" and statistics show that one in two people will have cancer at least once in their lifetime, so the existence of such a database has its own side.

[16] The purpose of this Act is, in light of the current situation where cancer is a serious problem for the lives and health of the people, such as that cancer is the largest cause of death due to the disease of the people, to improve the quality of medical care for cancer (Refers to the improvement of the quality of cancer medical care and cancer screening (Hereinafter referred to as "Cancer treatment, etc.") and the promotion of cancer prevention. The same shall apply hereinafter.), enhance the provision of information on cancer, medical care for cancer, etc. and prevention of cancer, and implement other cancer measures based on scientific knowledge, in accordance with the purpose of the Basic Act on Cancer Control (Act No. 98 of 2006), by stipulating matters concerning the implementation of the National Cancer Registration and the use, provision, and protection of information pertaining to the implementation of the National Cancer Registration, as well as matters concerning the promotion of in-hospital cancer registration, etc., and stipulating the utilization of information obtained through cancer registration, etc., to promote understanding and analysis of the status of cancer, medical care, outcomes, etc. and other cancer research and studies, thereby contributing to further enhancement of cancer measures.

Comprehensive Research Project on Cancer[17], and in 2007 a proposal was made to the effect that the local cancer registration system should be legislated in order to comprehensively implement the local cancer registration system, not as an exception to the local ordinances on the protection of personal information[18]. Against this background, the Basic Act on Cancer Control Measures was enacted on June 16, 2006[19]. Afterwards, the designation of the cancer medical care cooperation base hospital began to be made based on the idea of cancer fundamental law enacted in 2006. In addition, the Act on the Promotion of Cancer Registration was enacted as a legislature of the Diet in December 2013. This "Cancer Registration Act" was enforced in January 2016[20].

3.2 Overview of the Cancer Registration Act

The purpose of cancer registration is to collect, store, and analyze information on the diagnosis, treatment, and outcomes of cancer patients, to understand the occurrence of cancer and the actual conditions of cancer medical care, and to contribute to the improvement of cancer medical care itself and the formulation and evaluation of cancer countermeasure policies. The Cancer Registration Law defines national cancer registration information, prefectural cancer information, and in-hospital cancer information, and indicates the utilization of information by the national and prefectural governments, hospitals and clinics, researchers, etc., respectively.

The flow of the cancer registration is as follows[21]. (1) Medical information on all cancer patients diagnosed and treated at hospitals and designated clinics is collected and organized for use in national and prefectural cancer control. (2) Complementary registration of patients not included in the notification based on death information from cancer, etc., and patient death information is also registered. (3) The collected information will be used to develop cancer statistics and contribute to the survival rate, number of cases, extent of disease, and secondary prevention of cancer.

---

[17] Group leader was Eiji Maruyama, Professor, Graduate School of Law, Kobe University.

[18] Katsunori Kai, "Regional Cancer Registration Law System and Criminal Regulations: Focusing on Legislative Proposals" Waseda Law Review, Vol. 83, No. 4 (2008), p. 36.

[19] Act No. 98 of June 23, 2006.

[20] Act on Promotion of Cancer Registration (Act No. 111 of December 13, 2013).

[21] Graphic of the website of the Japan Cancer Registration Association "What is cancer registration?".

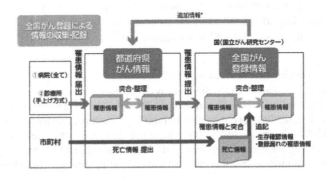

With the enactment of the Cancer Registration Act, it has become more and more recommended that not only the national government but also local governments (especially the prefectures) make use of the data of cancer registration as a framework of the Act, to actively plan and implement cancer countermeasures.

3.3 Limitations of the Cancer Registration Act

The limitation of the Cancer Registration Law is that it is limited to "cancer" as a matter of course. One of the limitations of the Cancer Registration Law is that it cannot be linked to information on diseases other than cancer, so that the medical information database has a defect that it cannot deal with diseases other than cancer, and it cannot deal with complex diseases including cancer.

4   Legal Structure on Medical Information in Japan

Based on the above issues, a bill submitted to the 193rd session of the Diet in 2017 was titled "Draft Law Concerning Anonymously Processed Medical Information to Contribute to Research and Development in the Medical Field[22]" and the purpose of the submission was to "Establishment of regulations for businesses that process medical information anonymously so that specific individuals cannot be identified, and promotion of advanced research and development on health and medical care and creation of new industries through safe and appropriate use of anonymously processed medical information, thereby contributing to the formation of a healthy, longevity society" (See footnote 23). In the following, the history of the examination on the utilization of medical information and the outline of the law are examined.

4.1   Awareness of the Need to Consider Personal Information in the Medical Field

Regarding medical information, the necessity of the utilization of the medical information was recognized for various needs in the field of medical treatment and nursing, that is, for efficient utilization of the insurance system by the related organizations and utilization by the administrative organizations, etc. as well as advance and development of the medical science.

Therefore, the Ministry of Health, Labour and Welfare held the review meeting for utilization and protection of information in the medical field from April to September, 2012, and the "Report on the ideal environment for the utilization and protection of information in the medical field" was summarized[23].

---

[22] Next Generation Medical Infrastructure Bill.

[23] Ministry of Health, Labour and Welfare, Study Group on the Protection of Personal Information at Medical Institutions Report, Report on the Utilization of Information in the Medical and Other Fields and the Establishment of an Environment for Protection, http://www.mhlw.go.jp/stf/shingi/2r9852000002k0gy-att/2r9852000002k0kz.pdf. At page 6–10 of the report, it is analyzed that accumulated anonymously processed data could be utilized in order to contribute to the improvement of medical care that enables the quality of medical service to be improved.

In this review meeting, although it is difficult to say that medical information made personal identification impossible only by mechanically masking personal identification information such as names, etc., the basic direction of the examination of the utilization of personal information in the medical field was discussed, including the discussion that the regulation of anonymization in the medical field should be divided into unlinkable anonymization and linkable anonymization in light of the fact that the provision of medical care, etc. and medical research itself would not be possible if information such as physical characteristics were not available.

4.2 Subsequent Review of Personal Information in the Medical Field

Prior to the examination of the next generation medical infrastructure bill, the following history existed. In other words, with the growing recognition of the importance of building digital infrastructures in the medical, nursing, and health fields, it is necessary to improve the efficiency of medical quality, improve the convenience of citizens and patients, promote research and development, and strengthen industrial competitiveness by building and utilizing information infrastructures in the medical, nursing, and health fields. In response, the "Next Generation Medical ICT Task Force" was established under the Health and Medical Strategy Promotion Headquarters of the Cabinet Secretariat in collaboration with the IT Strategic Headquarters.

After that, the "Next Generation Medical ICT Infrastructure Council" was established by adding related medical groups, related academic societies, and industries, etc. to the members of the task force, and the councils were held in April and December, 2015, and in March, 2016. Among them, working groups such as the Working Group for the Promotion of Standardization of the Collection and Exchange of Digital Data, the Working Group for the Adjustment of Medical Information Handling Systems, the Working Group for the Promotion of the Composition of Digital Data Collection and Utilization Projects, and the Working Group for the Promotion of the Introduction of Next Generation ICT to Medical Care were established. Especially, concerning the utilization of medical information, the summary of the "Working Group for the Coordination of Medical Information Handling Systems of the Next Generation Medical ICT Infrastructure Council" was issued in December 2016[24].

4.3 Utilization of Medical Information and Protection of Personal Information

The aforementioned summary of the "Working Group for the Coordination of Medical Information Handling Systems of the Next Generation Medical ICT Infrastructure Council" at present states the recognition that medical data that can be utilized on a nationwide scale in our country is based on receipt (medical fee schedule) data, which is the input of medical treatment acts (implementation information), and that the utilization of data concerning the results of medical treatment acts (Outcome) is not prepared, and that the data itself is held in a dispersed manner across the country due to the fact that

---

[24] The Working Group for Adjustment of the Medical Information Handling System of the Council for Next-Generation Medical ICT Infrastructure, summarized on December 27, 2016 http://www.soumu.go.jp/main_content/000462278.pdf.

medical institutions are mainly composed of the private sector and the separation of the insurance system.

In addition, as the Personal Information Protection Law was revised, it was analyzed that the burden of costs for the acquisition of personal information based on consent, the processing of data to be anonymized, the construction of systems, etc. increased. This is largely related to the fact that, as mentioned above, information including medical history, etc. was conceptualized as "Special care-required personal information" and as a result, provision to a third party by opt-out was prohibited.

Therefore, in order to appropriately utilize medical information in the future, it is necessary to establish a system that enables individuals and medical institutions to provide medical and other information with peace of mind, while carefully considering the protection of individual rights and interests.

4.4 So-called "Accreditation Body"

The main content of the Medical Big Data Act is that the so-called "accreditation body" system has been established as a new basis to collect clinical trial and inspection data widely, safely manage and anonymize them, and link them to the use for the promotion of drug discovery and research and development utilizing information in the medical field, etc.

In other words, the Act on the Use of Personal Information in Medical Care adopts a system to certify "Anonymously processed medical information preparation business operator" as "Medical Information Handling Business Operators"[25].

Specifically, the aim is to create a system that enables individuals and medical institutions, etc. to provide medical information with peace of mind while giving consideration to the protection of high rights and interests[26].

---

[25] Article8 A person who performs anonymously processed medical information preparation work (limited to juridical persons.) may, upon application, receive approval from the competent minister to the effect that it is recognized that the person is capable of conducting anonymously processed medical information preparation work properly and reliably.The present law provides a framework for the recognition of a so-called recognition organization, but it does not specify in detail what kind of information is collected and how it can be used by the recognition organization. These parts depend on future operation.

[26] Of the provisions of the relevant bills, the following are particularly important is Article 2.The term "anonymously processed medical information" as used in this Act means information about an individual that is obtained by processing medical information so that a specific individual cannot be identified by taking the measures specified in the following items according to the categories of medical information listed in those items and so that the medical information cannot be restored:(i) Medical information falling under Paragraph 1, Item (i): Delete a part of the description contained in the medical information (Including the replacement of a part of the description, etc. with another description, etc. by a method without regularity that can restore the description, etc.).(ii) Medical information falling under Paragraph 1, Item (ii): To delete all of the Individual Identification Codes included in the applicable medical institution (Including replacing the said personal identification code with other descriptions etc. by a method having no regularity capable of restoring the said personal identification code.). See also, Ishii, Sogabe, Mori ed., above note 7, pp. 954–977.

(1) A new system will be established to certify private organizations (= Certified Anonymously Processed Medical Information Producer) that can secure high information security, meet certain standards such as having sufficient anonymization processing technology, and conduct anonymization for the management and utilization of medical information in a secure and reliable manner.

(2) Medical institutions, etc. shall be able to provide medical information to accredited institutions if the person does not refuse to provide such information, and accredited institutions shall anonymize collected information and use it as big data for research and development as well as for medical administration, etc. (The provision of medical information from medical institutions, etc. to certified business operators is optional.)

Based on these systems, the national government is responsible for (1) the national government's responsibility to implement necessary measures and (2) a basic policy to comprehensively and integrally promote measures with regard to anonymously processed medical information to contribute to research and development in the medical field.

4.5 Consideration of the Situation in Japan

In Japan, the accumulation of information on cancer by the Cancer Registration Law and the preparation of some other databases have progressed to some extent. However, the cooperation between databases has not progressed, and how to utilize the databases has not been decided yet. Also, the COVID-19 and diseases other than cancers are not included in the database.

5 Exceptions to the Protection of Personal Information in Research and Development in Europe and Other Countries

The exceptions to the European rules, treatment in the United States, and other national databases are discussed below.

5.1 Exceptions to European Regulations

In Europe (EU), the EU General Data Protection Regulation (General Data Protection Regulation, GDPR) was passed in April 2016[27]. The new data protection rules recognize the right to data portability and other rights of reference in other countries (Article 22 on forgotten rights, etc.). Regarding medical information, Article 89, paragraph (2) allows exceptions when it is used for research and development. That is, as an exception to the new EU Data Protection Regulation, exceptions to protective measures for scientific

---

[27] Article 89 of the Regulation (EU) 2016/679 of the European Parliament and of the Council of 27 April 2016 on the protection of natural persons with regard to the processing of personal data and on the free movement of such data, and repealing Directive 95/46/EC (General Data Protection Regulation).

purposes are allowed, and exceptional treatment is allowed when personal data are handled for scientific or statistical purposes[28].

This regulation allows the EU and its Member States to assert the right of data subjects to scientific research[29] and to be exempt from the right to access and correct their data, to restrict or oppose the processing of their data, and to be informed of their use as patients[30].

It also states that exceptions can be made that require or do not require consent[31]. However, adequate safeguards should be applied to these exceptions, and the EU and its member states require the careful preparation of guidelines and the appropriate use of the data for research that is truly necessary in the application of exceptions to personal data of patients[32].

In this regard, it appears that COVID-19 is regarded as an exception based on this provision.

5.2 HIPAA Privacy Regulations in the United States

In the United States, there is a privacy rule of HIPAA (The Health Insurance Portability and Accountability Act of 1996), and in the privacy rule, the method of anonymization in the form which guarantees that the individual identifiability disappears is not used. Although the Federal Health Insurance Ministry has been criticized for its insufficient protection of privacy in the implementation of these regulations, it can be said that it is rather important to be able to identify patients in clinical practice[33].

5.3 Utilization of Medical Data in Other Foreign Institutions

For example, in U.S.A., the utilization of the database which accumulates enormous medical information such as CMS (Center for Medicare and Medicaid Services)[34] and SUS (Secondary Uses Service)[35] is advancing. Specifically, the SUS website explains that SUS is a single, comprehensive repository for medical data in the UK, enabling various reports and analyses to support the National Health Service (National Health Service) in providing medical services[36].

---

[28] Mayu Terada, Public Law on Advanced Technology and Regulation, Keiso shobo publishing 2020, pp. 46–70. See also, Ishii, Sogabe, Mori ed., above note 7, pp. 954–977.

[29] Paragraph 2 of Article 89.

[30] Paragraph 4 b of Article 14 and paragraph 3 b of Article 17.

[31] Paragraph 4 b of Article 14.

[32] Ibid.

[33] U.S. Department of Health & Human Services, Your Rights Under HIPAA, https://www.hhs.gov/hipaa/for-individuals/guidance-materials-for-consumers/index.html.

[34] https://www.cms.gov/.

[35] https://digital.nhs.uk/services/secondary-uses-service-sus/secondary-uses-services-sus-guidance.

[36] Ibid.

6   Medical Data Collection Relating to COVID-19 and Legal Structure in Japan

In China, the first COVID-19 cases from Wuhan City were reported for the first time on January 16, 2020. Furthermore, from February 1, 2020, COVID-19 10 positive patients were reported on cruise ships, and measures were taken to deal with the spread of infection.

In order to respond to COVID-19, a bill to partially revise the Act on Special Measures Concerning Countermeasures against Novel Influenza was approved by the Cabinet on March 10, 2020, and was passed and promulgated on the 13th of the same month.

This is an expansion of the special law, which was previously a law against H1N1 influenza, to COVID-19. Therefore, the COVID-19 is based on the Act on Special Measures Concerning Countermeasures against Novel Influenza (Act No. 31 of 2012, hereinafter referred to as "new flu law".). This was regarded as "New strains of influenza". In addition, the government ordinance (Cabinet Order No. 11 of 2020) that new type coronavirus infectious disease is decided as a designated infectious disease, etc. has been instituted. In addition, various provisions in the Act on Prevention of Infectious Diseases and Medical Care for Patients with Infectious Diseases (Act No. 104 of 1998, hereinafter referred to as "Infectious Disease Law".) now apply to COVID-19. These revisions also made it possible to take further measures, such as restricting the entry of buildings and requesting people to refrain from going out[37].

Furthermore, on March 26, 2020, the Minister of Health, Labour and Welfare reported to the Prime Minister that there was a high risk of the spread of COVID-19 based on Article 14 of the New Influenza Act, which is applied by replacing certain terms pursuant to Article 1–2, paragraphs (1) and (2) of the Supplementary Provisions of the New Influenza Act, because "In Japan, there have been sporadic outbreaks in areas where the number of patients with unknown routes of infection has increased, and infection has spread in some areas." On the same day, the Government established a government task force based on Article 15, paragraph (1) of the same Act, and on March 28 of the same year, the basic action policy for measures against the New Coronavirus Infection was established. On April 7, 2020, the Director-General of the Headquarters for Countermeasures for Novel Coronavirus Infection declared a state of emergency under Article 32, paragraph (1) of said Act (Until May 6 of the same year Saitama Prefecture, Chiba Prefecture, Tokyo Metropolis, Kanagawa Prefecture, Osaka Prefecture, Hyogo Prefecture and Fukuoka Prefecture). In addition, all prefectures were subject to emergency measures on April 16 of the same year[38].

In order to prevent the spread of COVID-19, the government has the basic recognition that "It is important to further promote the avoidance of "three dense" (Author's Note: "closed" "dense" "closely") and to contain the occurrence of clusters (The population in

---

[37] Cabinet Order enacted on January 28, 2020, Cabinet decision on revision of entry restriction, etc. decided on March 26, 2020.

[38] Basic Policy for Countermeasures against Novel Coronavirus Infection (March 28, 2020 (Changed on April 16, 2020): Decision of the New Coronavirus Infection Control Center in Japan).

which there was an association between patients[39]. Hereinafter referred to as "cluster".) through active epidemiological studies, etc., in order to prevent the occurrence of so-called overshoot, which is an explosive spread of infection (Hereinafter referred to as "overshoot".) and to minimize the number of infected, seriously ill, and dead persons." "In addition, it is important to limit the speed of the spread of infection as much as possible by implementing a combination of measures to reduce contact opportunities, such as requesting people to refrain from going out, as necessary, in order to achieve the containment described above and to prevent the collapse of the medical supply system."[40]

6.1   Gathering of Medical Information from the Government and Provisions of the Act Related to COVID-19

(1) Obtaining information from patients

In relation to medical information, the question is how to deal with it under the current law. First of all, when a patient with a COVID-19 (Confirmed patients, asymptomatic pathogen carriers, suspected disease patients, cadavers of infectious disease fatalities, cadavers of suspected infectious disease fatalities) is identified, the existing law has already mandated that the physician, etc. must report to the prefectural governor, etc. (Prefectural governors, mayors of public health centers and special ward mayors. In addition, the Infectious Disease Law) via the health center using the following form "immediately" (Article 12, paragraphs (1) and (6) of said Act). It was also stipulated that prefectural governors, etc. must report the content of the notification to the Ministry of Health, Labour and Welfare (Minister of Health, Labour and Welfare) "immediately" (Paragraph 2 of the said article)[41].

---

[39] It is explained as 'Avoid the Three Cs'. Government explained that particularly common contributory factors in outbreaks as "Closed spaces with poor ventilation," "Crowded spaces with many people nearby," and "Close-contact settings such as close-range conversations". See, https://www.mhlw.go.jp/stf/covid-19/kenkou-iryousoudan_00006.html.

[40] In Japan, because of the universal health insurance system, anyone can basically access low-cost, high-quality medical care at any time. However, because there is no spare capacity and limited medical resources to deal with infectious diseases that require special systems, such as coronavirus infection, the Ministry of Health, Labour and Welfare decided to call on the government to minimize the number of infected people in order to reduce the number of people accessing medical institutions. The Ministry of Health, Labour and Welfare website: Plan to Secure a System for Providing Health and Medical Care for COVID-19, https://www.mhlw.go.jp/stf/seisakunitsuite/newpage_00056.html.

[41] Prefectural governors, etc. may "When deeming it necessary for preventing the outbreak of an Infectious Disease or for clarifying the status, progress, and cause of the outbreak of an Infectious Disease, the prefectural governor may direct relevant officials to question the patients, Suspected Disease Carriers or Asymptomatic Carriers of a Class I Infectious Disease, a Class II Infectious Disease, a Class III Infectious Disease, a Class IV Infectious Disease, a Class V Infectious Disease or a Novel Influenza Infection, etc., a person with symptoms of a New Infectious Disease, the owners or managers of animals that are likely to transmit an Infectious Disease to humans, or other persons concerned, or to conduct necessary investigations." (Article 15, paragraph (1) of said Act, an aggressive epidemiological survey. Paragraph 8 of the same

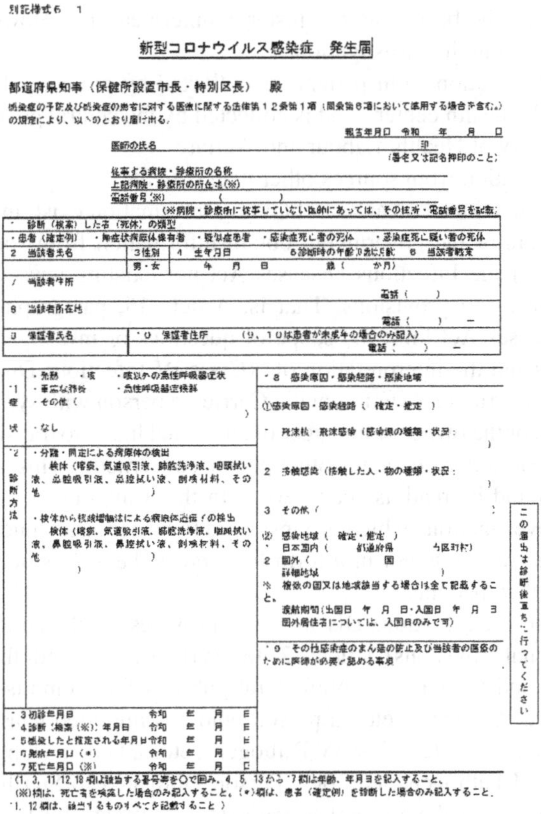

別記様式6－1

新型コロナウイルス感染症　発生届

都道府県知事（保健所設置市長・特別区長）　殿

感染症の予防及び感染症の患者に対する医療に関する法律第12条第1項（同条第6項において準用する場合を含む。）の規定により、以下のとおり届け出る。

報告年月日　令和　年　月　日

医師の氏名　印
（署名又は記名押印のこと）

従事する病院・診療所の名称
上記病院・診療所の所在地（※）
電話番号（※）　（　）
（※病院・診療所に従事していない医師にあっては、その住所・電話番号を記載）

1　診断（検案）した者（死体）の類型				
・患者（確定例）　・無症状病原体保有者　・疑似症患者　・感染症死亡者の死体　・感染症死亡疑い者の死体				
2　当該者氏名	3性別	4　生年月日	5診断時の年齢（0歳は月齢）	6　当該者職業
	男・女	年　月　日	歳（　か月）	
7　当該者住所　電話（　）				
8　当該者所在地　電話（　）　－				
9　保護者氏名	10　保護者住所　（9、10は患者が未成年の場合のみ記入）			
	電話（　）　－			

11 症状	・発熱　・咳　・咳以外の急性呼吸器症状 ・重篤な肺炎　・急性呼吸器症候群 ・その他（　） ・なし	18　感染原因・感染経路・感染地域 ①感染原因・感染経路（　確定・推定　） 1　飛沫核・飛沫感染（感染源の種類・状況：　） 2　接触感染（接触した人・物の種類・状況：　） 3　その他（　） ②　感染地域（　確定・推定　） 1　日本国内（　都道府県　市区町村） 2　国外（　国 詳細地域　） ※　複数の国又は地域該当する場合は全て記載すること。 渡航期間（出国日　年　月　日・入国日　年　月　日 国外居住者については、入国日のみで可）
12 診断方法	・分離・同定による病原体の検出 検体（喀痰、気道吸引液、肺胞洗浄液、咽頭拭い液、鼻腔吸引液、鼻腔拭い液、剖検材料、その他　） ・検体から核酸増幅法による病原体遺伝子の検出 検体（喀痰、気道吸引液、肺胞洗浄液、咽頭拭い液、鼻腔吸引液、鼻腔拭い液、剖検材料、その他　） ）	19　その他感染症のまん延の防止及び当該者の医療のために医師が必要と認める事項
	13初診年月日　令和　年　月　日 14診断（検案（※））年月日　令和　年　月　日 15感染したと推定される年月日　令和　年　月　日 16発病年月日（＊）　令和　年　月　日 17死亡年月日（※）　令和　年　月　日	

この届出は診断後直ちに行ってください

（1, 3, 11, 12, 18欄は該当する番号等を○で囲み、4, 5, 13から17欄は年齢、年月日を記入すること。
（※）欄は、死亡者を検案した場合のみ記入すること。（＊）欄は、患者（確定例）を診断した場合のみ記入すること。
11, 12欄は、該当するものすべてを記載すること。）

Fig. 1. Report of COVID-19 patient

Therefore, the public health center conducts the investigation on the contact tracing of so-called COVID-19, that is, close contacts, based on the above provisions. For details, "Procedures for the implementation of an aggressive epidemiological survey on patients with new coronavirus infections" (National Center for Infectious Disease Epidemiology, National Institute of Infectious Diseases, April 20, 2020 edition) is stipulated[42]. The forms reached (1) basic information and clinical information questionnaire of new coronavirus infectious disease (Include patients with suspected diseases), (2) new coronavirus infectious disease patient behavior questionnaire (source of infection), (3) new coronavirus infectious disease patient behavior questionnaire (contact person), (4) contact person list of new coronavirus infectious disease patient, (5) health observation questionnaire in the contact of new coronavirus infectious disease patient (For example, Fig. 2 shows the action questionnaire in (3).)[43]. These data obtained directly from

article reports to the Minister of Health, Labour and Welfare. Paragraph 2 of the same article in the case of the Minister of Health, Labour and Welfare).

42 See Fig. 1.

43 See Fig. 2.

patients, etc. become the basic data of cluster countermeasures. However, there is no penalty for not following the investigation.

In this way, information from patients is collected by prefectural governors (The actual site is a public health center.) and is collected by the central government through reports to the Ministry of Health, Labour and Welfare.

(2) Obtaining information from sources other than patients

Although the aforementioned means of obtaining information exist, in principle, when prefectural governors or the government obtain information from sources other than patients, etc., neither the Infectious Diseases Act nor existing laws such as the New Influenza Act have many provisions. That is, Article 15, paragraphs (1) and (2) of the Infectious Diseases Act limit the scope of questions or investigations. Therefore, it is difficult to expand the interpretation of "(Class IV Infectious Diseases) a patient, Suspected Disease Carrier or Asymptomatic Carrier, a person with symptoms of a New Infectious Disease, or the owner or manager of an animal likely to transmit an Infectious Disease to humans or its corpse, or any other person concerned;". This is because "Other related parties" should be read as "cadaveric". In this way, the so-called "aggressive epidemiological investigation" which is considered to be necessary under the Infectious Disease Law in the future, is not in a form that forces the acquisition of information from people other than patients.

Article 56 30 of the Infectious Diseases Act provides for the collection of reports accompanied by penal provisions (Article 72, item (vi)) on the grounds that "The Minister of Health, Labour and Welfare or a prefectural public safety commission may have a Holder of Specified Pathogens, etc., a person who has imported Class III Pathogens, etc., a person who has imported Class IV Pathogens, etc., a Person Obligated to Sterilize and Transfer Class I Pathogens, etc. or a Person Obligated to Sterilize and Transfer Class II Pathogens, etc. make a report to the extent necessary for the enforcement of the provisions of this Chapter (Provisions of Article 56 paragraph 27 (2) for prefectural public safety commissions)." However, this provision is limited to those possessing pathogens. Therefore, it can be said that this provision is not a provision widely used to obtain information from persons other than patients, etc.

Under these circumstances, Article 6, Clause 7 of the new flu law originally stated that "The national government may, when it finds it necessary for formulating the National Government Action Plan, request the heads of local governments and other executive agencies, designated public institutions, and other relevant persons to provide materials or information, state their opinions, and offer other necessary cooperation." Under this provision, it is possible to obtain information from people other than patients. However, "Other related parties" based on this law is not unlimited, though it is not as much as Article 15, Paragraphs 1 and 2 of the Infectious Diseases Act. In addition, since the purpose of collecting information is limited, as in the case of "To establish a government action plan" it is not a provision that can be expanded in the form of making predictions in the future and is used to collect a wide range of information. Furthermore, there is no penalty for this provision.

In this way, at present, there is no provision in a unified law or a special law for the government to obtain information from people other than patients.

新型コロナウイルス感染症患者行動調査票（接触者）　　（添付3-1）

NESID登録ID：　　　　　　　　　　　　　　　　　　　　　　患者氏名：

☆発症後の行動調査は、濃厚接触者を特定し、感染拡大を予防するために行う。原則として、診断されて症例として対応される直前までの行動について記載する。また、患者と同室であったり会話した者のうち、連絡や問い合わせが可能である者を優先的に記述する。

発症日より	日付	時刻	同居者以外の者との接触状況	接触場所	接触者氏名 ※	接触者の連絡先	備考
記載例	6/Y	9時〜12時 11時30分 〜 15時頃	①職場に出勤し、所属する部署2課の同僚と接触 ②取引先に訪問し、応対した社員や同席した社員等と接触	①〇〇物産株式会社 TEL：000-000-0000 ②〇×貿易株式会社 TEL：999-999-9999	①〇〇太郎、□□花子、△△次郎 ②〇×部長、△□主任	①は全て〇〇物産株式会社 ②は全て〇×貿易株式会社	
発症 2日前	/						
発症 1日前	/						
発症日	/						
発症 1日後	/						
発症 2日後	/						
発症 3日後	/						
発症 4日後	/						
発症 5日後	/						
発症 6日後	/						
発症 7日後	/						
発症 （　）日後	/						
発症 （　）日後	/						
発症 （　）日後	/						
発症 （　）日後	/						
発症 （　）日後	/						

接触者数が多数となる場合は、裏面の自由記載欄も活用して記載すること。

Fig. 2. Contact tracing report of COVID-19 patients

6.2 Laws and Regulations Concerning the Protection of Personal Information

(1) Personal Information Protection Law

In principle, the question is whether a private business operator can voluntarily provide information containing personal information to the government, etc. or in accordance with a request, etc. that is not based on laws and regulations, without special provisions on the acquisition of information from other than patients, etc. by the government, etc. In this regard, it is necessary to consider the use of personal information for purposes other than those specified in the Act on the Protection of Personal Information (Act No. 57 of 2003, hereinafter referred to as "Personal Information Protection Law".) and the provision of personal data to a third party. In particular, in the case where a private business operator intends to obtain a "Personal Information" without the consent of the person in question that the person is a new patient, etc. with a COVID-19, the acquisition without the consent of the person in question of Special Care-Required Personal Information (Article 2, paragraph 3 of the Act on the Protection of Personal Information "medical history") may become a problem.

The Act on the Protection of Personal Information stipulates the following four exceptional provisions concerning the use of personal information for purposes other than the intended purpose, provision to a third party, and acquisition of special care-required personal information (the items of Article 16, paragraph (3), the items of Article 23, paragraph (1), and the items of Article 17, paragraph (2) of said Act).

First of all, as mentioned above, there is no special law in the case where there is a provision concerning the acquisition of information from other than patients by the government, etc. In other words, (1) as a case based on laws and regulations, the question is whether or not there is a provision that can be read as a provision requiring provision to be provided, and whether or not there is a case where an exception naturally applies. However, there is no such provision.

The most likely exceptions are (3) public health improvements. The pandemic of COVID-19 is exactly a scene corresponding to "Public health improvement... Especially needed", and it is considered to be basically approved. In addition, in the guidelines of the Personal Information Protection Committee ("Guidelines for the Act on the Protection of Personal Information (General Rules)" (Public Notice No. 6 of the Personal Information Protection Commission of 2016) 3 -1 -5), there is an example of "Case 1 Cases in which information on the results of medical examinations conducted by insurers of health insurance associations, etc. is used for planning health promotion measures, improving the effectiveness of health services, epidemiological studies, etc. (The provisions of Sect. 4 shall not apply to cases that fall under Article 76 (1) (iii) of the Act.)". In addition, when the government, etc. conducts surveys to prevent the spread of COVID-19 infectious diseases and collects information for the planning of measures, responding to these surveys can be considered to fall under exceptional circumstances.

However, it should be noted that the above provisions also state that "if particularly necessary". Surveys and measures for COVID-19 require a certain level of concreteness, and when the purpose of use, etc. by the government, etc. is still at an abstract stage, there is a possibility that business operators will make risk judgments that it is more risky for them to comply with them.

In addition, there is an exception to this rule: (4) cooperation in the performance of government affairs. Examples listed in the Personal Information Protection Commission's guidelines (General Rule 3 -1 -5) also assume this exception. In other words, "Case 1 A business operator submits personal information in response to a voluntary request from a tax office or customs official, etc." "Case 2 When a business operator submits personal information in response to a voluntary request from the police" and "Case 3 Responses to general statistical surveys and statistical surveys conducted by local governments". In this way, it is possible to collect information in relation to the execution of administrative work related to the New Flu Law and the Infectious Disease Law. However, as in (3) above, it is necessary to provide cooperation in the execution of specific clerical work after organizing it in relation to risk judgment.

In addition to the above exceptions, statistical information (Data obtained by extracting items related to common elements from information of multiple persons and aggregating them for each of the same categories, which quantitatively grasp trends or characteristics of groups, etc., guideline anonymously processed information part 2 -1) and anonymously processed information may be used for other purposes or provided to a third party without the consent of the user.

With regard to the use of such exceptional circumstances, the Personal Information Protection Commission also publishes the Secretariat of the Personal Information Protection Commission "Handling of Personal Data for Preventing the Spread of New Coronavirus Infection" (April 2, 2020) and confirms that it can provide information in cases that fall under the provisions of (2) to (4) above. However, the same document also issued a warning that "In accordance with specific cases, take into consideration the items of data to be provided, their purpose of use, and safety management measures." In this way, it is assumed that the determination of the applicability of each exceptional event will be made on a case-by-case basis. As a result, there is a need to minimize the data provided and to take safety control measures when providing the data.

6.3 Government and Other Public Sector Personal Information Protection Legislation

In Japan, personal information held by public organizations and that held by the private sector are regulated by separate laws. Personal information in the public sector, including the government, is regulated by the Act on the Protection of Personal Information Held by Administrative Organs (Act No. 58 of 2003. Hereinafter referred to as "Act on the Protection of Personal Information by Administrative Organs".) and the Act on the Protection of Personal Information Held by Incorporated Administrative Agencies, etc.[44] ".). With regard to the restrictions on the use outside the intended purpose and the use outside the intended purpose, both of these stipulate, in addition to permitting the provision outside the intended purpose for the purpose of interpretation (Article 8, paragraph (1) of the Act on the Protection of Personal Information Held by Administrative Organs, and Article 9, paragraph (1) of the Act on the Protection of Personal Information Held by Incorporated Administrative Agencies, etc.), the following exceptions (Items of Article 8, Paragraph 2 of the Act on the Protection of Personal Information Held by Administrative Agencies, etc., and Items of Article 9, Paragraph 2 of the Act on the Protection of Personal Information Held by Incorporated Administrative Agencies, etc.).

In relation to measures to prevent the spread of infectious diseases, it is generally accepted that (2) use outside the purpose within an administrative organ is the execution of the affairs under the jurisdiction, and (3) external provision does not fall under the provision inside or outside the purpose, but for reasonable reasons.

6.4 Ordinance on the Protection of Personal Information by Local Governments

In addition, all local government ordinances for the protection of personal information have been enacted separately. Therefore, it is necessary to individually examine (so-called 2000 issues). The prefecture, etc. which controls the health center is not an exception, and the examination of individual personal information protection ordinance is necessary for the judgment of the exception reason.

---

[44] Act No. 59 of 2003. Hereinafter referred to as Act on the Protection of Personal Information Held by Incorporated Administrative Agencies, etc.

6.5   Provision of Statistical Information from Platform Operators

When government tries to utilize the big data of private business operators for measures to prevent the spread of infectious diseases, there are no special provisions concerning the acquisition of information from other than patients, etc. by the government, etc., and although the range of personal information and personal data that can be permitted due to exceptional reasons is wide to some extent, there are strict requirements concerning the confidentiality and location of communications.

In addition, it should be noted that the fact that it can be provided under exceptional circumstances does not mean that it must be provided, and whether or not it is provided by the project proponent is completely voluntary, so it can be said that it is not enforceable.

In response to the situation regarding COVID-19, the Ministry of Health, Labour and Welfare announced on March 27, 2020, "A call for the conclusion of an agreement on the provision of information contributing to measures against clusters of new coronavirus infections" and called for the conclusion of agreements among platform companies that can collect information. This is addressed to "To the press," and is not intended for a specific business operator.

7   Conclusion

The mechanism of utilization of medical information in our country is complicated by the mechanism of anonymously processed information itself, and it cannot be said that it is sufficiently arranged. Our country's system for protecting personal information is very comlicated. In addition, as we have already seen, no special system for the use of medical information has been established yet, even after the Personal Information Protection Law was revised in 2020 and 2021[45]. At present, a change in the system is under consideration. However, the framework for promoting the use of anonymously processed information is also unique, and it is not yet clear what constitutes "anonymously processed" even on the basis of multiple documents released by the Personal Information Protection Commission. In this context, in the special law on the use of medical information, there is an additional "anonymously processed medical information" on medical care.

As we have seen, the United States has HIPPA and GINA on the prohibition of genetic discrimination, but since the health insurance systems are completely different, there are many cases in which a comprehensive agreement is obtained before treatment. In cooperation with GOOGLE and other organizations, new AI technologies are being developed to link with medical care.

As reviewed in this paper, there is a cancer registration law in Japan, but it only covers cancer, and it is not relevant in this case, for example, COVID-19.

In the special law (Also known as the next-generation medical infrastructure law) for the medical big data, the mechanism of the accreditation of the accredited anonymously processed medical information preparation business on the anonymously processed information for contributing to the research and development in the medical field

---

[45] See above note 7, Ishii, Sogabe, Mori ed., Commentar for Personal Information Protection Law, pp. 19–26. See also, In the field of academic research.Principles of the Rules for the Protection of Personal Information.(Revised Personal Information Protection Act of 2021) (https://www.ppc.go.jp/files/pdf/210623_gakujutsu_kiritsunokangaekata.pdf).

is constructed. However, it is still unknown how medical information, which is supposed to be "Medical information that does not identify a specific individual" by this law, will contribute to research and development, since a certifying organization has just been certified. In addition, since there are no exceptional provisions for R&D, including the fact that it is not possible to deal with cases such as those in which the person concerned refuses to provide information, it is often unclear whether there will be a mechanism to flexibly provide information for R&D.

The Next Generation Medical Care Infrastructure law can be considered to have been formulated for the time being as a mechanism to certify "accreditation body" which intends to promote at least the utilization of medical information for research and development among various laws. However, in light of the fact that medical information should be utilized in a manner that helps to reduce the increase in medical costs as much as possible from a broader perspective and from a viewpoint other than research and development, a system should be established for the utilization of basic information, including the degree of anonymous processing, which allows more flexible utilization. In addition, since it is undeniable that the system is difficult to understand for the people, medical workers, and related persons, it is necessary to change the system as appropriate in order to make it easier to understand.

The Next Generation Medical Care Infrastructure was designed to do this, but it created a law to use anonymously processed information, which could prevent the use of anonymously processed information. (The law should be revised in this respect.)

Therefore, in view of the fact that medical information should be used in a manner that helps to control the increase in medical expenses as much as possible from a broader perspective and from a viewpoint other than research and development, a necessary system including a new law and administrative institution that governs the infrastructure should be established for the utilization of basic information, including the degree of anonymous processing, which allows more flexible utilization[46].

---

[46] Shimpo, above note 2, pp. 790–791.

Examining the Effective of Web Advertising on Pupil Size

Ryuta Yamashita[1]($\boxtimes$), Tadaaki Shimizu[2], Natsuki Yoshinaka[3], Rintaro Kataoka[4], and Naoki Sawada[4]

[1] Graduate School of Engineering, Tottori University, 4-101 Koyama-cho Minami, Tottori 680-8550, Japan
yamashita.ryuta@gmail.com
[2] Cross-Informatics Research Center, Tottori University, 4-101 Koyama-cho Minami, Tottori 680-8550, Japan
[3] Department of Engineering, Graduate School of Sustainability Science, Tottori University, 4-101 Koyama-cho Minami, Tottori 680-8550, Japan
[4] Department of Engineering, Information and Electronics Course, Tottori University, 4-101 Koyama-cho Minami, Tottori 680-8550, Japan

Abstract. The purpose of this study is to estimate the emotions that users experience when they see advertisements displayed by websites. It is possible to pro-vide users with the products and services they want by displaying web advertisements appropriately. This is a desirable situation for companies, users, and websites. We thought that users would have a physical reaction when they viewed a website. We especially focused on change of pupil size. In our experiment, the subjects were presented several types of web advertisements.

The types of web ads presented are: 3 types of ads display methods (banner-ad, front-ad, Click-ignore ad), 2 types of advertising images (positive and negative), for a total of 6 combinations.

We found a characteristic response of pupil size by ads types by use of golden cross and dead cross analysis. And we show possibility of estimating emotion by pupil size.

Keywords: Recommendation system · Pupil size · Web advertising · Multimodal information · Golden-cross

1 Introduction

The Internet has been widely used, and 80–90% of Japanese use it on a daily basis [1]. As a result, many web sites are published on the Internet, and many of them are provided by the benefits through the web advertisement. Many Web advertisements are posted on major web sites, such as "Google" and "Yahoo! Japan". These major websites are developing ways to present advertisements that are suitable for users [2]. One example is to build a recommender system using BIG-DATA. It uses the user's ID information and web operation history data to present advertisements suitable for the user.

© IFIP International Federation for Information Processing 2022
Published by Springer Nature Switzerland AG 2022
D. Kreps et al. (Eds.): HCC 2022, IFIP AICT 656, pp. 86–99, 2022.
https://doi.org/10.1007/978-3-031-15688-5_8

In this way, the environment of Web advertising is constantly evolving. However, according to the "Awareness Survey on Internet Advertising" [3], more than 80% of users responded that they "feel that advertising on the Internet is intrusive or annoying." This result shows that the user's impression of the web advertisement is bad, and it is not a good situation for websites, advertisers, and users. Web advertising connects users and products, and it is an important medium to promote better consumer behavior. For all three parties to get good results, the advertising system needs to serve ads more appropriately to the user.

We aim to build a recommendation system that displays advertisements that are more suitable for users. Therefore, we focused on the multimodal information of users while browsing a website. Multiple methods of communication, including visual and auditory, are referred to as multimodal information.

2 Related Study on Multimodal Information

In recent years, there has been a lot of study purposed at making systems understand the emotions of users. There are many studies that use multimodal information of users.

Kato's study is to develop a conversation system for users who were not experienced with ICT devices [4]. This system attempted to recognize facial expressions and estimate emotions from the subject's face image.

Furukawa's study [5] is an attempt to estimate emotions from pupillary responses and eye movements. This study is not target to Web advertising. However, the results showed that user's multimodal information tends to express the user's emotions.

Q. Zhao's study [6] purpose to estimate the user's next gaze direction and utilize it for recommendation functions. The study limited on the grid user interface of smartphones. However, this study is an example of the use of multimodal information for recommendation functions. In this study found that it is possible to estimate the user's next gaze even in the limited environment of a "grid-based UI" of a smartphone. The purpose of this study is to realize a system that can display recommendations efficiently by utilizing gaze.

The study by Simola examines the effect of advertising on reading web content [7]. Their study focused line of sight of subjects. In their study examines the effects of changing conditions, such as animating Web advertisements and adjusting display time intervals, on the line of sight. The subjects' gaze dwell time tended to be longer for animated ads than for static ads. Also, there is an effect between the appearance time of the advertisement and the movement of the gaze.

Yamanaka's study [8] proposes a convenient method of evaluating mental stress. An experiment was carried out to clarify the relation between changes in pupil diameter and autonomic nervous activity by measuring an electrocardiogram and pupil diameter. Several relationships between changes in pupil diameter and autonomic nervous activity were revealed and indicated that measurement of pupil diameter was an effective indicator of autonomic nervous activity.

3   Purpose

Based on related research, we hypothesized that "stimuli received from Web advertise-ments (hereafter referred to as "advertising stimuli") characterize users' multimodal information.

Total of six types of multimodal information were obtained in this experiment.

- Mouse clicks - Mouse cursor trajectory - Eye gaze - Pupil size - Emotion estimation from facial expression images - Posture estimation from body images.

The reason for targeting this multimodal information is that no medical knowledge or skills are required to handle them, and the data can be acquired with readily available devices.

In order to fairly describe the experimental environment, all multimodal information acquired in the experiment was enumerated, however this paper focused on "pupil size" and "mouse clicks". Other multimodal information is obtained for the co-experimenters. This multimodal information is not discussed in detail in this paper.

Therefore, the objective of this study was to "find characteristic changes in the magnitude of the tendency when users are exposed to advertising stimuli. If characteristic multimodal information can be found in the experimental results, it will be possible to estimate the subject's emotions based on these characteristics.

4   Experiment Details and Subjects

An experiment was conducted to obtain multimodal information about the subject's browsing of a Web site. For the experiment, we created our own two-choice quiz website (hereafter referred to as the "experimental website").

Subjects were given advertising stimuli while operating the experimental website. The details of the experimental website are described in Sect. 5.1. The types of advertising stimuli given to the subjects are described in Sect. 5.2. The details of the system for acquiring multimodal information are described in Sect. 6.

20 subjects (10 males and 10 females, aged 18–24) were asked to participate in this experiment. The subjects were told in advance that they would receive additional rewards (gift certificates) depending on their quiz performance. We created an environment in which the subjects could operate the quiz site seriously.

5   Experimental Website and Advertising Stimuli

5.1   Overview of the Experimental Web System

The experimental website has the following specifications: (1) to (5). The subjects were given advertising stimuli during the actions of (1) to (2).

(1)   Display the question text (see Fig. 1).
(2)   Click on the answer that the subject judges to be correct.
(3)   The experimental quiz system displays the correctness of the quiz (see Fig. 2).

(4) When the subject clicks the "Go to Next Question" button, the experimental quiz system returns to (1).

(5) After about 14 min, the experiment is finished.

Fig. 1. The question screen   **Fig. 2.** The correct answer screen

The total number of questions in the quiz on the experimental website was 738. The questions were randomized, but the same question was not displayed during one experiment. However, when all the questions have been submitted, they will be randomized again. The experimental website was built using an AWS (Amazon Web Service) [9]. Virtual server. The specifications of the virtual server used are shown in Table 1.

Table 1. Specifications of the virtual server.

AWS Spec (t2.micro)	Detail
OS	Amazon Linux release 2
Memory	1 GiB
Storage	8 GiB
Availability zone	us-east-2c

The experimental website was implemented using python (Django framework), html, CSS, and JavaScript. In addition, PostgreSQL was installed in the virtual server. In the experimental website, the question texts and correctness errors were saved in PostgreSQL.

5.2 Types of Advertising Stimuli and Stimulus Intensity

There are a wide variety of factors that interfere with the user's experience with ad displays. It is very difficult to investigate all factors. In this study, we investigated 1) images of advertisements and 2) methods of displaying advertisements.

1) Images of advertisements.

Various images are displayed in web advertisements. First, we decided to roughly investigate the relationship between the displayed images and multimodal information. For this purpose, we prepared two patterns of images that were thought to affect the user's pleasantness or unpleasantness.

In this experiment, OSAIS (Open Affective Standardized Image Set) [10] was used as an image that mimics an advertising image. OASIS is an open access online stimulus set that contains 900 color images of humans, animals, etc. Every image in OASIS is assigned two values: Valence value and Arousal. In addition, OASIS assigns a positive value and a negative value to every image. First, we selected images for our experiment that met the criteria based on two values, Arousal_mean and Valence_SD. The specific criterion is that Arousal_mean > 3.66 and Valence_SD < = 1.1. We selected 30 images that met the criteria of Arousal_mean and Valence_SD in the order of positive and negative values, respectively. However, we did not use those images that were offensive to public order and morals even though they met the criteria. (e.g., dead bodies, nudes, wounds, blood, etc.) Examples of positive and negative images, respectively, are shown in Fig. 3 and 4.

1a). Positive images: 30 images.

Fig. 3. Example of positive images

1b). Negative images: 30 images.

Fig. 4. Example of negative images

2) Methods of displaying advertisements.

In this study, the subjects were presented with three types of advertising stimuli: 2a) Banner ads, 2b) Front-page ads, and 2c) Click-ignore ads.

2a). Banner Ads.

Displays images like banner advertisements used in popular websites. This advertisement display will not interfere with the user's operation. An example is shown Fig. 5.

2b). Front-page Ads.

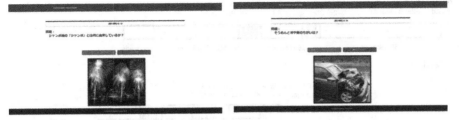

Fig. 5. Example of banner advertisement (Left: positive/Right: negative)

Front page advertisements are advertisements that are used on some websites. It is a display type that interferes with the user's operation of the web contents. An example of the advertisement display in this experiment is shown in Fig. 6.

Fig. 6. Example of front-page advertisement (Left: positive/Right: negative)

2c). Click-ignore Ads (Click-ignore + front page advertisement).
The third is a display pattern like the front-page advertisement, but with different click controls. This display pattern ignores the "Close" button in the Front-page advertisement with a certain probability. The specific process is as follows: First, a value between 1 and 6 is randomly determined when the Front-page advertisement is displayed. Then, ignore the click of the "Close" button for the number of times the value is determined. This means that the subject will have 1 to 6 clicks ignored. This display pattern is very disturbing to the user. This pattern will henceforth be referred to as "Click-ignore Ad".

Subjects were given a total of 7 different advertising stimuli (2 types of advertisement images * 3 display types + no advertisement stimuli) in an unbiased manner. Figure 7 illustrates how the advertisement stimulus is given to the test subject.

The following is an explanation of Fig. 7.

(1) The first 60 s after the subject started the experiment was the interval without advertisement stimuli. This is the interval for the subjects to get used to the display and operation of the experimental website. After 60 s, the first time the question is asked, the experimental website proceeds to (2).

(2) The experimental website provides advertising stimuli to the subjects. This advertising stimulus is randomly selected from the 7 types of displays already mentioned.

(3) The subject either closes the ad or answers the displayed questions.

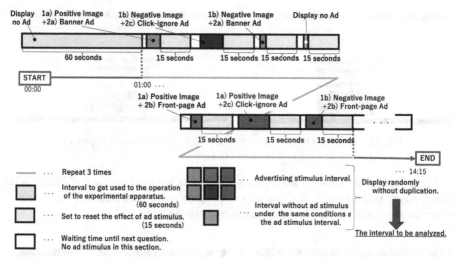

Fig. 7. Time chart of advertising stimulus

(4) After the operation of (3), the quiz is displayed without advertisement stimulus for 15 s. When the quiz is displayed for the first time after 15 s, the system proceeds to (5).

(5) The subject is again given the advertising stimulus. The advertisement stimulus to be given is randomly selected from the remaining display types.

(6) Repeat (3) through (5) until all 7 types of displays have been completed.

(7) Repeat (2) through (6) three times.

(8) After the completion of (7), the quiz will continue until the end of the experiment (14 min and 15 s). We set the experiment time to 14 min and 15 s so that all the ads could be displayed.

We also defined a measure of stimulus intensity for the four types of advertising displays in this experiment. The stimulus intensity was defined as the degree to which the advertisement interfered with the subject's operation. The stimulus intensity is shown in Table 2. In this paper, we also focus on the effect of stimulus intensity on multimodal information.

In addition, we focused analysis for difference of displayed positive and negative images. We hypothesized that there may be multimodal information that is featured only in positive or negative images.

In other words, we decided to focus on "stimulus intensity" and "positive/negative images" for our analysis.

6 Multimodal Information Acquisition System

The multimodal information of the subject's 6 points is obtained using the devices shown in (a)–(e) in Fig. 8 and Fig. 9 shows the scene during the experiment.

Table 2. The stimulus intensity of the advertisement

The stimulus intensity	Display type	Strength basis
Weak → Strong	No ads displayed	Because there are no ads on the screen
	Banner ad	Because the display of advertisements does not interfere with the subject's operation
	Front-page ad	Because advertisements that interfere with the operation of the experimental website are displayed
	Click-ignore ad	Because the process of ignoring the subject's click is performed in addition to the display of Front-ad

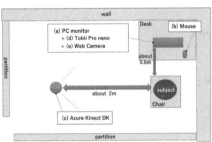

Fig. 8. Multimodal information acquisition system

Fig. 9. Scene during an experiment

Table 3 shows the specifications of the devices used in the multimodal acquisition system. As we described in Sect. 3, the devices (c) and (e) were prepared for co-experimenters.

There were no restrictions on the wearing of glasses in the above devices. Therefore, the wearing of the glasses was left up to the subject. On the other hand, wearing a thick jacket or a mask affects the data to be acquired. Therefore, we asked the subjects participating in the experiment not to wear them.

7 Pupil Size Analysis Method

7.1 Pretreatment

We performed preprocessing on the acquired pupil data. The purpose of the preprocessing is as follows:

– To standardize the scale between subjects
– To express a rough change rather than a detailed change

Table 3. List of devices used in the experiment

Device		Details
PC	CPU	Intel Core i9-9900X
	GPU	NVIDIA GeForce RTX 2060 SUPER
	OS	Windows10 Education
	Web Browser	Google Chrome
(a) PC monitor		iiyama ProLite XUB2792HSU
(b) Mouse		ELECOM M-BL27UBBK
(c) Azure Kinect DK		-
(d) Tobii Pro nano [11]		-
(e) Web Camera		Logicool C920n +

The detail of the preprocessing is as follows:
Original data (left and right pupil size).

- Interpolate missing data with data from the previous time
- Resampling process (60 Hz to 20 Hz)
- Average left and right eye data
- Normalize by 0 ~ 1

There were 20 subjects, but there was one subject for whom eye data could not be obtained due to the forelock. Therefore, the number of subjects for analysis was 19.

7.2 Analysis by Moving Average

A moving average of 10 s (5 s before and after) was calculated for the data that had undergone "7.1 Preprocessing". Figure 10 shows an example of the calculated moving average data and time trends. The areas with colored backgrounds in the figure are the areas where advertising stimuli are provided.

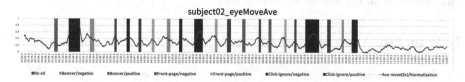

Fig. 10. An example of moving average data and advertising stimuli

The following trends were common among the 19 subjects

– Click-ignore ad has a large value. Ads with a long display time often have a large value.

- When an ad is displayed, pupil size rises and falls after the display, regardless of the type of advertising stimulus. This is especially noticeable for click-ignore and front-page.
- There is no feature difference due to the negative/positive influence of the displayed image.

7.3 Analysis by Golden Cross

The analysis in Sect. 7.2 allowed us to show the features in the moving average of pupil size. In addition, we focus on Golden Cross, which is one of the analysis methods using moving averages.

Golden cross is methods used especially when predicting stock price trends. Golden is calculated using two moving averages of different periods. This is one of the analysis methods using moving averages.

In Sect. 7.2, we used a 10-s moving average (5 s before and after). In this section, we added a 40-s moving average (20 s before and after) calculate the two crosses. Results of the calculated crosses are shown in Fig. 11.

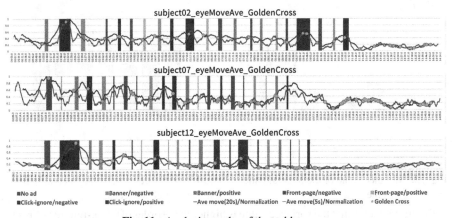

Fig. 11. Analysis results of the golden cross

Figure 11 shows that the Golden Cross tends to appear under the influence of the display of advertisements. This can be said from the fact that the frequency of appearance of the golden crosses during and after the display of advertisements is different.

When strong ads are displayed, both or one of the following two tend to occur.

- Pupil size is enlarged in the long-term moving average.
- A golden cross occurs.

However, a series of golden crosses indicates areas where pupil fluctuation is small.

The results of a detailed review of each advertising stimulus are as follows. In click-ignore ads, the pupil size is often large and there is often a golden cross. Banner ads tend to have a Golden Cross, although the pupil size is not large. Front-page ads tend to be somewhere in between.

As described above, by using golden cross, we were able to show the characteristics of pupil size. The above results suggest that advertising stimuli affect pupil size fluctuations.

7.4 Analysis by Variance Value Using MACD

MACD (Moving Average Convergence Divergence) is the difference between two exponential smooth moving averages, one short term and one long term. MACD is also an indicator to examine the movement of stock prices. It was introduced in this study to process time series data as well as stock prices.

We compared the MACD values of the advertising stimulus intervals for each advertising stimulus. We focused on the variance values of MACD.

The variance values for subject 02, which has been shown so far as an example is shown in Fig. 12, and the variance values for all 19 subjects are shown in Fig. 13.

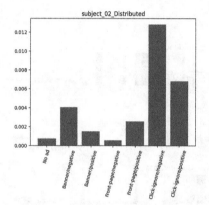 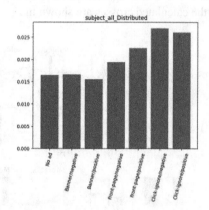

Fig. 12. Variance value of the interval under analysis for subject 02

Fig. 13. Variance value of the interval to be analyzed for all subjects

Figure 13 shows that the variance value is higher in the order of Click-ignore > Front-page > No ad ≥ Banner. There was no difference in the positive/negative images as in the analysis in Sect. 7.2. Therefore, the variance values were calculated by eliminating the difference between positive/negative images. As above, the variance values for subject 02 and all subjects are shown in Fig. 14 and 15, respectively.

Figure 15 clearly shows that the variance value of CDMA results in Click-ignore > Front-page > No ad ≈ Banner. In most subjects (16/19), Click-ignore had the highest variance value. However, as shown in Fig. 15, there were some subjects who had different size relationships.

The features calculated from the pupil size may be useful indicators for detecting the display of strong advertising stimuli.

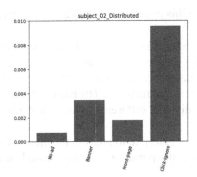

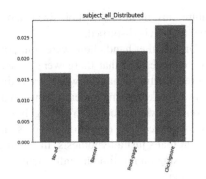

Fig. 14. Variance values for each display method for subject 02

Fig. 15. Variance values by display method for all subjects

8 Conclusion and Interpretation

8.1 Discussion

In this study, we asked subjects to operate a web browser and gave them advertising stimuli. Multimodal information was obtained and analyzed during the experiment. In this paper, we focus especially on the features of pupil size in our analysis.

The results of the analysis suggested that the advertisement display affected the pupil size of the subjects. Due to strong advertising stimuli, the size of the pupil tends to increase significantly.

Furthermore, we used golden cross to express the characteristics.

Golden Crosses tend to appear due to subjects' responses to advertising displays. Golden crosses tend to occur regardless of ad type. This revealed that a golden cross was displayed regardless of the complexity of the targeted ad avoidance behavior.

Especially when click-ignore ads were displayed, large fluctuating golden crosses occurred.

Therefore, the golden cross appears regardless of the type of ad display, however, it can be said that the appearance interval and pupil size at the time of appearance differed depending on the advertisement type.

We calculate the variance values were calculated from the MACD values of all 19 subjects. The results showed that the features by MACD variance values tended to appear in the order of Click-ignore > Front-page > No ad ≈ Banner.

Analysis by variance values shows a strong tendency for strong stimuli to have larger variance values than weak stimuli. However, it is not possible to separate whether this difference is due to the influence of the strength of the advertising stimulus or the complexity of the ad avoidance action.

8.2 Interpretation

Based on the rationale defined in Table 2, we believe that this feature of variance indicates the size of the perceived "disturbance" during web browser operation. In the future, I would like to use this feature to build in a recommendation system. By utilizing the feature movement of the pupil size discovered in this paper, it is possible to deter-mine if the user feels disturbed.

On the other hand, there were some subjects whose features were not easily visible. It is hypothesized that there were subjects who did not feel disturbed by the click-ignore advertisement even when it was displayed. Conversely, there were subjects who showed the feature movements shown in this paper in Banner ads. The reasons for these movements were thought to be largely due to individual differences based on the level of experience in PC operation and personality.

But that's just a hypothesis. In the future, we would like to analyze this hypothesis by focusing on multimodal information other than the pupil size feature focused on in this paper.

In addition, two types of images, positive and negative, were prepared for the experi-ment. As discussed in reference [7], there are many images in web advertising. We would like to refine the modeling of the effects of images by investigating various factors based on our findings.

From a medical point of view, it has been reported that the pupil size changes with stress, wakefulness, attention, and sleepiness [12]. The results were similar for the adver-tising stimuli in this study. We found that the pupil size was clearly changed by the web advertisement stimuli. Thus, we believe that the results of this experiment, including the medical findings, are generally valid.

8.3   Future Issues

Through this study, we found that a feature movement in pupil size appears depending on the type of web advertisement displayed. However, the following issues remain to be solved.

Issue 1: Features for positive/negative images have not been found.
Issue 2: Consideration of a judgment method that includes the individual differences indicated in Sect. 8.2.
Issue 3: Investigation of automatic decision-making methods using machine learning, etc.

First, for issue 1 and 2, we would like to use the pupil size data to study the calculation of features other than those concluded in this paper. Next, we would like to analyze multimodal information other than pupil size to show feature movements.

As for issue 3, we think it is necessary when building a recommendation system. Calculate other features based on the features concluded in this paper. Using these calculated features, we construct a machine learning model. As we continue to analyze the data acquired in this experiment, we will find new features of the movements and build a more robust machine learning model.

References

1. Ministry of Internal Affairs and Communications, 2020 Internet Usage Status. https://www.soumu.go.jp/johotsusintokei/whitepaper/ja/r02/html/nd252120.html. (in Japanese)

2. Yahoo! JAPAN Tech Blog, Introducing case studies of cross-sectional data utilization in the recommendation domain #machine learning. https://techblog.yahoo.co.jp/entry/202003318 26447/. (in Japanese)
3. Research Plus, Awareness Survey on Internet Advertising. https://www.research-plus.net/html/investigation/report/index127.html. (in Japanese)
4. Kato, T., Ishida, K.: A method for estimating emotional states for emotionally friendly dialogue using face images. In: Proceedings of the 81st National Convention, vol. 1, pp. 63–64 (2019). (in Japanese)
5. Furukawa, S., Kashino, M., Yoneya, M., Liao, H.-I.: Reading the mind through the eyes -heart-touching-AI key technology. NTT Tech. J. **28**(2), 22–25 (2016). (in Japanese)
6. Zhao, Q., Chang, S., Harper, F.M., Konstan, J.A.: Gaze prediction for recommender systems. In: Proceedings of the 10th ACM Conference on Recommender Systems, pp. 131–138 (2016)
7. Simola, J., Kuisma, J., Öörni, A., Uusitalo, L., Hyönä, J.: The impact of salient advertisements on reading and attention on web pages. J. Exp. Psychol. Appl. **17**(2), 174–190 (2011)
8. Yamanaka, K., Kawakami, M.: Convenient evaluation of mental stress with pupil diameter. Int. J. Occup. Saf. Ergon. **15**(4), 447–450 (2009)
9. AWS (Amazon Web Service). https://aws.amazon.com/?nc1=h_ls
10. OASIS (Open Affective Standardized Image Set). http://www.benedekkurdi.com/#!portfolio/project-4.html
11. Tobii Pro nano. https://www.tobiipro.com/product-listing/nano/
12. Hara, N.: Pupillographic stress, arousal and emotion assessments in visual stress. Jpn. J. Vis. Sci. **33**(2), 47–51 (2012)
13. Oyama, T., Kaneko, I., Ono, F., Sone, J., Hanamura, T.: Lecture evaluation using pupil diameter. In: FIT2011: The 10th Forum on Information Technology. 3rd vol., pp. 781–782 (2011). (in Japanese)

Digital–Sustainable Co-transformation: Introducing the Triple Bottom Line of Sustainability to Digital Transformation Research

Markus Philipp Zimmer[1,2](✉) and Jonna Järveläinen[2]

[1] Leuphana University, Universitätsallee 1, 21335 Lüneburg, Germany
markus.zimmer@leuphana.de
[2] University of Turku, 20014 Turku, Finland

Abstract. Organisations face two transformation challenges. They embark on their digital transformation (DT), while they also have to accomplish their sustainability transformation (ST). However, on an organisational level, existing information systems (IS) research has thus far treated both transformations separately. While we can observe calls for IS research that investigates the design and use of IT artefacts for ST, existing studies into DT emphasise economic sustainability. In fact, DT scholars hinge the success of DT on economic sustainability. We argue that this emphasis on economic sustainability is an opportunity missed; that DT can contribute to accomplishing the triple bottom line of sustainability (i.e., economic, social and environmental sustainability). We rest our argument on DT and ST's linchpin: innovation. Existing studies outline that both transformations stem from a sequence of innovations. Drawing on a typology of innovation for ST, we posit that sustainable digital innovations can contribute to both DT and ST. We conceptualise this proposition as a digital–sustainable co-transformation. We argue that this concept can sensitise both IS researchers and practitioners to introduce the triple bottom line of sustainability to DT and to conceive of DT and ST not as two transformations running in parallel but as one co-transformation.

Keywords: Digital transformation · Digital innovation · Sustainability · Sustainability transformation · Digital–sustainable Co-transformation

1 Introduction

Digital transformation (DT) receives grappling attention in both information systems (IS) practice and research [31, 36]. Existing work into this organisational transformation challenge suggests that DT alters organisations' value proposition and identity [33]. Defining DT, Vial outlines it as "a process that aims to improve an entity by triggering significant changes to its properties through combinations of information, computing, communication, and connectivity technologies." The underlying logic: organisations trigger significant changes, through infusing their value proposition with digital, to

D. Kreps et al. (Eds.): HCC 2022, IFIP AICT 656, pp. 100–111, 2022.
https://doi.org/10.1007/978-3-031-15688-5_10

maintain their economic sustainability. In this vein, IS scholars have studied changes to organisations' value proposition [31, 33], organisations' DT strategies [9, 40], and how digital innovations drive DT. However, organisations face not one but at least two transformation challenges.

Besides DT, they also face a sustainability transformation (ST) [13, 27, 28]. While they engage in the former in response to digital disruptions [31], they seek the latter in reaction to new laws and regulations that governments issue to accomplish the United Nations' (UN) Sustainability Development Goals (SDGs). These goals involve significant changes on an international, societal, organisational and individual level [7]. In practice, we can observe that organisations publish sustainability reports and announce sustainability strategies. Existing studies have termed this as ST [28], i.e., "organisational change efforts that are multi-layered, complex, and that relate to environmental societal, governmental, organisational, regulatory, and individual factors at the same time." The core notion of ST is that organisations improve their operations in accordance with the triple bottom line of sustainability. This triple bottom line comprises an economic, social and environmental dimension and conceptualises operations as sustainable, if they satisfy all three dimensions [30]. Thus, the ST captures organisational changes aimed at improving organisations' triple bottom line.

The SDGs and sustainability theme have also entered the field of IS research. For example, the Special Interest Group GREEN and International Conference on Information Systems 2021 requested manuscripts that investigate IS and sustainability [15]. Moreover, journals announced special issues on IS and sustainability [18]. These calls for research indicate IS scholars increasing interest in studying IS and sustainability. However, first, this research focuses on environmental sustainability [14, 27] and second, we find little research that introduces sustainability to the research theme of organisational DT. Indeed, existing DT studies have focused on economic sustainability [2, 31]. We argue that this is an opportunity missed; that DT can contribute to ST, if we introduce the triple bottom line of sustainability to DT and tackle both transformations as one co-transformation. Hence, we ask the research question of *how can we conceptualise the digital- and sustainability transformation as one co-transformation?*

To answer this question, the remainder of this article first outlines the key premises of existing DT and ST literature as well as their linchpin: sustainable digital innovations. Afterwards, we present an empirical example illustrating a sustainable digital innovation presenting a digital–sustainable co-transformation initiative. The subsequent discussion closes this article presenting two contributions. First, we propose the concept of a digital–sustainable co-transformation that rests on digital sustainable innovations. We argue that this concept can sensitise both researchers and practitioners to understand DT and ST not as two transformations running in parallel but as one co-transformation. Second, we argue that it introduces the triple bottom line of sustainability to DT research.

2 Conceptual Background: Digital Transformation, Sustainability Transformation and Their Linchpin

In this section, we present the conceptual background for answering our research question. We first present existing studies on DT with its focus on economic sustainability.

Afterwards, we outline the concept of ST. Subsuming that both DT and ST stem from innovation, we draw on a typology of innovation for ST to conceptualise sustainable digital innovations as the linchpin between the two transformations.

2.1 Digital Transformation

DT receives significant attention in practice and research. DT is "a process that aims to improve an entity by triggering significant changes to its properties through combinations of information, computing, communication, and connectivity technologies." [31] Scholars and practitioners have engaged in understanding and mastering DT [9, 16]. They found that when embarking on their DT, organisations seek economic sustainability [2, 16, 31]. They transform their value proposition and internal structures to accomplish future-oriented economically sustainable modes of organising [9, 33]. To accomplish this goal, they formulate DT strategies [19, 22].

DT strategies serve as blueprints for organisations' transformation activities. They sketch a path from organisations' established business models to digital business models [22, 26]. In these strategies, organisations build on grass-root level digital innovations [4, 9, 40]. They organise innovation events to which they invite employees who then suggest and afterwards implement digital innovations. These realised digital innovations then constitute organisations' realised DT strategy. Thus, organisations' intended DT strategy serves as a blueprint but the realised DT takes an emergent form that unfolds from a sequence of digital innovations [9, 39, 40]. Indeed, Hinings et al. define DT as a sequence of digital innovations that accumulates to organisation-wide changes [20]. While the presented existing work on DT provides answers to "what it is" and "how it unfolds", it remains silent on when we can deem organisations' DT successful.

Reviewing IS studies on DT success, Barthel identifies a set of four clusters that reflect different notions of DT success [2]. The first, *company value and performance*, comprises studies that measure the impact of DT at the macro level (e.g., stock market price, company reputation, cost reductions, employee or customer satisfaction). The second, *digital business performance*, rests DT success on external performance measures of the new digital business that organisations create for their DT (e.g., revenue or profitability of the digital business models). The third, *realised external transformation*, suggests to measure DT success in the progress of the realised external changes (e.g., transformation of value proposition, customer interaction etc.). The fourth, *realised internal transformation*, discusses maturity models that capture the progress of the internal transformation of processes, structures, etc. Thus, while the first and second cluster present a notion of DT success that hinges on achieving organisational objectives, the third and fourth rest on accomplishing the DT process [2]. According to Barthel, DT success criteria are thus contribution to organisational objectives and degree of completion, which can feature an internal or external orientation (see Fig. 1).

All DT success clusters pin DT's success to economic sustainability. The DT success criteria indicate an emphasis on accomplishing sustained competitiveness and profitability. However, with sustainability entering the field of IS research, we must ask whether economic sustainability should be or can be the sole dimension for assessing DT success? In the triple bottom line of sustainability, economic sustainability presents one of three dimensions. This suggests that DT could support organisations' ST and that the

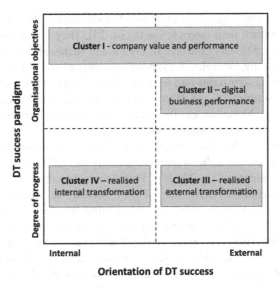

Fig. 1. Overview of DT success factors (adapted from [2])

triple bottom line of sustainability offers an alternative to assessing DT success. Thus, we next consult existing work on ST to identify a conceptual linchpin between DT and ST.

2.2 Sustainability Transformation

Sustainability development refers to taking decisions that "[meet] the needs of the present without compromising the ability of future generations to meet their own needs" [35]. In an act of global governance, the UN has defined the SDGs. The most pressing issues that the SDGs address: social and environmental sustainability [24, 30]. Setting the SDGs, the UN ask national governments to take action toward social and environmental sustainability [1, 7, 24]. However, besides governments, organisations take a central role in sustainability development [1, 14, 24]. They source, process, and re-use environmental resources. They employ workers, act in local and global communities and most importantly, they drive innovation and thus change [24, 30]. They are central actors in our societal processes and mechanisms requiring sustainability development.

The definition of sustainability evolved from a focus on environmental sustainability to a triple bottom line of sustainability [11, 14, 30]. The triple bottom line defines actions as sustainable, if they satisfy the three dimensions of economic, environmental and social sustainability [11, 12]. This renders sustainability a complex challenge because it demands actors to consider multiple parameters and their interdependencies when taking decisions for ST. In this vein, Seidel et al. define organisational STs as "a special case of organisational change efforts that are multilayered, complex, and that relate to environmental societal, governmental, organisational, regulatory, and individual factors at the same time." [28] Thus, ST, next to DT, presents a major transformation challenge for organisations [14, 24].

Interested in the convergence of these two transformation challenges, sustainability scholars have studied their interrelation [8, 14, 24]. They found four interrelations. Researchers and practitioners conceive of digital and sustainability as (1) standalone challenges, (2) neutrally interrelated, (3) positively interrelated or (4) negatively interrelated [8]. Despite these insights into the interrelation between DT and ST, their nexus remains subject to scrutiny [8, 14]. Noteworthy, DT can also have deteriorating effects on sustainability [14]. Moreover, existing work focuses on the contribution of digital to economic and environmental sustainability [8, 14, 24].

Existing IS studies reflect these observations. IS researchers postulate two perspectives on IS and ST. IS can either support organisations' ST or offer direct solutions to sustainability challenges [17, 27, 28]. At the core of both perspectives, organisations' innovation capabilities drive their ST [3, 25]. However, similar to sustainability research, prior work focuses on environmental sustainability. For example, Seidel et al. report design principles and affordances that can support environmental ST [27]. Similarly, Hanelt et al. show how IS can support the effectiveness of eco-innovations (namely, electric vehicles) [17]. Also, Seidler et al. propose an eco-sustainability logic to support pro-environmental behaviour [29]. While this indicates that the phenomenon of ST is a subject of interest in IS research, existing work (in IS and other research fields) focuses on environmental sustainability.

Concluding, we define ST as an organisational change process that aims at significant changes to improve organisations' triple bottom line – economic, social, and environmental – sustainability. We further highlight three observations. First, existing studies in IS on the research theme of DT and into ST emphasise the economic and environmental dimensions. This suggests that we require research that takes a holistic view at sustainability. Second, the interrelation between digitalisation and sustainability remains unclear. Scholars argue for neutral, positive and negative interrelations. In any case, they argue for sustainability being a strategic imperative for DT since organisations' ST is critical for sustainability development [24].

2.3 Sustainable Digital Innovations: The Linchpin of a Digital- and Sustainable Transformation

DT and ST both present organisations with transformation challenges. While the first requires organisations to infuse their value proposition and identity with digital [31, 33], the second involves organisational changes for contributing to the SDGs [12]. Both require significant changes [7, 33] that entail qualitatively different organisations [5]. Thus, we can subsume that DT and ST alter the inner workings – the deep structure – of organisations. Further, both transformations rest on innovation [3, 20, 25, 30, 31].

Scholars have argued that DT emerges from a sequence of digital innovations [20]. Digital innovations are combinations of innovative digital business concepts and digital technological solutions [34]. Indeed, prior studies present cases of realised DT strategy emerging from a grass-root level process of generating and implementing digital innovations [4, 9, 40]. Thus, we can understand digital innovations to be at the core of organisations' DT.

Similarly, innovations are at the core of ST [25, 30]. In ST, we can observe practitioners and scholars seeking innovations that satisfy the triple bottom line of sustainability.

Silvestre and Tirca suggest a typology of innovation for ST [30]. They differentiate between four types of innovation: traditional, social, green and sustainable innovations (see Fig. 2).

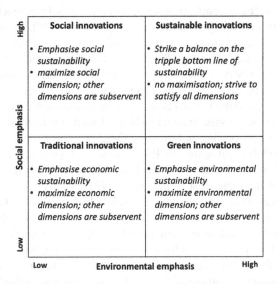

Fig. 2. Typology of innovations for ST (adapted from [30])

Traditional innovations present the basic type of innovation that offers economic gains, e.g., an increase in market share, returns or earnings. Social innovations address societal differences, e.g., poverty, hunger, health issues and inequality. Green innovations contribute to the preservation of our planet, e.g., clean production, circular economy, etc. Since sustainability presents a triple bottom line, innovations often require trade-offs. For example, emphasising an innovation's social sustainability may drop its economic sustainability. However, sustainable innovations strike a balance on the triple bottom line of sustainability [30]. Silvestre and Tirca note that sustainable innovations must not be new to the world but account for an organisations' ST, if they are new to that organisation [30]. Hence, sustainable innovations play a significant role for organisations' ST.

Building on scholars studying DT and ST, we can understand both transformations as stemming from a sequence of innovations [20, 30, 31]. This makes innovation the linchpin of the two transformations. In this vein, we suggest the concept of sustainable digital innovations as a type of innovation that contributes to accomplishing both DT and ST. We define sustainable digital innovations as digital innovations that satisfy the triple bottom line of sustainability. Sustainable digital innovations transform organisations into digital but also sustainable organisations. Next, we illustrate the concept of sustainable digital innovations presenting the exemplary case of Bext360.

3   Exemplary Case Bext360: Sustainable Digital Innovation for Digital–Sustainable Co-transformation

Bext360 is an example of a sustainable digital innovation. Bext360 is a service platform that combines digital technological solutions (i.e., blockchain, machine vision and software) to improve the supply chain transparency of coffee [10]. Most of the world's coffee is produced by small farms, who receive only a fraction of the consumer prices for coffee but carry climate risks (e.g., flooding or draughts) or suffer from middlemen manipulation [21, 41]. The bext360 machine, as a sustainable digital innovation, tackles these sustainability issues. It evaluates the coffee cherries' quality using machine vision, presents real-time offers to the farmers based on their coffee cherrie's quality and stores the respective coffee batch's information to a blockchain that is later amended with new records on the batch's processing and shipping [24, 37].

Positioning bext360 in Silvestre and Tirca's framework [30], we conceive of it as a social innovation. For the owners of the small farms, bext360's independent evaluation and real-time payment create trust in the process [21]. Indeed, the farmers trust the machine over humans [38]. The roastery can select high-quality coffee cherries and verify the journey of a certain batch to the roastery based on the blockchain [23]. This information can be presented to consumers and wholesale customers, but also to any other stakeholder of the process, which creates supply chain transparency [21, 43]. This transparency alters the power distribution between farmers and purchasers (often large multinational corporations) making exploitation of farmers more difficult [21].

Bext360 is also a green innovation since the blockchain also monitors the environmental footprint of a coffee batch [42]. For instance, based on the location of origin, shipping steps and details on the used transportation stored to the blockchain, it is possible to calculate the emissions for transportation and to evaluate the transportation method [44]. Further possibilities involve measuring herbicides or pesticides in the coffee cherries. Moreover, based on the farm locations (if known), comparison of satellite images can reveal whether farmers fire-cleared forests to grow coffee, how often the crop has been irrigated artificially or the farms' waste management.

Coda Coffee, a US coffee roastery, uses the bext360 platform to increase transparency of its supply chain [14]. Previously, the Coda Coffee owners travelled around the world and worked closely with coffee farmers and cooperatives to ensure both the quality of coffee cherries, but also ethical work conditions and environmental sustainability [38]. Bext360 allows Coda Coffee to achieve the same organisational goals but sustainably. Thus, introducing bext360 as a sustainable digital innovation to its supply chain, Coda Coffee accomplished a digital–sustainable co-transformation initiative.

4   Discussion

In this article, we cast the research question of *how can we conceptualise the digital- and sustainability transformation as one co-transformation?* Building on the tenets of both DT and ST, we have argued that innovations are the linchpin between the two. In this vein, we suggested the concept of sustainable digital innovations. We then illustrated this concept using an exemplary case: Coda Coffee introducing bext360 to its supply chain. We next extend the concept of sustainable digital innovations to the concept of digital–sustainable co-transformation. Afterwards we present implications to research and practice.

4.1 The Concept of Digital-Sustainable Co-transformation

Drawing on the presented conceptual background, we propose the concept of digital–sustainable co-transformation. The digital–sustainable co-transformation is a process that involves significant changes to an organisation based on a sequence of sustainable digital innovations. Prior studies suggest that both DT and ST rest on a sequence of innovations [20, 30, 31]. Building on Silvestre and Tirca's typology of innovations, we conceptualised sustainable digital innovations as digital innovations (innovative combinations of digital business concepts and digital technological solutions [34]) that satisfy the triple bottom line of sustainability. With the concept of digital–sustainable co-transformation, we adapt this typology to DT. That is, DT can provide grounds for organisations to accomplish their ST through sustainable digital innovations. We stress the plural in "innovations" since a single innovation makes no transformation but a sequence of innovations does. As a strategic imperative, ST subsumes the strategic objective of DT, i.e., economic sustainability. Therefore, we present this as a typology of DT for ST (see Fig. 3).

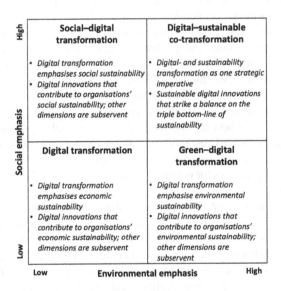

Fig. 3. Typology of DT for sustainability

The typology differentiates between four types of DT for sustainability. First, DT as studied in prior work with an emphasis on organisations' economic sustainability. Second, social-DT as capturing a transformation process that rests on digital innovations that emphasise the social dimensions of sustainability. Third, green-DT that emphasises digital innovations that contribute to environmental sustainability. Last, the digital–sustainable co-transformation that understands both DT and ST as one strategic imperative and introduces the triple bottom line of sustainability to DT. This last type of DT for sustainability strikes a balance on the triple bottom line without seeking maximisation of any of the dimensions.

We argue that this typology, and particularly the concept of digital–sustainable co-transformation, introduce the triple bottom line of sustainability to organisational DT research. Moreover, it asks scholars and practitioners to conceive of DT and ST not as separate, but as one transformation challenge. Scholars pose that DT and ST require significant changes [8, 30, 33]. DT alters organisations' value proposition and identity [31, 33] and ST has significant impact on value creation and society. If DT research retains its prevalent focus on economic sustainability, scholars and practitioners miss the opportunity to leverage DT for ST. The concept of digital–sustainable co-transformation puts forth this argument and calls for research that considers DT and ST as one co-transformation. It suggests that when altering their value proposition and identity to digital, organisations could simultaneously alter both to digital–sustainable.

4.2   Research Implications

We outline four research implications. First, the concept of digital–sustainable co-transformation acts as a sensitising device [32] that introduces the triple bottom line to DT research. This adds to existing DT studies' considerations of how and whether DT contributes to organisations' economic sustainability [2, 9, 22]. We thus argue that the digital–sustainable co-transformation invites IS scholars to take a critical approach to studying DT and organisational change that ventures beyond economic values; to take a critical-turn in studying DT and question whether the economic dimension should be the major dimension or whether – and how – organisations can accomplish a dig-ital–sustainable co-transformation. In this vein, the concept calls for future research that investigates how the digital–sustainable co-transformation manifests in organising empirically. For example, how this perspective alters internal organising and strategic alignment between digital and business? Specifically, how can organisations utilise dis-tinct metrics to evaluate the co-transformation's success in accomplishing sustainability? These are exemplary questions for potential critical research into the digital–sustainable co-transformation.

Second, besides these empirical questions, the concept requires scholars to criti-cally reflect their research approaches. At times, our research approaches run risk of reproducing the values inscribed in the real-world phenomenon without questioning these values against what is at stake – here sustainability. Hence, considering that exist-ing DT studies tilt toward economic sustainability, we argue that the digital–sustain-able co-transformation suggests employing critical research approaches to DT research that, opposed to reproducing the field values, scrutinises the field values against a pre-defined set of values (e.g., sustainability), if we strive for our research to facilitate accomplishment of the SDGs.

Third, the triple bottom line is not only absent in DT research but also in IS research on sustainability. IS scholars studying ST have thus far focused on how IS can support ST (IT enabled ST) with a focus on environmental sustainability [17, 27, 29]. Since the digital–sustainable co-transformation stresses the triple bottom line, we argue that future research should take a holistic view on IS and ST. That is, to extend the existing emphasis on economic and environmental sustainability to investigate how IS can support (or offer solutions for) social and environmental sustainability. If we consider existing literature on digital, however, the focus should be on "offering solutions". With digital, we can observe the fusion of business and IT to one digital business strategy and an organising logic of digital [6, 37]. The digital–sustainable co-transformation sets digital and sustainable on par. Thus, we argue that scholars should study them (digital and sustainable) as integral – inseparable – parts of business.

Lastly, existing sustainability research deals with DT and ST as two separate phenomena that – occasionally – converge [8, 14]. The concept of digital–sustainable co-transformation shifts this view. Opposed to speaking of convergence and interrelation, the concept suggests to conceive of both as one co-transformation that emphasises a balance on the triple bottom line. This alters questions of how DT disrupts – positively or negatively – sustainability to how DT and ST can synergically accomplish sustainability development.

4.3 Practical Implications

The proposed concept of a digital–sustainable co-transformation holds practical implications. In public discourse, DT and ST appear as two separate concerns. Introducing the digital–sustainable co-transformation sensitises public discourse – involving practitioners – to think of and address these two transformations as one. That is, to generate not digital innovations for DT and then sustainable innovations for ST but to craft, articulate and execute digital–sustainable co-transformation strategies that foster sustainable digital innovations that strike a balance on the triple bottom line. This suggests the consideration of how practitioners can merge their DT and ST strategies into one strategy. This merger offers the prospect of hitting two birds with one shot, i.e., to save resources on both transformations while accomplishing them jointly.

References

1. Amui, L.B.L., et al.: Sustainability as a dynamic organizational capability: a systematic review and a future agenda toward a sustainable transition. J. Clean. Prod. **142**, 308–322 (2017). https://doi.org/10.1016/j.jclepro.2016.07.103
2. Barthel, P.: What is meant by digital transformation success? Investigating the notion in IS literature. In: Ahlemann, F., Schütte, R., Stieglitz, S. (eds.) WI 2021. LNISO, vol. 48, pp. 167–182. Springer, Cham (2021). https://doi.org/10.1007/978-3-030-86800-0_13
3. Bengtsson, F., Gerfalk, P.J.: Information technology as a change actant in sustainability innovation: insights from Uppsala. J. Strat. Inf. Syst. **20**(1), 96–112 (2011). https://doi.org/10.1016/j.jsis.2010.09.007
4. Berghaus, S., Back, A.: Disentangling the fuzzy front end of digital transformation: activities and approaches. In: Proceedings of the ICIS 2017, Seoul, South Korea, pp. 1–17 (2017). https://doi.org/10.1057/9780230512771_16
5. Besson, P., Rowe, F.: Strategizing information systems-enabled organizational transformation: a transdisciplinary review and new directions. J. Strat. Inf. Syst. **21**, 103–124 (2012). https://doi.org/10.1016/j.jsis.2012.05.001
6. Bharadwaj, A., et al.: Digital business strategy: toward a next generation of insights. MIS Q. **37**(2), 471–482 (2013)

7. Biermann, F., et al.: Global governance by goal-setting: the novel approach of the UN Sustainable Development Goals. Curr. Opin. Environ. Sustain. **26–27**, 26–31 (2017). https://doi.org/10.1016/j.cosust.2017.01.010

8. Brenner, B., Hartl, B.: The perceived relationship between digitalization and ecological, economic, and social sustainability. J. Clean. Prod. (2021). https://doi.org/10.1016/j.jclepro.2021.128128

9. Chanias, S., et al.: Digital transformation strategy making in pre-digital organizations: the case of a financial services provider. J. Strat. Inf. Syst. **28**, 17–33 (2019). https://doi.org/10.1016/j.jsis.2018.11.003

10. Cook, E.: Bext360: start-up in sustainable supply chain digitization. https://supplychaindigital.com/supply-chain-risk-management/bext360-start-sustainable-supply-chain-digitization. Accessed 24 Jan 2022

11. Elkington, J.: Capitalism 25 years ago I coined the phrase "triple bottom line." Here's why it's time to rethink it (2018)

12. Elkington, J.: Towards the sustainable corporation: win-win-win business strategies for sustainable development. Calif. Manag. Rev. Winter **36**(2), 90–102 (1994)

13. Elliot, S.: Transdisciplinary perspectives on environmental sustainability: a resource base and framework for IT-enabled business transformation. MIS Q. **35**(1), 197–236 (2011)

14. Feroz, A.K., et al.: Digital transformation and environmental sustainability: a review and research agenda. Sustainability **13**(3), 1–20 (2021). https://doi.org/10.3390/su13031530

15. Graf-Drasch, V. et al.: Call for papers: sustainably digital. In: SIG GREEN Pre-ICIS Workshop (2021)

16. Hanelt, A., et al.: A systematic review of the literature on digital transformation: insights and implications for strategy and organizational change. J. Manage. Stud. **58**(5), 1–39 (2020). https://doi.org/10.1111/joms.12639

17. Hanelt, A., et al.: Driving business transformation toward sustainability: exploring the impact of supporting IS on the performance contribution of eco-innovations. Inf. Syst. J. **27**(4), 463–502 (2017). https://doi.org/10.1111/isj.12130

18. Henriksen, H.Z., et al.: Special issue: sustainable development goals in IS research: opening the agenda beyond developing countries' research. Scand. J. Inf. Syst. (2020)

19. Hess, T., et al.: Options for formulating a digital transformation strategy. MIS Q. Exec. **15**(2), 17–33 (2016). https://doi.org/10.1108/10878571211209314

20. Hinings, B., et al.: Digital innovation and transformation: an institutional perspective. Inf. Organ. **28**, 52–61 (2018). https://doi.org/10.1016/j.infoandorg.2018.02.004

21. Kshetri, N.: Blockchain's potential impacts on supply chain sustainability in developing countries. In: Academy of Management Annual Meeting Proceedings. Academy of Management Briarcliff Manor, NY, p. 10510 (2020). https://doi.org/10.5465/AMBPP.2020.40

22. Matt, C., Hess, T., Benlian, A.: Digital transformation strategies. Bus. Inf. Syst. Eng. **57**(5), 339–343 (2015). https://doi.org/10.1007/s12599-015-0401-5

23. Pavlić Skender, H., Zaninović, P.A.: Perspectives of blockchain technology for sustainable supply chains. In: Kolinski, A., Dujak, D., Golinska-Dawson, P. (eds.) Integration of Information Flow for Greening Supply Chain Management. EcoProduction, pp. 77–92. Springer, Cham (2020). https://doi.org/10.1007/978-3-030-24355-5_5

24. del Río Castro, G., et al.: Unleashing the convergence amid digitalization and sustainability towards pursuing the Sustainable Development Goals (SDGs): a holistic review. J. Cleaner Prod. **280**, 1–40 (2021)

25. Schaltegger, S., Wagner, M.: Sustainable entrepreneurship and sustainability innovation: Categories and interactions. Bus. Strateg. Environ. **20**(4), 222–237 (2011). https://doi.org/10.1002/bse.682

26. Sebastian, I.M., et al.: How big old companies navigate digital transformation. MIS Q. Exec. **16**(3), 197–213 (2017)

27. Seidel, S., et al.: Design principles for sensemaking support systems in environmental sustainability transformations. Eur. J. Inf. Syst. (2017). https://doi.org/10.1057/s41303-017-0039-0

28. Seidel, S., et al.: IT-enabled sustainability transformation-the case of SAP. Commun. Assoc. Inf Syst. **35**, 1–17 (2014)

29. Seidler, A.-R., et al.: Encouraging Pro-environmental behaviour: affordances and institutional logics in IS-enabled organisational sustainability transformations. In: European Conference on Information Systems, pp. 1–12 (2018)

30. Silvestre, B.S., Țîrcă, D.M.: Innovations for sustainable development: moving toward a sustainable future. J. Clean. Prod. **208**, 325–332 (2019). https://doi.org/10.1016/j.jclepro.2018.09.244

31. Vial, G.: Understanding digital transformation: a review and a research agenda. J. Strat. Inf. Syst. **28**(2), 118–144 (2019). https://doi.org/10.1016/j.jsis.2019.01.003

32. Walsham, G.: Doing interpretive research. Eur. J. Inf. Syst. **15**(3), 320–330 (2006). https://doi.org/10.1057/palgrave.ejis.3000589

33. Wessel, L., et al.: Unpacking the difference between digital transformation and IT-enabled organizational transformation. J. Assoc. Inf. Syst. **22**(1), 102–129 (2021). https://doi.org/10.17705/1jais.00655

34. Wiesböck, F., Hess, T.: Digital innovations. Electron. Mark. **30**(1), 75–86 (2019). https://doi.org/10.1007/s12525-019-00364-9

35. World Commission of Economic Development: Our Common Future. Oxford University Press, New York City, NY (1987)

36. World Economic Forum: The Digital Enterprise: Moving from experimentation to transformation (2018)

37. Yoo, Y., et al.: Research commentary—the new organizing logic of digital innovation: an agenda for information systems research. Inf. Syst. Res. **21**(4), 724–735 (2010)

38. Youngdahl, W.E., Hunsaker, B.T.: Coda coffee and bext360 supply chain: machine vision, AI, IoT, and Blockchain (2018)

39. Zimmer, M.P.: Digital Transformation in an Incumbent Organisation: The Co-Enactment of Digital Transformation Through Macro- and Micro-Level Activities. Annales Universitatis Turkuensis, Turku, Finland (2021)

40. Zimmer, M.P.: Improvising digital transformation: strategy unfolding in acts of organizational improvisation. In: 2019 Proceedings of the Americas Conference on Information Systems (AMCIS), Cancun, pp. 1–10 (2019)

41. About Coffee - Fairtrade Foundation. https://www.fairtrade.org.uk/farmers-and-workers/coffee/about-coffee/. Accessed 25 Jan 2022

42. Bext360: Blockchain for a Transparent, Sustainable Supply Chain. https://www.techstars.com/the-line/startup-profile/bext360-blockchain-for-a-transparent-sustainable-supply-chain. Accessed 25 Jan 2022

43. Bext360: Blockchain for the Coffee Suppl(AI) Chain - Technology and Operations Management. https://digital.hbs.edu/platform-rctom/submission/bext360-blockchain-for-the-coffee-supplai-chain/. Accessed 25 Jan 2022

44. Bext360 Releases New Sustainability Features to its. https://www.globenewswire.com/news-release/2018/10/11/1620138/0/en/Bext360-Releases-New-Sustainability-Features-to-its-Traceability-SaaS-Platform-in-order-to-Empower-Organizations-to-Meet-Corporate-Social-Responsibility-Policies.html. Accessed 27 Jan 2022

Law

Don't be Caught Unaware: A Ransomware Primer with a Specific Focus on Africa

Joey Jansen van Vuuren[1]([⊠]), Louise Leenen[2], and Anna-Marie Jansen van Vuuren[1]

[1] Tshwane University of Technology, Pretoria, South Africa
{jansenvanvuurenjc,Jansenvanvuurena1}@tut.ac.za
[2] University of the Western Cape and CAIR, Cape Town, South Africa
lleenen@uwc.co.za

Abstract. Ransomware attacks have become the fastest growing and most serious type of cybercrime. A ransomware attack does not only capture victims' data, but also prevents victims from accessing their own data until a ransom has been paid. The prevention of and recovery from a ransomware attack have become a major concern for governments and organizations. This paper presents guidelines for institutions to secure their systems from ransomware attacks and to put steps in place for recovery if their systems have been attacked. The human is often the weak link in allowing an intrusion into a network. African countries are at even greater risk because their populations are often not sufficiently trained nor aware of cybersecurity risks.

Keywords: Ransomware · Cybersecurity culture · Cybercrime combatting culture · Cyber-attacks · Cybersecurity in Africa

1 Introduction

Ransomware attacks are currently considered to be one of the most serious cyber threats to businesses and governments, and the severity of their impact is constantly increasing. Ransomware is a type of malware that encrypts a victim's data or steals personal data of the victim, and the attacker then demands a ransom to release the data [1]. IBM Security published a guide to ransomware in 2020 in which they note that as ransomware is evolving, the ransom demands are increasing in value - up to US $80 million have been claimed. Attackers are now also using extortion methods. They may threaten a target if ransom is not paid to escalate the attack, release captured data publicly, or to auction confidential data to the highest bidder [2]. Ransomware can cause irreversible damage to the Operating System (OS) or user files even after its removal. Prevention or early detection of ransomware is important [1].

Our methodology consists of a literature search on ransomware attacks combined with our knowledge in cybersecurity and cybersecurity culture, in order to present a primer for the prevention of or recovery from a ransomware attack.

Published by Springer Nature Switzerland AG 2022
D. Kreps et al. (Eds.): HCC 2022, IFIP AICT 656, pp. 115–131, 2022.
https://doi.org/10.1007/978-3-031-15688-5_11

2 Ransomware

Ransomware is defined as "malware" (malicious software) with the primary aim to extort money from users [3, 4]. It is software code that blocks access to a computer system, or gains access to private information [5]. The captured information is encrypted so that authorized users loose access to their own data until a ransom is paid. In summary, ransomware blocks users' access to their own resources and the attacker coerces victims to pay (usually) to regain access to their data files or, in some cases, to prevent the attacker from releasing private information on different platforms on the web.

Attackers gain access to computers by using different techniques such as "Social Engineering" where an authorized user is manipulated to give the attacker access to their systems. This is mostly done via phishing emails where attackers use fake emails, e.g. a supposed emails from a bank, to lure users into providing sensitive information which may include passwords [5]. These emails often encourage users to open malicious attachments, or the email body contains links to malicious websites. As part of their attack, attackers can create a website which contains code capable of exploiting unpatched security vulnerabilities on a site visitor's system [6]. Social media platforms are often used to gather personal information about potential victims. Attackers also use vulnerabilities in a network service or unpatched software. Sometimes the attacker falsely claims that the user system is locked and coerces the victim to pay the ransom.

2.1 Types of Ransomware

The following types of ransomware are frequently employed during attacks:

- **Scareware or hoaxware** is fake ransomware presented on the user interface to demand ransom payments even if there is no threat [7]. The attacker pretends to belong to a technical support team and falsely informs users that their computers have been infected with malware and that they can remove the supposed malware if the victims purchase his "removal" or (fake) antivirus services. After the purchase, the attacker removes his presence. An unsophisticated user may believe his system is protected by an antivirus program. Scareware normally do not damage the files or other information on the system and can usually be halted by killing the process in the computer's memory and in its startup entries.
- **ScreenLocker or Locker Ransomware** is software that locks a target's computer interface. The attacker blackmails the victim into paying a ransom [4] to unlock the computer. The attack can also be on the OS level to disable user operations and block the user from accessing the operating system. Normally the attacker displays warnings (ransom note) that the user's system is being attacked. These warnings cover a significant part of the user's screen. In most cases this ransomware can be removed without losing files or private information by terminating the process and deleting the payload.

- **Crypto Ransomware** deletes important data of the user [8]. The ransomware searches through a victim's computer or network in search of specific data including images, PDFs and text files which may be important to the victim and collects these selected items. Strong cryptography is used to encrypt the relevant files. If the victim fails to comply with the ransom demands, the encrypted data is lost permanently. Some variants such as the Petya-ransomware attacks the Master File Table (MFT) of the file system which makes it very difficult to recover the files without paying the ransom [1].
- **Doxware,** also called "Ransomware with Data Exfiltration", behaves similarly to other types of ransomware by encrypting files and presenting its demands to the victim, but it also steals sensitive files and photos, and sends copies back to whoever controls the malware. The attacker threatens to expose sensitive information on the internet unless the victims pay the ransom amount. The attacker is thus able to make a twofold threat for payment - to return the encrypted files to the victim as well refraining from publishing the victim's sensitive information online [6]. Examples of data exfiltration ransomware are the Maze and the DoppelPaymer ransomware [1].

Most of the above ransomware examples use executable files that are run on the victims' computers. A new phenomenon is **Fileless ransomware** that executes an attack without placing malicious software on a victim's computer. Rather than using executable files, an attacker uses Command Scripts or Remote Desktop Protocol (RDP) connections. Poshcoder mimicks Locker ransomware by using PowerShell scripts on Windows, and SamSam and CryptON attack via RDP connections [1].

Another option is **VM-Based Ransomware** that deploys a Virtual Machine (VM) on the victim's system and hides itself in this virtual machine to avoid detection. It then maps host folders as shared folders into the VM. The folders inside the VM are then encrypted. Ragnar ransomware was the first of this type of ransomware [1].

2.2 A Framework for Ransomware Attacks

Figure 1 captures the process an attacker follows during a ransomware attack. The attacker first has to gain initial access into a target system. This initial access is escalated to take control of a target system by means of infiltrating a higher level of access to file systems. During the exploitation phase, can go ahead and encrypt the data so that he can issue a ransom note.

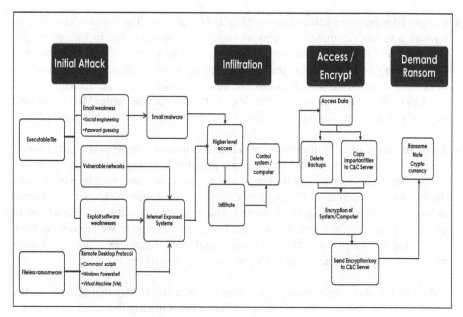

Fig. 1. A ransomware attack framework

3   Major International Ransomware Attacks in 2021

Over the past years, ransomware attackers have shifted their targets from individuals to larger corporations due to the possibility of higher ransom profits. By 2020, the increase in ransom payments grew by 300% in the United States, and attacks shifted to exfiltrating company information - the more sensitive, the better [9]. The damages that companies or governments suffer globally due to cybercrime was expected to reach US $6 trillion and for ransomware alone was expected to reach $20 billion by the end of 2021. Ransomware is now the fastest growing and most damaging type of cybercrime. [10]. Most ransomware payments are done in cryptocurrencies, which makes it more difficult to trace the attackers [1].

The Touro College & University System [11] identified the ransomware attacks that had the biggest impact on the USA in 2021. These include attacks on the Colonial Pipeline, Brentagg, Acer, JBS Foods, Aunata, the National BasketBall Association, AXA, CAN, CD Project and KIA Motors. The attackers that demanded the ransom amounts are given in Table 1.

Table 1. Ransomware attackers 2021

Attacker	Victim	Ransom
DarkSide gang	The Colonial Pipeline is part of the USA's critical infrastructure systems and supplies gas along the East Coast of the country. The billing system of the Colonial Pipeline was attacked, and this resulted in the company not able to bill its customers. Not having access to this system influenced the supply of gasoline, resulting in gasoline shortages, chaos and panic. Customers panicked and tried to hoard the gasoline and ignored safety precautions. Colonial Pipeline paid the ransom because they were afraid that personal information of customers will be leaked [11]	Attackers demanded more than $4.4 million The FBI cold-traced the digital wallets and crypto currency $2.3 million of the paid ransom amount was recovered [12]
	Brentagg is a world leading chemical distribution company with 670 sites and headquarters in Germany. Attackers targeted the North American division by encrypted devices on the company's network and stealing unencrypted files (150 GB). An attacker created a private leak for proof of the stolen data [13]	Attackers demanded $7.5 million dollars Brentagg paid $4.4 million and nothing was recovered.
REvil or Sodinokibi hacker group	ACER is a multinational computer manufacturer. Attackers exploited the Microsoft exchange server to get access to Acer's files, and leaked images of sensitive financial documents and spreadsheets In another attack in 2021, not ransomware-related, ACER's Indian offices were also attacked and 60 GB of files were stolen. [14]	Attackers demanded $50 million. Acer counteroffering $10 million, a 20% discount was allowed. It is not known how much ACER paid

(continued)

Table 1. (*continued*)

Attacker	Victim	Ransom
	JBS FOODS is one of the biggest meat processing companies supplying to restaurants and grocery stores in North America. The company was forced to halt cattle-slaughtering operations at 13 of its meat processing plants. Consumers were warned not to do panic buying [11, 15]	Attackers demanded $11 million. JBS paid in crypto currency and this was the largest ransomware payment by June 2021 [11]
	QUANTA, the Computer Manufacturer and Apple's business partner, was attacked and the apple product blueprints and other sensitive information were stolen. After the firm refused to negotiate with the attackers, they targeted Apple instead [11]	Attackers demanded $50 million, but the ransom was not paid [11]
	KASEYA, the enterprise technology company, experienced the first instance of a supply chain attack. Kaseya provides IT solutions, a management tool for handling networks and endpoints, compliance systems, service desks, and a professional services automation platform. Because Kaseya managed their customers networks and endpoints, the attack on Kaseya also gave the attackers access to the networks and endpoints of their customers [16]. Companies in 17 countries and more than a thousand businesses were affected by this attack. Some victims, such as Swedish supermarket, Coop, remained closed for business on the day of the attack [17]	Attackers demanded $70 million but no ransom was paid [17]
Babuk	The National Basketball Association (NBA) was attacked, and the attackers claimed they had stolen 500 GB of data about the Houston Rockets. This included confidential documents, such as financial info and contracts [18]	The ransom amount was probably $85 million but it has not been confirmed [19]

(*continued*)

Table 1. (*continued*)

Attacker	Victim	Ransom
Avaddon	AXA was attacked soon after the company announced important changes to their insurance policy such as halting reimbursement for ransomware payments to many of their clients in France. The attackers gained access to 3 TB of data [20]	The ransom amount is unknown but this attacker group's ransom is normally about $40 million [20]
Evil Corp	The network of CNA, an insurance company, was attacked and the attackers encrypted 15,000 devices, including many computers of employees working remotely and logged in via a VPN. The malware used was Phoenix CryptoLocker	A ransom amount of $40 million was paid [21]
HelloKitty gang	CDProjekt Red is a popular videogame development firm based in Poland. Attackers accessed source code for Cyberpunk and Witcher 3 games which was in development, and encrypted some devices [22]	The attackers wanted $7 million and sent the ransom note via Twitter. The victim company did not pay ransom because they had backups and was able to restore their data. They did not recover completely from the attack and the games that were attacked presented some errors. [22]
DoppelPaymer	KIA MOTORS, a subsidiary of Hyundai, reported a widespread IT and systems outage, but they did not confirm the hack. The system outage affected its Mobile UVO link apps, payment services, phone services, owner portal, and dealerships' internal systems. The attackers claimed they attacked Hyundai Motor America [23]	Attackers demanded $20 million or 800 bitcoins (worth $30 million) [23]. Because KIA did not confirm the hack, it is speculated that they did pay the ransom

4   Ransomware Attacks in Africa

A report released by the International Criminal Police Organization (Interpol) on cyber-crime in Africa, identified ransomware as one of the top five prominent threats in Africa [24] (Fig. 2). The report further indicated that South Africa is the most hard hit country in Africa with Egypt being second and Tunisia third [24].

South Africa's figure of 52 victims per one million internet users is around 92 times lower than that of the UK, which has 4,783 victims per one million internet users, and about 29 times lower than that of the USA. South Africa is listed as seventh highest in terms of number of attacks in the world, behind France with the Netherlands in the next spot [25].

In a global survey by Sophos, the state of response to ransomware attacks in South Africa showed that about 49% of organisations are paying the requested ransom. The amount of ransom paid is not the total cost, as the cost of recovery can be up to $710,000 (R11.5 million). Insurance policies covered 99% of the costs of the 77% of organisations that had cyber insurance [26]. However, these attacks are becoming even more serious in South Africa due to the Protection of Personal Information (PoPI) Act of 2013 that came into effect on 1 July 2020. Non-compliance with the PoPI Act, for example not securing personal information, can result in a fine of R10 million or a 10 year jail sentence [27]. The PoPI Act also prescribed to companies that they have to alert users or customers when the company falls victim to a cyberattack. Therefore, when the South African retail giant, Dis-Chem, suffered from an incident where a third-party service provider of the company was attacked, it notified its customers of the breach of their personal information.[28] At this moment there is no confirmation if it was a ransomware attack on the service provider, yet the data-breach resulting from this could potentially lead to future attacks.

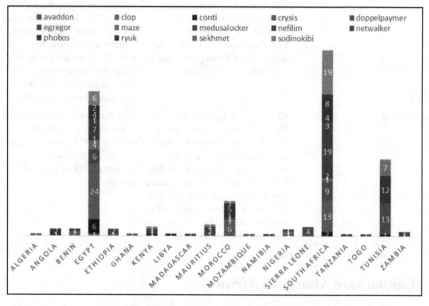

Fig.2. Ransomware attacks in Africa [24]

4.1 Major Ransomware Attacks in Africa in 2021 and 2022

Almost all reports of ransomware attacks in Africa contain information of attacks against South African companies or government institutions. Other African countries are also attacked but there is less information available about them. The reports on ransomware attacks in Africa also tend to contain less information than reports on attacks in the USA, UK and Europe. According to a report by Interpol, published in October 2021, African organisations experienced the highest increase in ransomware attacks, at 34%, during the first quarter of 2021, compared to the rest of the world [29].

Several South African government departments and institutions were attacked during 2021. This country's Department of Justice was attacked in September 2021. All online services, including email and the department's website, became inoperable [30]. Information on the servers was encrypted and became unavailable to employees and the public. Consequently, the department could not issue of letters of authority, render bail services or respond to emails [31]. The department immediately activated a contingency plan, preventing the ransomware from spreading to other government systems. Their systems only returned back to service one month after the attack. According to media reports, no ransom was paid [30]. At about the same time another government institution, the South African National Space Agency (SANSA), also suffered an attack, from a group called "CoomingProject." Although SANSA's network was not affected, data of the agency was found in the public domain [32].

Two months earlier, in July 2021, the "Hello Kitty"-gang attacked Transnet. Transnet is a public entity who reports to the Department of Transport. They manage the port in Durban. This attack on them affected many other African countries, because Durban is used for the shipment of their products, including copper and cobalt mined in Zambia and the Democratic Republic of Congo [30]. This supply chain attack paralysed the port for more than 10 days, resulting in trucks standing idle while waiting for goods to be released, perishable goods expiring, businesses facing late deliveries and penalties due to delayed goods. Many ships were anchored for days or weeks waiting to offload cargo at the port [33]. These attacks were not all the same; Transnet and the justice department were locked out of their systems but SANSA's data was made public. In none of these cases it was reported that the ransom was paid.

The private sector and financial services have also suffered from these type of attacks. Curo, one of South Africa's best-known asset management firms controlling more than 2 trillion South African Rand in its overall portfolio, was attacked in January 2022. The attackers prevented the company from accessing their data for five days. Fortunately, the attack did not affect highly sensitive customer information, and Curo did not lose control of its financial assets at any stage. Curo's management decided to ignore the attackers and focused on restoring their systems to full functionality [34].

The latest attack was against TransUnion, a company with 3 million consumers and 600000 businesses. The attacker, N4ughtySecTU, allegedly stole 4TB of data that included identity numbers, personal and email addresses, telephone numbers, etc. Even the member database of the governing ANC party was leaked. TransUnion refused to pay the ransom amount of $15 million [25].

One of Egypt's oldest and largest publishing houses was attacked by ransomware in August 2021, and the attack resulted in a loss of access to electronic copies of reference books [35].The Nigerian Guardian reports that about 71 percent of Nigerian organisations were hit by ransomware in 2021 [36].

4.2   Causes of Ransomware Attacks in South Africa

A study done by ITWEB and KnowBe4 on 378 South African organizations showed that 34% of the organizations fell victim to ransomware and 48% of the victims experienced a severe impact on their business operations [5]. Kaspersky saw a 24% increase in ransomware attacks in the second quarter of 2021 in South Africa. Sophos found that the average cost to rectify a ransomware attack in South Africa is about ZAR 6,7M ($0.45 Million), and that 24% of businesses that formed part of the survey indicated they were hit by a ransomware attack during the past year. Only 11% of those businesses were able to recover all their data in a reasonable timeframe [5]. The attacks on South African entities were launched by a variety of ransomware including Crysis, Nefilim, Ryuk, Clop and Conti (BUSINESSTECH, 2021). The methodologies of the ransomware intrusions are shown in Fig. 3.

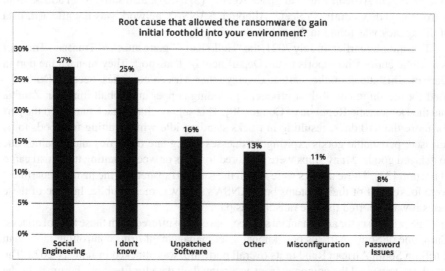

Fig. 3.   Root causes for ransomware access [5]

5   Preventing a Ransomware Attack

In this section, the authors provide guidelines that can be followed by organizations to prevent ransomware attacks. There are steps for managers to follow, as well as guidelines for employees. Some of the guidelines form part of a general cybersecurity culture to be fostered in any organization (Fig. 4).

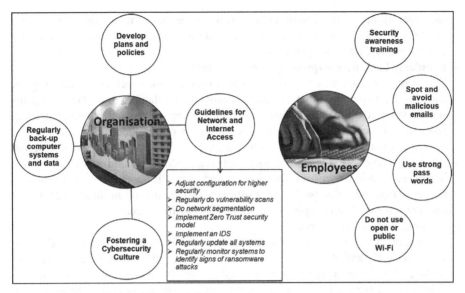

Fig. 4. Framework for prevention of ransomware attack

5.1 Steps for Organizations

- **Develop plans and policies**

  Every organization should have a Cybersecurity Policy that includes the raising of cybersecurity awareness within the organization [37]. There must be specific guidance for raising ransomware awareness.

  A Cyber Incident Response Plan is crucial. This plan depicts steps to be followed by the company's IT security team during a ransomware event. It should include response and notification procedures when attacked, as well as the roles and responsibilities and communications that should be shared, during and after an attack. When designing this plan, remember to include partners, vendors and CSIRTs (Cyber Incident Response Teams) that would need to be notified of an attack. A resilience plan that includes data recovery and addresses, the procedure on what to do if the organization has lost control of critical functions, is also necessary.

- **Fostering a Cybersecurity Culture**

  ENISA, the European Union Agency for Network and Information Security, defines the term "Cybersecurity Culture" (CSC) as "the knowledge, beliefs, perceptions, attitudes, assumptions, norms and values of people regarding cybersecurity and how they manifest themselves in people's behavior with information technologies" (ENISA, 2017). ENISA also advises to raise cybersecurity awareness and to implement an information security framework. A Cybersecurity Culture framework was developed by Leenen, Jansen van Vuuren & Jansen van Vuuren [38] where they advised that a CSC should be integrated in the employee's job, habits and conduct, including all the socio-cultural measures that support technical security methods, for cyber actions to become a natural aspect of the daily activity. Awareness and education are also important pillars of the CSC. The International Telecommunications Union regards the fostering of a cybersecurity culture as a core aspect of maintaining cybersecurity [39]. ENISA provides a very useful guide to advise organizations in creating Cybersecurity Culture programs [40].

- **Regularly back-up computer systems and data**
  The most important way to recover from a ransomware attack is to make regular backups of all your important data and to ensure the availability of backups. Backups should be stored offline or in a cloud-based file hosting service with automatic backup processes to prevent attackers from accessing it. A policy should be drafted on the correct procedures for making backups. External storage device must be disconnected and only be connected when backups are being made. If a cloud service is used, it is advised to disconnect from the cloud storage when it is not required for making backups. Routinely test backups for efficacy. In the case of an attack, verify that backups have not been tampered with before rolling back data.

- **Network and Internet Access**
  It is important to create Best Practice Guidelines for the use of a Remote Desktop Protocol (RDP) and other remote desktop services. Disable unused RDP Server and Message Block (SMB) ports for both cloud and company usage, and remove or disable outdated versions of SMBs. Secure configuration settings can help to limit an organization's threat surface and close security gaps left from default configurations. Regularly perform vulnerability scans of the network and especially for internet facing devices [41]. Devices must be properly configured, security features must be enabled, and vulnerable plugins as well as file extensions must be disabled. Filter network traffic to stop incoming and outgoing communications with known malicious IP addresses [42]. Do network segmentation to allow only certain users onto the network, and implement a Zero Trust Security model to protect the most critical applications and data [42].

- **Implement an IDS**
  An Intrusion Detection System (IDS) identifies malware activity by comparing network traffic logs to signatures that detect known malicious activity. A good IDS updates signatures often and will send alerts if it detects potential malicious activity.

- **Regularly update all systems**
  Ensure that all the organization's operating systems, applications, and software are updated regularly and turn on auto updates for security patches including updates on the firmware and systems. Prioritize the patching of critical vulnerabilities on systems, and vulnerabilities on Internet-facing servers including software that processes Internet data, such as web browsers, browser plugins, and document readers [42]. A Privileged Access Management (PAM) solution can be implemented where used and changed passwords can be verified. [5].

- **User device and account management**
  All user devices must have antivirus and anti-malware solutions with up-to-date signatures installed. Limit user and privileged accounts through "account use"-policies, user account control, and privileged account management. Employ multi-factor authentication for all services, logins, particularly for web mail, virtual private networks (VPNs), and accounts that access critical systems. Adopt solutions that will force an immediate review of the account escalation attempts and implement applications that allow block listing. Enable strong spam filters to reduce the risk of phishing emails

being distributed to employees [42]. Use deceptions such as the creation of fake file repositories (honeypots) that look like legitimate repositories which hackers can target. These deception systems can alert the company that there is suspicious behavior on the network. In this process the hacker activity can be identified and the company can act in time [5, 43].

- **Regular monitoring of systems to identify signs of ransomware attacks**
  Use behavioural analysis to monitor networks systems for anomalous traffic flows and patterns [5]. Look for anomalous file system activity, such as numerous failed file modifications (due to the ransomware attempting to access those files). Investigate if the computer or system suddenly gets slower, or if there is an increase in CPU and hard disk activity for no apparent reason. This can be due to the ransomware searching for files, encrypting files, and removing data files. Sudden unavailability of some of these files could be due to the encryption, deleting, renaming or relocation of files. There can also be suspicious network communications that is caused by interaction between the ransomware and the attackers' command and control server [43].

- **Cyber insurance policy**
  Consider getting a Cyber insurance policy and check whether the policy covers ransomware losses. As described above, with ransomware attacks increasing this could be a viable way to prevent huge losses.

5.2 Employees

- **Security awareness training**

Security awareness training is an important factor of a cybersecure culture. Training must cover hacking and phishing techniques, and in general, make employees aware of Social Engineering attacks to extract information from individuals.

- **Emails**

Employees must be able to spot and avoid malicious emails – this is a key factor to stop ransomware attacks. Employees must remain vigilant and check the source of any email before downloading an attachment.

- **Passwords**

Employees must be encouraged to use strong passwords that should not be reused across multiple accounts or stored where others can get access to it. Employees should not use information generally available on social networks, such as their birthdays or family members' names, to create passwords.

- **Open or public Wi-Fi**

Employees must be discouraged to use open or public Wi-Fi or networks because hackers can easily infiltrate these networks.

6 Recovery After a Ransomware Attack

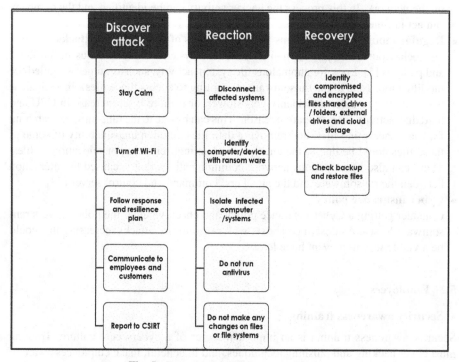

Fig. 5. Recovery after Ransomware attack

What should one do if you fall victim to such an attack? Here are some suggested guidelines an individual or an organization should follow (Fig. 5):

- Stay calm. Stick to the response and resilience plans and do not make any rash decisions. Contact the organization's CSIRT or sector CSIRT at the earliest opportunity.
- Identify and disconnect all affected systems from any network or isolate them and unplug storage devices such as USB or external hard drives. Do not erase any information or make any changes on your file systems. Do not run the antivirus programs. Check the file properties of the infected or encrypted files to identify on which computer the ransomware is installed.
- Turn off any wireless capabilities such as Wi-Fi or Bluetooth.
- Determine the size of the attack including the number of files that is compromised or encrypted on the shared drives or folders, cloud storage or external hard drives. Check which files were backed up and what needs to be restored.

- Encourage open and honest communication, internally to the company and users, as well as externally to vendors and clients. Issue a public statement that explains what had happened, the information available on the attack and your plan to recover the files. Notify law enforcement and regulatory bodies of the attack [5].

7   Conclusion

This paper considers the growing threat of ransomware internationally, with a specific focus on Africa. Ransomware has become the cybercrime with the biggest impact on governments and businesses. The authors presents a primer for institutions to strengthen their cybersecurity measures against ransom ware attacks. It is often human error that leads to ransomware attackers gaining a first entry into a system, and thus cybersecurity training and awareness become crucial. African companies are particularly vulnerable against ransomware because cybersecurity awareness tends to be lower in African countries, compared to the rest of the globe.

References

1. McIntosh, T., Kayes, A., Chen, Y.-P.P., Ng, A., Watters, P.: Ransomware mitigation in the modern era: a comprehensive review, research challenges, and future directions. ACM Comput. Surv. (CSUR) **54**(9), 1–36 (2021)
2. IBM Security, The definitive guide to ransomware: Readiness, response, and remediation. IBM Security. https://www.ibm.com/downloads/cas/EV6NAQR4. Accessed 12 Feb 2020
3. Barak, I.: How Does Ransomware Work?. https://www.cybereason.com/blog/how-does-ransomware-work#:~:text=Ransomware%20is%20a%20type%20of,ransom%20payment%20to%20restore%20access. Accessed 25 Sep 2017
4. Kharraz, A., Robertson, W., Balzarotti, D., Bilge, L., Kirda, E.: Cutting the Gordian Knot: a look under the hood of ransomware attacks. In: Almgren, M., Gulisano, V., Maggi, F. (eds.) DIMVA 2015. LNCS, vol. 9148, pp. 3–24. Springer, Cham (2015). https://doi.org/10.1007/978-3-319-20550-2_1
5. Van der Walt, C., Collard, A., Grimes, R.A., Pillay, K.: Defending Against Ransomware - An Advisory by the South African Cybersecurity Hub. www.orangecyberdefense.com/za/contact/. Accessed 10 May 2021
6. SecureMac, What is Doxware?. https://www.securemac.com/blog/what-is-doxware. Accessed 15 Jan 2020
7. Brewer, R.: Ransomware attacks: detection, prevention and cure. Network Security **2016**(9), 5–9 (2016)
8. COMODO, Ransomware Attacks 2021. https://enterprise.comodo.com/blog/recent-ransomware-attacks/. Accessed 4 Oct 2022
9. Harvard Business Review, Ransomware Attacks Are Spiking. Is Your Company Prepared?. https://hbr.org/2021/05/ransomware-attacks-are-spiking-is-your-company-prepared. Accessed 15 Jan 2021
10. Morgan, S.: Cybercrime to cost the world $10.5 trillion Annual by 2025. Cybercrime Magazine (2020)
11. The Touro College & University System, The 10 Biggest Ransomware Attacks of 2021. https://illinois.touro.edu/news/the-10-biggest-ransomware-attacks-of-2021.php. Accessed 25 Nov 2021

12. Macias, A., Wilkie, C.: U.S. recovers $2.3 million in bitcoin paid in the Colonial Pipeline ransom. CNBC. https://www.cnbc.com/2021/06/07/us-recovers-some-of-the-money-paid-in-the-colonial-pipeline-ransom-officials-say.html. Accessed 10 Oct 2021

13. Din, A.: Chemical Distributor Brenntag Says What Data Was Stolen During the Ransomware Attack. HEIMDAL. https://heimdalsecurity.com/blog/chemical-distributor-brenntag-says-what-data-was-stolen-during-the-ransomware-attack/. Accessed 15 Sep 2021

14. Greig, J.: Acer confirms second cyberattack in 2021 after ransomware incident in March. ZDNET. https://www.zdnet.com/article/acer-confirms-second-cyberattack-in-2021/. Accessed 5 Nov 2021

15. Morrison, S.: Ransomware attack hits another massive, crucial industry: Meat. Vox. https://www.vox.com/recode/2021/6/1/22463179/jbs-foods-ransomware-attack-meat-hackers. Accessed 15 Sep 2021

16. Osborne, C.: Updated Kaseya ransomware attack FAQ: What we know now. ZDNET. https://www.zdnet.com/article/updated-kaseya-ransomware-attack-faq-what-we-know-now/. Accessed 20 Oct 2021

17. Tung, L.: Kaseya ransomware attack: 1,500 companies affected, company confirms. ZDNET. https://www.zdnet.com/article/kaseya-ransomware-attack-1500-companies-affected-company-confirms/. Accessed 9 Sep 2021

18. Mehrotra, K.: NBA's Houston Rockets Face Cyber-Attack by Ransomware Group. Bloomberg. https://www.bloomberg.com/news/articles/2021-04-14/nba-s-houston-rockets-face-cyber-attack-by-ransomware-group. Accessed 15 Sep 2021

19. Goud, N.: https://www.cybersecurity-insiders.com/babuk-ransomware-attack-on-nba-houston-rockets/. https://www.cybersecurity-insiders.com/babuk-ransomware-attack-on-nba-houston-rockets/. Accessed 28 Jan 2021

20. Ikeda, S.: Ransomware Attack Reported at Insurance Giant AXA One Week After It Changes Cyber Insurance Policies in France. CPO Magazine, Rezonen Pte. Ltd. https://www.cpomagazine.com/cyber-security/ransomware-attack-reported-at-insurance-giant-axa-one-week-after-it-changes-cyber-insurance-policies-in-france/. Accessed 15 Nov 2021

21. Mehrotra, K., Turton, W.: CNA Financial Paid $40 Million in Ransom After March Cyberattack. Bloomberg. https://www.bloomberg.com/news/articles/2021-05-20/cna-financial-paid-40-million-in-ransom-after-march-cyberattack. Accessed 15 Sep 2021

22. Keane, S., Gonzalez, O.: Cyberpunk 2077 developer CD Projekt hit by ransomware attack, source code leaked. Cnet. https://www.cnet.com/tech/computing/cyberpunk-2077-developer-cd-projekt-hit-by-ransomware-attack-source-code-leaked/. Accessed 15 Sep 2021

23. Hope, A.: Kia Motors America Suffers a $20 Million Suspected DoppelPaymer Ransomware Attack. CPO Magazine, Rezonen Pte. Ltd. https://www.cpomagazine.com/cyber-security/kia-motors-america-suffers-a-20-million-suspected-doppelpaymer-ransomware-attack/#:~:text=Automaker%20Kia%20Motors%20America%20%28KMA%29%20suffered%20a. Accessed 15 Nov 2021

24. BUSINESSTECH, South Africa under cyber attack: Interpol reveals top threats in South Africa (2021). https://businesstech.co.za/news/it-services/531990/south-africa-under-cyber-attack-interpol-reveals-top-threats-in-south-africa/

25. Myles, I.: Cybercriminals love South Africa -Study. MyBroadband. https://mybroadband.co.za/news/security/443090-cybercriminals-love-south-africa-study.html. Accessed 9 May 2022

26. Myles, I.: South African companies getting nailed by ransomware — and they are paying up. MyBroadband. https://mybroadband.co.za/news/security/443728-south-african-companies-getting-nailed-by-ransomware-and-they-are-paying-up.html?msclkid=da174ab7d075 11ecadd77ffe4139712e. Accessed 9 May 2022

27. Money Expert South Africa, What-is-the-POPI-Act-a-simple-summary. https://www.moneyexpert.co.za/broadband/what-is-the-popi-act-a-simple-summary/. Accessed 9 May 2022

28. Moyo, A.: Dis-Chem prescription service outage after cyber attack. ITWeb. https://www.itweb.co.za/content/8OKdWqDXNezqbznQ. Accessed 11 May 2022
29. ITWeb, Hornetsecurity global ransomware survey reveals the 'stinging' truth. https://www.itweb.co.za/content/kLgB17e8QnNv59N4. Accessed 10 May 2022
30. Thomas, I.: The State of Ransomware Attacks in Africa. Ironscales. https://ironscales.com/blog/the-state-of-ransomware-attacks-in-africa. Accessed 9 Feb 2022
31. Moyo, A.: Justice department battles to contain ransomware attack. ITWeb. https://www.itweb.co.za/content/DZQ58vVPOB1MzXy2. Accessed 9 Oct 2021
32. Moyo, A.: SA's govt entities under attack as space agency hit by data breach. ITWeb. https://www.itweb.co.za/content/6GxRKMYJy1bqb3Wj. Accessed 9 Oct 2021
33. ITWeb, Lessons from Transnet: Is your business prepared for a ransomware attack. https://www.itweb.co.za/content/GxwQDq1ZJQLvlPVo. Accessed 29 Sep 2021
34. Soteria, Ransomware attack hits financial services firm Curo. http://soteriacloud.co.za/news/financial-services-ransomware-attack-ransomware/. Accessed 9 Feb 2022
35. Tayea, H.: Ransomware Virus Hits One of Egypt's Largest Publishing Houses. SEE-egy. https://see.news/ransomware-virus-hits-one-of-egypts-largest-pub/. Accessed 10 May 2021
36. Guardian, Nigeria, Ransomware hits 71% of Nigerian organisations. https://guardian.ng/technology/ransomware-hits-71-of-nigerian-organisations/. Accessed 10 May 2022
37. Government Technology, 7 Steps to Help Prevent & Limit the Impact of Ransomware. https://www.govtech.com/security/7-steps-to-help-prevent--limit-the-impact-of-ransomware.html. Accessed 15 Aug 2020
38. Leenen, L., Jansen van Vuuren, J., Jansen van Vuuren, A.M.: Cybersecurity and cybercrime combatting culture for african police services. In: David Kreps, Taro Komukai, T V Gopal, Kaori Ishii, (ed.) Human-Centric Computing in a Data-Driven Society. IFIP Advances in Information and Communication Technology, vol. 590, pp. 248–261. Springer, Cham (2020). https://doi.org/10.1007/978-3-030-62803-1_20
39. ITU, International Telecommunications Union Corporate Annual Report 2008. International Telecommunications Union. https://www.itu.int/osg/csd/stratplan/AR2008_web.pdf. Accessed 8 Nov 2008
40. ENISA, Cyber Security Culture in Organisations. European Agency for Network and Information Security (ENISA) (2017)
41. Piper, D.: Cybersecurity and infrastructure security agency releases guidance regarding ransomware. Internet Law 25(1), 1–17 (2021)
42. CISA, Protecting sensitive and personal information from ransomware-caused data breaches. https://www.cisa.gov/sites/default/files/publications/CISA_Fact_Sheet-Protecting_Sensitive_and_Personal_Information_from_Ransomware-Caused_Data_Breaches-508C.pdf. Accessed 10 Jan 2021
43. Melnick, J.: How to Detect Ransomware. https://blog.netwrix.com/2020/09/03/how-to-detect-ransomware/. Accessed 28 Jan 2020

A Study on AI Creations and Patent Law Protection

Ayuki Saito[1(✉)], Michele Baccelli[2], Kazuto Kobayashi[3] , and Mitsuyoshi Hiratsuka[4]

[1] Japanese Patent Attorney, Matsumoto-shi, Nagano, Japan
Ayuki.Saito@outlook.jp
[2] HOFFMANN EITLE, Munich, Germany
mbaccelli@hoffmanneitle.com
[3] Tokyo Institute of Technology, Meguro-ku, Tokyo, Japan
Kobayashi@sangaku.titech.ac.jp
[4] Tokyo University of Science, Shinjuku-ku, Tokyo, Japan
hiratsuk@kb3.so-net.ne.jp

Abstract. The process of conceiving an invention, how AI may contribute to the conception process, and how AI inventions should be protected by patent law are examined. In our approach and analysis, AI remains in the category of sophisticated tools used by natural persons to create inventions. The approach is assessed against a decision by the Australian Federal Court acknowledging that the AI machine DABUS can be held as an inventor. As a result of our study, however, we believe that it is at least questionable whether DABUS can be considered an autonomous inventor. Thus, in those cases where someone names an AI machine as the inventor, we propose setting a high standard of proof in requesting to produce as evidence the actual machine output claimed as the invention and to illustrate how the machine operates to arrive at such output.

Keywords: Inventorship · AI · Patent

1 Introduction

Today, with the rapid progress of AI technology, the debate on AI creations is increasingly alive with attention being paid to the case of DABUS, a patent application filed in many countries around the world and naming AI as the inventor. In the DABUS application, several jurisdictions have denied the possibility of naming a machine as the inventor, while other jurisdiction like Australia have allowed it, thus further fueling the discussion as to whether patent rights shall be granted to an AI invention, and, if so, to whom the patent rights should belong. However, there are very few cases where AI has autonomously made inventions. In this paper, we examine the process of conceiving an invention, how AI can invent or contribute to the conception process, and then consider how AI inventions should be protected by patent law.

The present article reflects only the personal opinion of the authors and not necessarily those of the organizations with which they are affiliated. Further, the authors do not endorse any product or service herein mentioned.

© IFIP International Federation for Information Processing 2022
Published by Springer Nature Switzerland AG 2022
D. Kreps et al. (Eds.): HCC 2022, IFIP AICT 656, pp. 132–143, 2022.
https://doi.org/10.1007/978-3-031-15688-5_12

2 Definition of Inventor

Japanese Patent Law stipulates that a person who has made an invention that can be used for industrial purposes is entitled to a patent, see Article 29, paragraph 1. Under this provision, it is understood that a natural person who truly invented can be an inventor [1]. However, the definition of an inventor is not stipulated in the Patent Law and is left to academic theories.

Nakayama [2] states that "An inventor is only a person who has actually participated in the creative act of the invention".

Regarding the criteria for judging joint inventors, Yoshifuji [3] writes: "Since invention is the creation of a technical idea, the existence of substantial cooperation must be judged exclusively from this perspective. A person who is not involved in the creation of the idea itself, such as a mere administrator, assistant, or patron, is not a joint inventor.

3 Examination by the Japanese Government

In Japan, in response to the recent rapid development of AI technology, the "Next Generation IP System Study Committee Report" was compiled in 2016 [4]. Figure 1 shows the treatment of AI creations in the current IP system. Based on this report, creations and rights to be named as inventor are classified as follows:

(a) Creation by a natural person: Rights arise.
(b) Creation using AI as a tool: Rights for the natural person arise when the AI is generated by the creative intention and creative contribution of a natural person.
(c) Creation by AI: If human involvement cannot be regarded as a creative contribution (e.g., mere encouragement of creation) and AI is not evaluated to have generated the work autonomously, no rights arise.

The report further states that it is usually difficult to distinguish between a creation by a natural person and by AI. The difference between the two is in the process of creation, and not in the creation itself. For this reason, unless it is clearly stated that the work is an AI creation, it is treated as if it were a creation by a natural person. At any rate, given the increased availability and performance of AI tools, there is a possibility that IP rights may increase exponentially. The report also states that, since IP rights are exclusive, by treating AI creations in the same way as those made by natural persons, there is a concern that those who have access to such AI tools may more easily monopolize vast amount of information and knowledge, importantly – we add – without requiring the endeavors, dedication and time (more precious to man than to a machine) that a human would need to arrive at a creation.

In short, the report raises the concern that the use of AI may unnecessarily inflate the number of inventions and related patents possibly without sufficiently justified efforts.

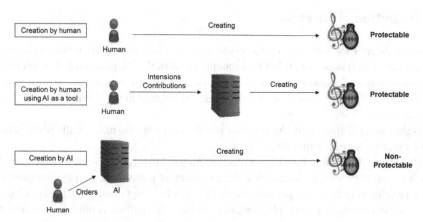

Fig. 1. Treatment of AI creations in the current IP system

4   Conception of Inventions and AI

4.1   Assumptions

In this paper, we focus on AI inventions created by natural persons using AI as a tool, see case (b) above, presently being a technologically realistic scenario. The analysis will proceed as follows: Firstly, we examine the processes that lead to the conception of an invention. Secondly, we analyze which processes can be carried out by a natural person or by AI. Then, we attempt to examine the creation of inventions from the perspective of creative intention and creative contribution. In this way, we believe that it is possible to find a solution to the concerns expressed above.

4.2   The Processes Leading to an Invention

In general, conception and reduction to practice are present when a natural person comes up with an invention. Leaving aside the reduction to practice, and simplifying, the activities leading to an invention and to the filing of a patent application may be considered to consist of the following processes (1) to (7) [5]:

(1) Identification of the facts to be solved
    The facts may include technical issues, social needs, and mere human desires. In reality, there may be various mental steps that lead to these facts. However, we are herein not concerned with the thinking steps as such, but rather with the facts to be solved thanks to the invention.
(2) Investigation of conventional technology and clarification of related problems
    Most inventions are created based on conventional technologies. In this process, conventional technology is investigated, the problems that cannot be solved are clarified, and preparations for the conception are made.

(3) Conception

Conception represents directions for solving a problem and means for arriving at the solution to a problem beyond the idea. This process is the core of the activity leading to one or more inventions.

(4) Reduction to practice

This is the process of considering how to realize the solution to the problem that has been conceived.

(5) Realistic production of the problem-solving means

The feasibility of the problem-solving means is confirmed through actual experiments and/or verifications.

(6) Invention discovery and pre-filing search

Through a pre-filing search, the part of the conceived solution that is perceived to overcome the problems of the conventional technology and to satisfy patentability requirements (novelty, inventive step, etc.) is extracted as the invention.

(7) Conceptualization (of technical ideas)

The invention is completed by expressing the technical features of the conceived solution in the form of claims.

4.3 Examination of the Roles of Natural Persons and AI when Conceiving Inventions

Before Conception.

In process (1), we consider that not only a mere command to "invent" but also "specific instructions" are necessary. The specific instructions are equivalent to the "motivation" for the invention, and include technical issues, requirements of natural persons, etc. For example, in the currently realized automatic composition device [6], it is necessary to input the "motif" of a piece of music when the device composes it. This motivation is recognized as the creative intent of a natural person.

In process (2), a natural person is required to provide an algorithm to the AI in order to come up with an idea, the algorithm causing e.g. to learn conventional technology, understand and clarifying problems. For example, in the project where an AI called "TouRobo-kun" solves a university entrance exam problem, a natural person designs the algorithm for the AI to come up with the solution to the problem [7]. In other words, through the design of the algorithm, the natural person contributes to the process by which "TouRobo-kun" comes up with the answer. Usually, it is not easy for an AI to come up with an algorithm by itself, but it must be provided by a natural person so that the AI can learn. We will call this process "pre-learning", which is necessary for AI to come up with an idea. Pre-learning is done by a natural person for an AI, and we believe that part of the "creative contribution" of a natural person is recognized here.

Conception.

The idea in process (3) is conceived by AI based on the conventional technology obtained by applying the algorithm from process (2). It is not possible to describe exactly what kind of actions the AI take, but we believe that such actions are based, for example, on the optimal combination of a huge amount of information that cannot be handled by a natural person.

Reduction to Practice.
In process (4), the AI presents how to materialize the idea, and in process (5) it actually conducts experiments and verifications. An invention is a "creation of a technical idea" (Article 2(1) of the Japanese Patent Act), and in this regard, Takabayashi [8] states that an invention "must be feasible and repeatable as a means to achieve a certain goal, since it is a technology".

The fact that a natural person provides specific instructions to an AI means that the natural person naturally expects to implement the AI invention. However, in process (5), it is necessary for a natural person, who is the subject of implementation of the invention, to verify the possibility of implementation. This work is considered to be part of the creative contribution of a natural person.

In U.S. case law [9], the idea requires recognition of both existence and appreciation of value. Applying this precedent to the case under examination, the moment when the AI understands the idea output from the AI itself is the moment when the "existence" is recognized, and the moment when the feasibility of the idea is confirmed as a result of verification is the moment when the "value" is recognized. In other words, process (5) is usually carried out by a natural person, and the natural person is considered to be involved in the conception of the AI.

After Reduction to Practice.
In processes (6) and (7), AI extracts patentable parts (mainly the novel parts with attempts to guess the possibly less obvious parts) based on the learned conventional technologies. As for the preparation of documents like a patent application, a semi-automatic specification generation system may be used [10].

4.4 Discussion

Table 1 summarizes the processes leading to an invention and the roles assumed in each process. Specifically, the natural person provides specific instructions in process (1), prior learning in process (2) (e.g. provision of algorithms leading to conception and learning of conventional technology), and verification of an embodiment in process (5). The creative intention of natural persons is recognized in process (1), and the creative contribution of natural persons is recognized in processes (2) and (5). We believe that processes (1), (2), and (5) are the roles of natural persons that are indispensable, perhaps no matter how advanced AI technology becomes, at least for certain types of inventions; the DABUS case seems to challenge this assumption and we will discuss it later. Thus, we believe that at least based on present evidence it should not be expected that an AI machine will be able to invent autonomously anything based on mere instructions from a natural person, ie. inventions should still be treated as made by humans assisted by highly sophisticated AI tools. To those naming AI as the autonomous inventor, a high standard of proof should be requested to show that this is the actual case. If the number of autonomous-AI inventions should then significantly increase, further policy considerations may have to be taken into consideration as to which type of rights might arise.

Table 1. Invention process and assumed role assignment

Invention process		Assumed division of roles	
1	Identification of the fact to be solved	Human	Input assignments into AI
2	Investigation of conventional technology and clarification of problems in conventional technology	Human AI	Human to AI to perform pre-training
3	Conception	AI	Combining vast amounts of literature, etc.
4	Reduction to practice	AI	Output the concept
5	Realistic production of the problem-solving means	Human	Demonstration by a natural person
6	Invention discovery and pre-filing search	AI	Confirmation of patentability
7	Conceptualization (of technical ideas)	AI	Output the completed invention

4.5 The "USE AS A TOOL" Requirement: A Comparison with a Circuit Simulator

The previous section discusses the case of a natural person using AI as a tool, which may be compared to a simulator used as a tool for generating an electronic circuit.

A circuit simulator of this type can be described as a device to which a desired function or a higher-level logic circuit is input. The simulator then automatically outputs an optimized circuit by taking into account constraints or conditions, like e.g. the number of transistors, the size of the circuit, calculation speed of the critical path, etc. In the process of designing a circuit using such a simulator, a natural person may design an initial circuit; the simulator solves various constraints to realize and finalize the circuit. In this respect, circuit simulators and AI have something in common in that they automatically output optimal results.

In the case of an AI outputting an invention, a natural person provides the creative intention, in particular by imputing algorithms leading to the facts to be solved, and the creative contribution, in particular the prior learning, so the AI is used as a tool.

By comparison, in the case of a circuit simulator, a circuit is completed by optimizing some numerical calculations against the design by a natural person. In this case, the natural person gives the circuit simulator the creative intention (constraints to be solved) and the creative contribution (circuit design), so that we can say that the circuit simulator is used as a supplementary tool.

Hence, both the AI and the circuit simulator are essentially software tools used by man to more quickly complete certain tasks.

5   Examination of Inventors and Right Holders

5.1   Setting of the Model

From the development of the AI platform to the completion of the AI related inventions, several actors intervene:

(A)   Developer: A programmer who develops the AI platform.
(B)   Owner: A provider of the AI platform, e.g., a company to which the developer belongs.
(C)   Purchaser: A person who purchases the AI platform and owns the AI that has been pre-trained.
(D)   Educator: A person who provides pre-training to the AI platform.
(E)   User: A person who intends to use the AI to make inventions.
(F)   Verifier: A person who verifies the output of the AI.
(G)   Big data owners (as represented by the managers).
(H)   Owner (managers) of AI parameters.

In this paper, we assume that the above to be all different actors.

Figure 2 shows the flow from the development of an AI platform to the completion of an AI invention. The left side of the figure corresponds to the developer and the right side corresponds to the user. First, the developer (A) develops the AI platform, which is owned by the owner (B). The platform is then transferred to an individual or company (C) that intends to use it. The platform is pre-trained by an educator (D) so that it is suitable for a specific type of use. After the pre-learning is completed, the platform is used by the user (E). The output generated in the process of use is verified by a verifier (F). The big data and AI parameters generated in the process of pre-training and the invention are managed by their respective owners (G, H).

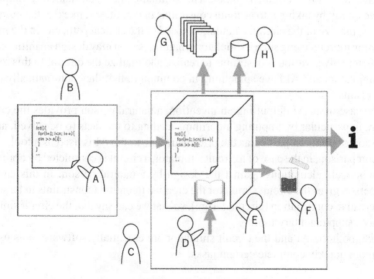

Fig. 2. Study model

5.2   The Role of Natural Persons

In Sect. 4.3, we considered that processes (1), (2), and (5) are performed by or involve natural persons. In this section, we examine which of the agents are specifically responsible for these processes.

In process (1), a natural person, the user (E) of AI, inputs specific instructions to the AI.

In process (2), it is necessary to provide prior learning to the AI. The essence of pre-learning is the construction of learning data and tuning of AI parameters to obtain optimal AI parameters. We believe that the role of the educator (D) is extremely important in this process.

Process (5) is to verify the feasibility of the idea based on the AI output. The verifier (F) is involved in this process.

However, the developer (A) and the owner (B) are involved in the AI platform, but they are not involved in the invention itself. As for purchasers (C) and owners (G, H) of big data or AI parameters, it cannot be said that they are substantially involved in the invention, since they are mere owners or administrators.

5.3   Inventors and Patentees

AI inventions as herein considered are in the category of "use as a tool" available to natural persons. Therefore, we assume that the inventor is also a natural person who uses AI as a tool. In the case of "use as a tool," it is necessary to give creative intention and creative contribution to the AI invention. Specifically, the former is the input of specific instructions, and the latter is the provision of prior learning and verification of the feasibility of the idea. From the discussion in the previous section, the educator (D), the user (E), and the verifier (F) fall into this category. Since each of them is assumed to be a different actor, it is appropriate to consider all of these actors (hereinafter referred to as "users") as joint inventors. In addition, based on the U.S. precedent that "if a computer cannot be an inventor, a natural person who recognizes the existence and value of the invention can be an inventor" [11], it is appropriate to consider the users as inventors.

With respect to the patentee, according to the Patent Law, unless the right to obtain a patent is transferred (Article 33, Paragraph 1) or special provisions regarding employee inventions (Article 35) are applied, the right to obtain a patent arises with the inventor, and the inventor is given the patent. As applied to this case, the patent right belongs to the user, from the beginning.

For completeness, we note that usage patterns different from the above may also be considered, in which case the person who made a substantial contribution to the invention will also be different. Further, depending on the starting point of the model, one may also view the developer of the AI platform as an inventor because of his/her contribution being essential to the conception of the invention.

Therefore, while maintaining the principle that the patent belongs to the original user, we believe that it should be allowed to determine who should be recognized as the inventor in each mode of use through contracts or agreements.

6 Examples of Patent Applications Naming AI as Inventor

In 2018, two patent applications were filed with the European Patent Office (EPO) naming DABUS, a non-natural person, as the inventor. These applications have since been filed in many countries around the world. Many patent authorities, including the EPO, rejected the applications because the naming of the inventor did not meet the legal requirements. On the other hand, the Republic of South Africa [12] and Australia recognized DABUS as an inventor.

DABUS is a complex software architecture that may be described as the combination of two artificial neural networks. The first network generates notions as a consequence of internal or external perturbations. The second network analyzes the output of the first network and assesses its novelty, utility or value, and selectively reinforces the way the first network is perturbated so that notions having higher prospects of being novel, useful or valuable can be produced. Simplifying, the first network may be thought as a sort of chaotic generator of ideas, with the second network judging the output from the first and educating the first to produce better results so that ultimately the creation of valuable and non-random ideas is achieved. Allegedly, the system – once trained – can freely run to produce notions in the sense of inventions [13].

6.1 Judicial Decision of the Australian District Court

On July 30, 2021, the Australian Federal Court annulled the decision of the patent authorities to reject the DABUS application and referred the application back to the Patent Office [14].

In the judgment, the Court addresses the technology behind DABUS stating that it is an autonomous system and its output is the claimed invention, see marginals 30–47. The Court also states that constraints on the concept of inventorship would stifle innovation in various fields, based on the example of the use of AI in the pharmaceutical field, see 56.

Additionally, the district court finds that AI can be recognized as an inventor mainly because of the following reasons (for additional details, refer also to [15, 16]).

There is no specific provision that explicitly denies the proposition that AI can be an inventor, see 119.

Unlike copyright law, which includes the requirement of human authorship and the existence of moral rights, there is no specific aspect of patent law that encourages an interpretation that excludes non-human inventors, see 120.

The term "inventor" is not defined by law or regulation and thus has its ordinary meaning, see 121.

It is consistent with the purpose of the Act to construe the term "inventor" in a manner that encourages the publication and dissemination of innovations and their inventions by means of rewards, regardless of whether the innovation was made by a human being or not, see 124.

Similar to Article 2A, the right to computer inventions will encourage the development of creative machines by computer scientists and developments in the facilitation and use of the products of such machines by others, leading to new scientific advantages, see 125.

The Court assumes that DABUS would be autonomous, including the selection of input data, the setting of goals, and the choices and paths to reach those goals, see 127. It then states that such AI systems are not mere tools but operate at least semi-autonomously, see 128. Furthermore, the district court states that it would be better to recognize the AI as the inventor, rather than the programmer, owner, or other person associated with the AI, to avoid uncertainty in the recognition of the inventor, see 131.

It is perhaps important noting that the Australian Court was not apparently concerned with the question of whether DABUS actually generated the invention, but rather with the legal point of whether the machine could be named as inventor. In this legal framework, it might suffice only a preliminary assessment as to whether DABUS can be reasonably held to be the actual inventor.

6.2 Our Proposed Model and Comparison with the Australian District Court Decision

In the following we compare our above model and assumptions, namely that AI remans a tool available to humans for making inventions, against the Australian decision.

Regarding process (1), we considered that the facts to be solved are input by natural persons, without which AI cannot operate. On the other hand, the Federal Court acknowledges that DABUS autonomously invents. Furthermore, since it is "capable of adapting to new scenarios without additional human input," the Court apparently acknowledges that the facts to be solved were also proposed by DABUS. To generate a notion or idea, DABUS is trained based on a knowledge domain, as far as one can derive from US5,659,666 that Applicant submitted to the EPO as one of the documents describing how DABUS operates [17]. Based on this, it is questionable that the machine – and not a person – is the one to have directly chosen the facts, i.e. the knowledge domain on which to work towards an invention. The Australian decision seems to mainly follow Applicant's submissions, in particular that after an initial learning aiming at verifying correctness of first notions by a human, then DABUS can freely run to arrive at the invention. It is however highly desirable ascertaining the boundary of where the human-assisted learning ends and where the machine free-run starts. As a side remark, we wonder whether the outcome of the judicial case would have been different, had it involved an opposing party capable of challenging Appellant's submissions on solid technical grounds. In summary, we believe that it is fair questioning whether and how far it is credible that DABUS can choose the facts on its own.

Regarding process (2), this paper considers that prior learning is the role of natural persons. On the other hand, the decision acknowledges that at least an initial training needs to take place, which may need to be tailored to a specific technical domain, see e.g. US 5,659,666. Also here, it is in our view questionable the credibility that DABUS can autonomously perform process (2). Further, the judgment acknowledges that DABUS was designed by the applicant, namely Mr. Thaler. Therefore, this process involved a natural person.

Regarding process (5), this paper considers that the verification of feasibility is the role of a natural person. On the other hand, there is no express reference to this point in the judgment, which rather seems to accept the Appellant's submissions. However, we believe that it is dubious or at least unclear whether this process was conducted by natural persons or by DABUS. The doubts are fueled by the fact that the invention at issue relates to a food or beverage container including a wall having a fractal profile. A fractal is a never-ending pattern that appears the same at different scales, i.e. it is an infinitely small detailed profile that cannot be machined in practice. In this regard, the application states that "It is to be understood that these fractal elements 18–28 have fractal characteristics within practical considerations determined for example by the limits of the chosen manufacturing/forming process, the material [...] In practice, the fractal elements 18–28 will typically reach a minimum practical dimension determined by such constraints.". It is in our view unclear whether such recognition, crucial to the reduction to practice of an abstract – probably artistic – idea, was actually output by DABUS, by a natural person evaluating the output or even by the patent attorney in anticipation of possible objections of an otherwise insufficient disclosure. Probably an analysis of the actual output by DABUS, which would represent the invention disclosure in the case at issue, may help answering this question.

Hence, we believe that there are at least some open questions and legitimate doubts as to whether processes (1), (2) and (5) can be considered to be performed by DABUS. A more detailed and thorough analysis of the actual functioning of DABUS, as well as observation and documentation of its functioning and output seem at least desirable in order to more comfortably conclude that technology is ready to have a machine being the sole inventor.

7 Conclusion

In this paper, we analyzed the inventive acts of AI and concluded that AI remains in the category of sophisticated tools used by natural persons. In addition, we evaluated our approach against a decision by the Australian Federal Court acknowledging that the AI machine DABUS may be legally named as an inventor when accepting the assertion that the claimed invention was indeed the autonomous output of the machine. As a result of our study, however, we believe that it is at least questionable whether DABUS can be considered an autonomous inventor. Thus, in those cases where someone names an AI machine as the inventor, we propose setting a high standard of proof in requesting to produce as evidence the actual machine output claimed as the invention and to illustrate how the machine operates to arrive at such output.

In the future, AI research will progress at an accelerated pace, and groundbreaking inventions may be created using vast amounts of information that cannot be handled by natural humans. Such inventions may contribute to the development and progress of the world, but may also lead to destructive, illegal or detrimental applications. In such cases, it is the reasoning of the natural person who uses AI as a tool that must be questioned; only with the appropriate use of AI can inventions lead to industrial development. Natural persons should take into account the impact of AI-related inventions on the development of industry and the cumulative progress of technology, and work and apply for patents on their inventions in a responsible manner.

References

1. JPO. Regarding the indication of inventors (2021). https://www.jpo.go.jp/system/process/shu tugan/hatsumei.html. Accessed 29 Jan 2021
2. Nakayama, N.: Industrial Property Law, (1) Patent Law, 2nd edn., Enlarged Version. Kobundo (2000)
3. Yoshifuji, K., Kumagai, K.: Introduction to Patent Law, 13th edn. Yuhikaku, Tokyo (1998)
4. Verification, Evaluation and Planning Committee, Intellectual Property Strategy Headquarters, Report of the Next Generation IP System Study Committee: Toward the Construction of a Next Generation IP System Corresponding to Digitalization and Networking (2016)
5. Okochi, A.: Inventive Action and Technological Thought: The Business Historical Phase of Technology and Patents. University of Tokyo Press (1992)
6. http://www.dtmstation.com/archives/51929623.html. Accessed 29 Jan 2021
7. Arai, N.: Can Robots Enter the University of Tokyo? East Press (2014)
8. Takabayashi, R.: The Standard Patent Law, 5th edn. Yuhikaku, Tokyo (2014)
9. Invitogen Corp. v. Clontech Labs., Inc. Anon., 429 F.3d 1052, 1064 (Fed. Cir. 2005)
10. https://specif.io/. Accessed 29 Jan 2021
11. Abbott, R.: I think therefore I invent: creative computers and the future of patent law. Boston Coll. Law Rev. **57**(4), 1079 (2016)
12. JETRO Dubai Office, Africa IP Information: World's First Patent Granted in South Africa for Application Naming AI as Inventor (2021). https://www.jetro.go.jp/ext_images/_Ipnews/afr ica/ip_aripo_20210802_3.pdf. Accessed 29 Jan 2021
13. Marginals 30 to 43 of Thaler v Commissioner of Patents [201] FCA 879, File Number VID 108 of 2021
14. Thaler v Commissioner of Patents [201] FCA 879, File Number VID 108 of 2021. https://www.judgments.fedcourt.gov.au/judgments/Judgments/fca/single/2021/2021fca0879
15. Yamamoto, E.: On AI-related inventions in Australia. Patent **74**(9), 12–16 (2021)
16. Nakayama, I.: Inventors of AI-related inventions. Bessatsu Patent (26), 49–69
17. The Designation of Inventorship (EPO Form 1002) submitted to the EPO on 24 July 2019
18. Hiratsuka, M., Saito, A., Kobayashi, K.: A study on the entity of inventions related to AI and protection by patent law. Intellect. Prop. J. **1** (2017)
19. Saito, A., Kobayashi, K., Hiratsuka, M.: Patent applications with AI as an inventor and its invention process. Patent **73**(10) (2020)

General Monitoring and Constructive Knowledge? Issues of Automated Content Moderation by Hosting Service Providers Under Japanese Law

Toru Maruhashi[✉]

Department of Law, Meiji University, Tokyo, Japan
`torumaruhashi@meiji.ac.jp`

Abstract. This article reviews the current state of Japanese legal system regarding Content Moderation including automated or AI-based system operated by Hosting Service Providers (HSPs) and its relationship with knowledge-based limitation of liability of and injunctions against HSPs. We have been careful enough not to legislatively impose HSPs general monitoring obligations due to concerns on de facto censorship, significant chilling effect on freedom of expression and cost burden on HSPs. However, recent discussion was leaning towards proactive monitoring of illegal information with expectation that introduction of Content Moderation equipped with AI will become easier due to the progress of technology diffusion and cost reduction. This Japanese legal status and discussions are evaluated in comparison with global legal system especially recent EU legal system updates and judicial precedents. Finally, it concludes with extraction of issues such as prohibition of general monitoring and imposing excessive cost burdens on HSPs and need for confirming effect of proactive Content Moderation on knowledge-based limitation of liability.

Keywords: Automated content moderation · Intermediary Liability · Hosting service

1 Introduction[1]

An internet intermediary service classified as a hosting service provider, especially a platform service such as a large-scale Social Network (collectively, an "HSP") which moderates a large amount of content uploaded by users. This so-called "Content Moderation[2]" operation may involve monitoring all uploads of users, suppressing before

---

[1] This article is a product of further elaboration of my previous articles, "Intermediaries' Liability - Transformation of Limitation of Liability Legislation", 1554 Jurist 19, and "Content Moderation and the Use of AI, and Injunction - Comparison with EU Trends", 132 Hanrei-Jiho no. 2508 (both in Japanese).

[2] This terminology has become used in recent years. *See* Grimmelmann J, "The Virtues of Moderation" (2015) 17 Yale Journal of Law and Technology 42, which analyzed generally online moderation practices, but does not use the two-word phrase "content moderation".

© IFIP International Federation for Information Processing 2022
Published by Springer Nature Switzerland AG 2022
D. Kreps et al. (Eds.): HCC 2022, IFIP AICT 656, pp. 144–158, 2022.
https://doi.org/10.1007/978-3-031-15688-5_13

their publication, deleting them after publication, and/or freezing and deleting the users' accounts.

It may be a global trend[3], as a policy agenda for coping with illegal and harmful content[4], to impose the de jure or de facto requirement for HSP to implement automated Content Moderation i. e. automatic screening and filtering or blocking content process using automated tools implementing advanced technology including artificial intelligence (such advanced technology is hereinafter called collectively "AI" and AI-based Content Moderation is called "ACM")[5].

In fact, it is certainly an urgent global common issue that as a measure against illegal or harmful information, whether to allow, promote, obligate, or conversely to limit use of ACM by HSP legislatively or administratively, taking into consideration that using ACM is becoming more efficient, but still leaves limits in the accuracy and trustworthiness. Furthermore, the issue extends to the way of enforcement by courts or administrative authorities, especially how far they can/shall award injunctive orders reflecting the HSPs' ability of suspension of illegal content using ACM.

There have been various discussions on the risk of excessive deletion of legal information by Content Moderation and mitigations of this risk[6] and how to avoid actions affecting fundamental rights such as private censorship[7] and the overall chilling effect on freedom of expression by Content Moderation.

This article does not go deep into the policy principles and legislation to protect against these over- or erroneous removals and mitigate their adverse systemic effects.

Instead, since HSPs' use of advanced technologies to avoid under-removal for the measures against illegal information is expected, we mainly focus on the issue of whether HSP can be required to generally (and comprehensively) monitor their users' content uploads and how HSP's limitation of liability is affected by the Content Moderation, especially ACM. When the illegal information is detected accurately by ACM, if such detection is considered as knowledge or awareness of an HSP, the HSP is forced to delete

---

[3] G. Frosio and S. Mendis, "Monitoring and Filtering: European Reform or Global Trend?" in Oxford Handbook of Online Intermediary Liability, G. Frosio, Ed. May 2020. https://doi.org/10.1093/oxfordhb/9780198837138.013.28.

[4] Both terminology of illegal content and harmful content harms society at large or individuals. In this article, "harmful content" is used to mean "legal but harmful" or "harmful but not illegal or unlawful" in terms of criminal or civil proceedings. For example, not all discriminately content is unlawful or illegal, but unethical. *See* e. g. ACM Code of Ethics and Professional Conduct, where "harm" is broadly defined as negative consequences, especially when those consequences are significant and unjust.

[5] *See* e. g. R. Gorwa, R. Binns, and C. Katzenbach, "Algorithmic content moderation: Technical and political challenges in the automation of platform governance," Big Data & Society, vol. 7, Art. no. 1, Jan. 2020, https://doi.org/10.1177/2053951719897945.

[6] Envisaged remedial actions include how to achieve transparency and accountability related to the Content Moderation, how to mitigate technical limitations of accuracy and reliability of the diagnostic results of AI used in ACM especially for context-dependent expressions, the availability of remedial scheme for users whose post and/or account is suspended or deleted due to erroneous diagnosis and determination in the Content Moderation process.

[7] *See* e. g. K. Langvardt, "Regulating Online Content Moderation" Georgetown Law Journal, vol. 106, Art. no. 5, Jun. 2018.

the detected illegal information. If ACM is reasonably effective (with little systemic risk of over- and erroneous removals and other biproducts), naturally it becomes an option for the legislature to require or for the court to order the HSP to implement and utilize the ACM within the range of its effectiveness by a legislation or an injunction.

In this article we first define problem involving Content Moderation, then review the current state of Japanese legal system regarding Content Moderation including ACM by HSP and its relationship with limitation of liability of and injunctions against HSP. Next, the Japanese status will be evaluated in comparison with recent EU legal system updates and judicial precedents. Finally, it concludes with extraction of issues.

2 Problem

2.1 Definition of Content Moderation

The proposed EU Digital Services Act[8] ("DSA") Article 2(p) defines Content Moderation as follows:

> "… the activities undertaken by [HSPs] aimed at detecting, identifying and addressing illegal content …, provided by recipients of the service, including measures taken that affect the availability, visibility and accessibility of that illegal content …, such as demotion, disabling of access to, or removal thereof, or the recipients' ability to provide that information, such as the termination or suspension of a recipient's account[9]".

In the DSA, Content Moderation is not required to be automated, but as we will see later, it is assumed to be ACM that effectively uses AI.

2.2 General Monitoring

In the process of ACM, an HSP systematically determines (flags) targets or candidates for filtering or blocking from all texts, images, and other information.

If we would allow voluntary ACM by HSPs, that means whether we accept HSPs' general, exhaustive and comprehensive monitoring all such information posted by us and following automated judgment.

On the other hand, even if we can rely on the ability of HSPs through ACM to make accurate judgments, when such a general monitoring is a legal requirement, constitutional or other higher norms become issues.

---

[8] Proposal for a Regulation of the European Parliament and of the Council on a Single Market for Digital Services (Digital Services Act) and amending Directive 2000/31/EC COM(2020) 825 final.

[9] The definition of Content Moderation covers not only illegal content, which directly affects the civil and criminal liability of HSPs, but also information incompatible with their terms and conditions. Wilman F, The Responsibility of Online Intermediaries for Illegal User Content in the EU and the US (Edward Elgar Publishing 2020) paras. 8.21–8.33 discusses intermediaries contractually prohibiting users from providing certain types of content and actively enforcing the prohibitions but distinguishes it from 'privatized' enforcement of illegal information by intermediaries for satisfying their legal requirement or for obtaining limitation of liability.

Although the Japanese Provider Liability Limitation Act (hereinafter "PLLA")[10] does not provide explicitly for whether there is a duty to generally monitor, it is interpreted that HSPs do not owe such a duty by confirming that there is "no awareness of information distribution" as an eligibility for limitation of liability under Article 3(1) PLLA[11].

The DSA maintains (Article 7) the prohibition of the general monitoring obligation in Article 15(1) of the Electronic Commerce Directive[12] ("ECD") which states: no general obligation to monitor the information which [HSPs] transmit or store, nor actively to seek facts or circumstances indicating illegal activity shall be imposed on those [HSPs] The first subparagraph of Article 17(8) of the Digital Single Market Copyright Directive[13] ("DSMCD") also states that: the application of [Article 17] shall not lead to any general monitoring obligation.

Under Sect. 512(m) of the U.S. Digital Millennium Copyright Act[14]("DMCA"), which is entitled "Protection of Privacy", nothing in that Section should not be interpreted as a condition for the application of the exemption for monitoring of services or active detection of infringement by HSPs.

In other words, neither Japan, the EU member states, nor the U.S. imposes a general monitoring obligation on HSPs.

Nevertheless, in fact, "voluntary" Content Moderation conducted by HSPs are prevalent, and specific laws e. g. regulation on terrorist content[15] require the proactive removal of certain specific information.

2.3 Effect on Recognition by Detection

According to the DSA definition, Content Moderation is a content monitoring activity that starts with the detection of illegal information. Since the monitoring is done by human or automated systems, the question is whether it is possible or not, and the legal effect of the recognition of facts on the distribution of the information and detection and judgment of its illegality on the part of HSPs.

If HSPs are made aware of illegal information by the Content Moderation but leave it undeleted, they can be held liable for tort of omission against the victim or criminal liability for the omission. As a general consequence, HSPs are more likely to be reluctant to detect illegal information in order to avoid encountering illegal information. HSPs

---

[10] Act on the Limitation of Liability for Damages of Specified Telecommunications Service Providers and the Right to Demand Disclosure of Identification Information of the Senders (Act No. 137 of November 30, 2001).

[11] *See* Explanatory Note (in Japanese) by Ministry of Communication and General Affairs at.https://www.soumu.go.jp/main_content/000671655.pdf (last accessed 2022/5/15).

[12] Directive 2000/31/EC of the European Parliament and of the Council of 8 June 2000 (OJ L 178/1). *See* generally Wilman (fn.9) Chapter 3.

[13] Directive (EU) 2019/790 of the European Parliament and of the Council of 17 April 2019 on copyright and related rights in the Digital Single Market and amending Directives 96/9/EC and 2001/29/EC (OJ L 130/92).

[14] 17 U. S. C. s512.

[15] *See* e.g. Regulation (EU) 2021/784 of the European Parliament and of the Council of 29 April 2021 on addressing the dissemination of terrorist content online (OJ L172/79).

face less legal risk if they do not encounter illegal information in order to avoid obtaining knowledge or awareness of illegal information. Also, in the case of a legal system in which the provider's liability is limited if there is no knowledge or awareness of illegal information (knowledge-based-liability), the provider loses its immunity upon obtaining it. This is a situation described as the Good Samaritan paradox or the moderator's dilemma, but if we want to strengthen the countermeasures against illegal information via HSPs, we need to maintain the immunity and allow HSP's Content Moderation with certain monitoring activities.

Article 6 DSA prohibits HSPs from being deemed ineligible for immunity solely due to carrying out voluntary own-initiative investigation. Preamble 25 DSA states policy reason to clarify this effect "[i]n order to create legal certainty and not to discourage activities aimed at detecting, identifying and acting against illegal content that providers of intermediary services may undertake on a voluntary basis".

In addition, it would be useful to limit the liability of HSPs to the user such as removal or disabling access to content posted by the user. Article 3(2) PLLA, and Sect. 230(c)(2) of the U.S. Communications Decency Act are examples of legislation that limits the liability of HSPs against information content provider. However, if there is a contractual relationship with the user, the effect is limited to confirming the validity of the exercise of contractual rights.

3 Content Moderation and Interference Preventive Injunction Claims in Japan

3.1 The Prohibition of Censorship and the Inviolability of the Secrecy of Communications Under the Japanese Constitution and the Telecommunications Business Act

The Constitution of Japan guarantees the freedom of expression in Article 21, paragraph 1, prohibits censorship in the first half of paragraph 2, and states in the second half that the secrecy of communications shall not be violated.

Our Supreme Court has narrowly construed that a censorship prohibited under the Constitution is limited to prohibition after the administrative authorities' conduct of the comprehensive and general examination of the specific matters of expression prior to its publication[16].

In the Hoppo Journal Case[17], the Court applied that precedent to determine whether a preliminary injunction on publication could be issued and held that a court injunction on publication does not constitute the censorship, but as a prior restraint, the strict scrutiny standard applies.

In response to Article 21 Constitution, the Telecommunications Business Act[18] (hereinafter "TBA") prohibits censorship of communications handled by telecommunications carriers in Article 3 and does not allow anyone to violate the secrecy of such communications in Article 4 (1).

---

[16] Sup. Ct., December 12, 1984, 1982 (Gyo Tsu) 156, 38 Minshu 12, p.1308).

[17] Sup. Ct., June 11, 1986, 1981 (O) 609 of 1982, 40 Minshu 4, p.872).

[18] Telecommunications Business Act (Act No. 86 of December 25, 1984).

3.2 Provider Liability Limitation Act

The PLLA was enacted referring the US CDA, DMCA and ECD as mother laws.

An HSP cannot be exempted for damages under article 3(1) PLLA[19] if an HSP has knowledge of the distribution of information by telecommunications intended to be received by unspecified persons and knows that the rights of others have been infringed (actual knowledge) or has reasonable grounds for believing that he or she could have known that the rights of others were being infringed (constructive knowledge). It is not an article that forces HSPs to engage in private censorship, violates Article 21(1) Constitution, nor conflict with Article 3 TBA.

Article 3(2) PLLA is a safe harbor clause that exempts an HSP from liability for damages if the HSP takes measures such as deleting the sender's postings but only to the extent necessary to prevent transmission (i) where the HSP has reasonable grounds to believe that the rights of others have been unjustly infringed by the distribution of the information via the specified telecommunications, and (ii) where the HSP inquires the sender of the infringing information as to whether the sender agrees to take down the information when the person who claims that his or her rights have been infringed requests the HSP to take down the information. The former is so-called Good Samaritan Takedown immunity, while the latter is Notice-Notice & Takedown (NN&T) immunity.

Although the PLLA does not exempt HSPs from criminal liability, it is understood that they will not be held criminally liable unless there is a special involvement with a crime such as opening a BBS specializing in child pornography.

There is no statute that explicitly allows a victim to request for an injunction against HSPs from publication of user postings that infringes the victim's rights, but as described below, future interference by such a posting may be prevented from recurring by an injunctive order of the courts.

3.3 Guidelines for the PLLA and Illegal Information and Model Terms and Conditions

HSPs in Japan are not held liable for damages[20] for leaving or removing infringing information as long as the Content Moderation complies with the PLLA.

In Japan, there are soft-law-guidelines and standard terms and conditions that can be referred to in each field (Table 1).

Regarding information infringing rights covered by PLLA, in 2002 a self-regulatory body was established by rightholders' organizations and business organizations such as providers': guidelines on defamation and privacy, copyright infringement, trademark infringement[21].

---

[19] Even if an HSP is not exempted for damages under PLLA, it can still be held that the HSP is not liable under general tort law principle.

[20] In the EU, as defined by the DSA, Content Moderation is not only for information that infringes civil rights, but also for information that is criminally illegal or harmful (legal-but-harmful) that does not fall under these categories.

[21] *See* these Guidelines (in English) Provider Liability Limitation Act Guidelines Review Council at https://www.telesa.or.jp/consortium/provider/pconsortiumproviderindex_e-html.

In 2006, telecommunications-related organizations established a self-regulatory consortium[22] and formulated the "Guidelines for Dealing with Illegal Information on the Internet," and their member providers have implemented self-regulatory measures to takedown illegal information, including information that infringes on social interests. In addition, the "Model Terms and Conditions for Internet Services Concerning Response to Illegal and Harmful Information"[23] has been formulated, which lists information that is offensive to public order and morals in addition to illegal information and describes how to respond to such information.

Table 1. Soft-law-guidelines relating to content moderation in Japan

Subject of content moderation by HSP	Source of rights/violations	Source of hard law	Style of softlaw/Self-regulation
Infringing information covered by PLLA	Defamation/ privacy violation	Civil code	Codes of conduct
	Copyright infringement	Copyright act	Codes of conduct (Notice and takedown)
	Trademark infringement	Trademark act	Codes of conduct (Notice and takedown)
Illegal information other than infringing information	Obscene materials etc	Penal code	Codes of conduct
harmful information	—	Civil code	Model terms and conditions

However, these softlaw-guidelines do not assume that HSPs will actively engage in voluntary Content Moderation or utilize AI in Content Moderation.

3.4 Recommendations for the Decade Review of PLLA

The Recommendation for the Decade Review of PLLA (hereinafter "Review Recommendation")[24] states that, since the ECD does not impose a general monitoring obligation on providers and such monitoring is not a condition for liability limitation under the US DMCA, it is necessary to consider the following points:

1. it is not legally appropriate to require [HSPs] to monitor information in circulation, including by technical means, as it may result in de facto censorship, and be liable to invite a significant chilling effect on freedom of expression,
2. may infringe the secrecy of communications, and
3. it is often impossible for providers to bear the burden of monitoring.

---

[22] *See* https://www.telesa.or.jp/consortium/illegal_info.

[23] *Ibid.* English version of model terms and conditions and explanatory guide is available.

[24] Published in July 2011.

Review Recommendation continues: if imposing the monitoring obligation is denied, the introduction of technical monitoring means should not be a requirement for the limitation of liability under the PLLA.

Further, as for the monitoring of information for which there was a demand to prevent retransmission of the infringing information, it is sufficient to take measures to prevent transmission when the information becomes known to be circulated *ex post* because of chilling effect on freedom of expression and the reality of feasibility of implementation of such monitoring measure.

In addition, technical measures at [that] point can only confirm the identity of the copyright infringing material, and it is difficult to make the introduction of such measure mandatory from the viewpoint of cost.

Furthermore, it is not reasonable to easily expand the interpretation that [HSPs] who does not know the circulation of individual information is liable as a sender under PLLA as a person who placed the information in circulation[25].

The Review Recommendation also rejected the voluntary monitoring and deletion, introduction of technical measures such as filtering of illegal uploads, and implementation of reasonable measures such as suspension of service for users who repeatedly and continuously commit infringement as the requirements for limitation of liability of providers.

3.5 Cases Requesting for Preventive Injunction Against HSP

In Japan, there is no judicial precedent that an HSP was ordered to prevent its users from posting in the future while holding that it is a typical HSP whose liability for damages are limited under PLLA.

As to specificity of injunction, although it is technically closer to a search engine than HSP, we shall refer File Rogue (Napster-like Hybrid P2P system) case[26]. The file for which the P2P file exchange should be suspended is copied in the MP3 format with the file information in which both the "original title" column and the "artist" column of the music list are described. It seems to be a simple specification to pay attention to, but it is necessary to use advanced text filtering technology because it includes all the combination of letters (Kanji, Hiragana, Katakana, and uppercase and lowercase letters of the alphabet are not specified in the judgment). On the other hand, the suspension of transmission and reception of all the managed works requested by the plaintiff the Japanese Society for the Rights of Authors, Composers, and Publishers (JASRAC) was not allowed as the request for abstract prohibition of copyright infringement itself.

In the TV Break (initial name was Pandora TV) video posting service case[27], the defendant was technically an HSP like YouTube, but the IP High Court held that copies were made by the HSP using the copying act by the user and deemed a subject who directly infringes the copyrights of plaintiff JASRAC for making the public transmission of the music listed and provided by JASRAC. The court also enjoined future reproduction and public transmission without narrowing down the attributes of the target files of the

---

[25] Expressing concerns on TV Break case (fn.27) below.

[26] Tokyo Dist. Ct. December 17,2003, 2002 (Wa) 4237.

[27] IP High Ct. September 8, 2010, 2009 (Ne)10078.

copyrighted work. Defendant = Appellant HSP argued that such an injunction was a comprehensive injunction effectively ordering deletion of legitimate files and has a chilling effect on the freedom of expression of video posting sites and the development of the culture that is the purpose of Copyright Act. However, the court dismissed it because it limited to video files that were copies of JASRAC managed works uploaded without a license. In addition, the fact that technical infringement avoidance measures and deletion measures such as hash matching of video files that infringe copyright and audio fingerprint matching are not adopted by HSP was taken into consideration as a negative factor in the judgment of infringement. In other words, it is a case where the injunction order is affected by not doing ACM using automated technology.

As to personality rights infringement, in the Animal Hospital case[28], it was confirmed that an infringement preventive injunction against a bulletin board operator was possible by citing the Hoppo Journal case[29], but under the fact of the case, the request for injunction of reappearance of the same wording as the defamatory statements was rejected.

3.6   Urgent Recommendations on How to Deal with Slandering on the Internet

"Urgent Recommendations on How to Deal with Slandering on the Internet" (August 2020)[30] (hereinafter "Urgent Recommendation") calls for proactive voluntary efforts in combating slander and defamation, considering the role that HSPs play in daily life and social and economic activities.

Regarding Content Moderation (deleting or hiding illegal[31] posts and suspending accounts by HSPs), the following responses and ideas are given (emphasis by the author):

- In addition to setting up an easy-to-understand system for reporting deletion requests, etc., [HSPs] will take prompt action such as deletion in response to reports from affected users.
- Since a large amount of information is circulated on [HSP's] service, it is assumed that [HSPs] will **at their own initiative generally and always monitor a large amount of information, find infringing information** (illegal information), and **take prompt action without waiting for reports from users.**

---

[28] Tokyo Dist. Ct. June 26, 2002, 2001 (Wa) 15125. On appeal, Tokyo High Court also found that the deletion operation of the bulletin board, including the deletion guidelines set by the operator, was extremely inadequate as a remedy for victims and does not affect his liability. Tokyo High Ct. December 25, 2002, 2002 (Ne) 4083.

[29] (n.17).

[30] The Study Group on Platform Services of the Ministry of Internal Affairs and Communications.

[31] "In the case of defamatory information that is short of constituting infringement of rights (legal-but-harmful information), while taking measures **to prevent the chilling effect on freedom of expression due to over-removal** etc., and to avoid **unreasonable private censorship**, it is expected that various countermeasures will be taken **autonomously** by HSPs according to the scale and specifications of the service." Surprisingly, it names HSPs as the entity who should consider and care the balance between merits of countermeasures and, "chilling effect on freedom of expression" or "unjustified private censorship.

- Although it is not appropriate to uniformly require implementation of [AI-based ACM], **when** in the future technology that utilizes **AI** algorithms **becomes widespread and progresses**, and **costs are reduced**, making it easier to introduce it, it is also expected that **information will be deleted at its own initiative based on the rules and policies** stipulated in the freely designed service of the platform operator **without a report from the user or a third party**...
- [HSPs] will **promptly determine whether to remove information** in response to reports from users as well as **reports from government agencies with legitimate authority and expertise**.

The government will work with HSPs and develop an environment to support the smooth implementation of various initiatives related to slander and libel in HSPs, including a certain legal framework.

In relation to Content Moderation, although making [content removal through ACM] mandatory will require extremely careful judgment, the application of the PLLA will be reconsidered in a timely manner, considering the spread and progress of [AI], the accompanying changes in the cost burden of HSPs, and the changes in users' expectations of the roles required of HSPs.

3.7 Summary: Content Moderation in Japan

Except for the File Logue and TV Break cases, there is no case law suggesting the relationship between Content Moderation and injunctive relief, but courts have no hesitation in issuing an injunction which would require general monitoring once the defendant is found to be out of the scope of HSP under PLLA, in other words, is deemed a publisher, even if the injunction in effect requires the HSP's implementation of AI.

As for the legislative mandate for general monitoring of HSPs, the reluctance of the Review Recommendation to impose such a mandate because it is "de facto censorship" due to the significant chilling effect on freedom of expression, the risk of infringement of the secrecy of communications, and the cost of monitoring HSPs, has not been completely reversed until now.

On the other hand, regarding the voluntary Content Moderation of illegal information by HSPs, it is expected that it will be accompanied by the constant monitoring of a large amount of information in circulation, provided that the introduction of AI, will become easier due to the progress of technology diffusion and cost reduction.

4 Recent EU Legislation and Case Law

For comparison, we shall examine below recent legislative and judicial trends in the EU that relate to Content Moderation or envisage the use of AI.

4.1 DSMCD Article 17

Article 17(3) DSMCD excludes the application of the limitation of liability under Article 14(1) of the ECD to certain HSPs.

Article 17(3) DSMCD excludes certain HSPs from the limitation of liability under Article 14(1) ECD. Article 17(4)(b) of DSMCD states that HSPs must use their best endeavours, with professional diligence and high industry standards, to implement upload blocking of works for which relevant and necessary information is provided by the right holder. In effect, the right holders are expected to provide data or finger-prints of their works for automatic matching by HSP. In addition, the Article (4)(c) imposes on HSPs a best-effort obligation for prompt removal of individual works from websites (takedown) and future upload blocking (stay-down) in accordance with (4)(b) upon receipt of a sufficiently specific notice from the right holder.

However, according to Article 17(7), upload blocking of non-infringing works due to exceptions or limitation must be avoided. For this reason, in its guidance on the application of Article 17 based on Article 17 (10)[32], the European Commission stated that automated blocking should in principle be limited to cases of manifest infringement, and that other cases should in principle be first published subject to ex-post human review based on notification by the right holder.

As mentioned above, since the first subparagraph of Article 17(8) states that it should not lead to the obligation of general monitoring, it clarifies the position that ACM is "specific" monitoring as opposed to "general" one.

4.2 YouTube and Cyando Joined Cases[33]

In the *YouTube and Cyando* joined cases, CJEU held that Article 8(3) Information Society Copyright Directive[34] (hereinafter "ISCD"), which obliges Member States shall ensure that rightsholders are in a position to apply for an injunction against [HSPs] whose services are used by a third party to infringe a copyright or related right does not preclude the fulfilment of a prerequisite for a claim for an injunction under the national law of a Member State, such as German interferer liability (Störerhaftung), which before court proceedings are commenced, that infringement has first been notified to [an HSP] and [the HSP] has failed to intervene expeditiously in order to remove the content in question or to block access to it and to ensure that such infringements do not recur.

The rightsholder will be given the opportunity to terminate the infringement out of court and prevent its recurrence and will not lose the right to seek an injunction. In addition, HSPs do not need to proactively monitor uploaded user content to avoid injunction claims, thus complying with Article 15(1) ECD.

Article 17 DSMCD seems to be formulated by incorporating German interferer lia-bility (Störerhaftung) system which requires the private enforcement of out-of-court removal and staydown request against HSPs before court proceedings. Article 17

---

[32] COMMUNICATION FROM THE COMMISSION TO THE EUROPEAN PARLIAMENT AND THE COUNCIL Guidance on Article 17 of Directive 2019/790 on Copyright in the Digital Single Market COM/2021/288 final.

[33] *YouTube and Cyando*, Joined Cases C-682/18 and C-683/18, ECLI:EU:C:2021:503, 22 June 2021.

[34] Directive 2001/29/EC of the European Parliament and of the Council of 22 May 2001 on the harmonisation of certain aspects of copyright and related rights in the information society (OJ L 167/10).

DSMCD will facilitate such an out-of-court enforcement against HSPs, when it is expected that they have efficient ACM systems.

4.3 Glawischnig-Piesczek Case[35]

Eva Glawischnig-Piesczek (EGP), a senior official of the Green Party in Austria, requested Facebook Ireland (FB) to remove the defamatory remarks commented with the portrait photo of EGP. The Court of First Instance issued an interim order to remove the words that had the same or equal meaning as the comments, and after an appeal, the Austrian Supreme Court referred the case to the CJEU for a preliminary ruling.

CJEU found that the ECD, in particular, Article 15(1), did not preclude national courts from (emphasis added):

–ordering [an HSP] to **remove** information which it stores, the content of which is identical to the content of information, which was previously declared to be unlawful, [(**stored identical information [Ii]**)] or to block access to **[Ii]**, **irrespective of who requested the storage** of that information,

–ordering [an HSP] to remove which it stores, the content of which is equivalent to the content of information which was previously declared to be unlawful [(**stored equivalent information [Ie]**)], or to block access to **[Ie]**,

- provided that the monitoring of and search for the information concerned by such an injunction are **limited to information conveying a message the content of which remains essentially unchanged** compared with the content which gave rise to the finding of illegality and **containing the elements specified in the injunction**, and
- provided that the **differences in the wording** of that equivalent content, compared with the wording characterizing the information, which was previously declared to be illegal, **are not such as to require [HSP] to carry out an independent assessment** of that content.

As there is a genuine risk that information which was held to be illegal is subsequently reproduced and shared by another user of that network, an injunction ordering the deletion or blocking of **[Ii]** is justified, irrespective of who requested the storage of that information[36].

For granting an effective remedy, the Court held that the injunction must be extended to **[Ie]** but avoid imposing excessive burden on HSP in so far as the monitoring of and search for information which it requires are limited to information containing the elements specified in the injunction, and its defamatory content of an equivalent nature does not require the host provider to carry out an independent assessment, since the latter **has recourse to automated search tools and technologies**[37].

The injunction of both **[Ii]** and **[Ie]** cannot be regarded as general monitoring in violation of ECD Article 15(1)[38].

---

[35] CJEU, C-18/18, *Glawischnig-Piesczeck*, ECLI:EU:C:2019:821, 3 October 2019.

[36] Id. Para. 36–37.

[37] Id. Para. 46.

[38] Id. Paras 37, 47.

The significance of CJEU findings regarding ACM is that the court seems to believe that AI is enough advancing, and it is easy for a national court to understand AI algorithm and can easily depend on HSP's recourse to AI specifying injunction order.

4.4 Dsa

As mentioned above, the DSA defines Content Moderation and maintains the Article 15(1) ECD which prohibits the Member States from requiring HSPs to conduct general monitoring.

4.5 Summary: Content Moderation in the EU

We believe both YouTube and Cyando and Glawischnig-Piesczek[39] judgements will facilitate out-of-court request for removal and staydown content identical to and equivalent to illegal information using AI.

The main legal interest protected by Article 15(1) ECD is the freedom to conduct of business by avoiding excessive burden on HSPs, but it is also considered to function to protect, at least indirectly, the fundamental rights of users' personal data, privacy and freedom of expression[40].

Article 6 and preamble 25 DSA will be expected to create legal certainty and not to discourage good faith voluntary own-initiative Content Moderation by HSPs for illegal information or for compliance. We need to see if this level of assurance for immunity works well.

5 Comparison: ACM Environment Between the EU and Japan

This section compares the legal systems from Content Moderation to injunction and their discussions in the EU and Japan, as, again, discussion in Japan has referred to EU status.

What has controlled legitimacy of monitoring and filtering in a mandatory fashion in Content Moderation process is, in the case of the EU, Article 15(1) ECD, which protects the legal interests of freedom to conduct business of HSPs and (indirectly) fundamental rights of users, while in the case of Japan, "de facto censorship," "significant chilling effect on freedom of expression," "secrecy of communication," and "burden on [HSPs]" have been also lined up.

The EU has so far decided not to make Content Moderation general obligation except for individual legislations, but Japan will consider it according to the spread and progress of AI, the reduction of cost burden of HSPs, and changes in users' expectations, although it requires "extremely careful scrutiny".

In Japan, if we take the direction to make upload blocking best effort obligation and to incorporate private out-of-court injunction into Content Moderation practice as

---

[39] The Glawischnig-Piesczek case is also cited in the DSA and remains valid even after the law is enacted as an interpretation of the legality of the injunction in Article 7 DSA.

[40] *See* Wilman, fn.9, paras.3.25–3.31.

private law enforcement measures like Article 17 DSMCD, an extremely careful scrutiny is necessary. Even if it is not mandatory, a government mandated system that promotes "voluntary" deletion by Content Moderations but follows administrative authorities' *ex post* control to avoid under-removal would have similar effects. The current debates can be regarded as a legitimate direction to the extent that it aims to increase the transparency and accountability of HSPs regarding the risk of over- and erroneous removals by ACM and to ensure relief for users, at the same time it aims to promote ACM in order to make measures against a large volume of illegal information more effective.

While Article 18(1) ECD has limited the scope of injunction requests for infringing information, there is no case in Japan where such a restriction has been applied to typical HSPs. We may expect few cases will continuously be reported, if ACM advances. As seen from YouTube and Cyando judgment, the spread and advancement of ability of AI-based Content Moderation will increase the ratio of out-of-court dispute resolution. That means courts will handle only difficult cases, which requires issuing injunction with detailed (algorithmic) instruction to prevent infringement. In order to avoid the risk of over- and erroneous removals by AI on the part of HSPs, as a natural result from the Glawischnig-Piesczek precedent, judges and courts will be required to have literacy on and technology related to AI preferably inhouse.

6 Conclusion: Issues for Japanese Law

6.1 General Monitoring

In Japanese law, general monitoring by HSPs is not mandated by the Constitution or TBA but rather prohibited in principle. However, we have not discarded the option of ordering HSPs to be proactive in Content Moderations, as discussed in our Urgent Recommendations. It would be necessary to reconfirm the necessity of proactive Content Moderation. Since the Japanese Constitution prohibits censorship and judicial precedents require that prior restraint meet the strict scrutiny standard, "extremely careful scrutiny" is required, but referring to the global trend especially in the EU, the following issues need to be cleared for such consideration.

6.2 Confidentiality of Communications

There is no issue of secrecy of communication in the first place if the Content Moderation takes place only *ex post* (after posting). If the proactive *ex ante* Content Moderation can be legalized after strict scrutiny, the violation of the secrecy of communication under TBA should be exempted.

6.3 Excessive Burden on HSPs

HSPs shall not be required to implement specific type of AI for Content Moderation, which requires excessive burden on and significant investment from HSPs, whether based on an individual legislation or injunctions ordered by a court.

6.4 Development of Tools to Limit Liability for Proactive Measures

It is desirable to clarify legislatively the impact of the execution of ACM on knowledge-based civil and criminal liability.

More specifically, Article 3(1) PLLA clarifies that without awareness or constructive knowledge of infringing information, there is no liability for damages. In this regard, if it is confirmed that awareness under Article 3(1) PLLA do not arise solely because of the execution of voluntary Content Moderation, the range of options for HSPs will be further expanded, because they are free to design up to the stage of mechanical detection of illegal information using AI. For example, based on the "manifestly" illegal criterion, i.e., the certainty that the information is illegal, as stated in the Article 17 DSMCD Guidance[41], HSPs will be able to distinguish between cases where the information should be removed immediately, cases where it should be flagged and manually checked again, and cases where it should not[42].

The above knowledge and design standard should be supplemented by existing softlaw-guidelines in detail preferably with the participation of very large global HSPs.

---

[41] fn. 32.

[42] The limitation of liability to the sender for erroneous removals may be considered already covered in Article 3(2) PLLA. It would be desirable to clarify the relationship between "reasonable grounds" in Article 3(2) and erroneous-removals in AI-based Content Moderation in the soft-law guidelines.

Comparison of Legal Systems for Data Portability in the EU, the US and Japan and the Direction of Legislation in Japan

Mika Nakashima[✉] [iD]

Faculty of Global Informatics, Chuo University, Tokyo, Japan
nakashima.77h@g.chuo-u.ac.jp

Abstract. The General Data Protection Regulation (GDPR) is legislation for the protection of personal data that applies in the EU. Article 20 of the GDPR stipulates the Right to data portability as one of the rights of data subjects. The monopoly on data held by digital platforms, such as GAFA (Google, Amazon, Facebook, Apple), is becoming a significant issue, and in this context, there is a need for the right to data portability in terms of not only the right of data subjects to reclaim their personal data but also promoting competition among businesses. The California Consumer Privacy Act (CCPA) of 2018 is the first comprehensive legislation for the protection of personal data in the US, albeit at the state level, with provisions similar to the EU GDPR; the CCPA establishes the Right of access and portability in Section 1798.100 as one of the rights of consumers. The California Privacy Rights Act (CPRA), passed in 2021, amends the CCPA to further strengthen the rights stipulated therein. The Bill of the Consumer Online Privacy Rights Act of 2019 (CORPA) was introduced in the Congress in 2019 and may become the first comprehensive legislation for the protection of personal information in the US at the state level. In recent years, in addition to the GDPR in the EU and the CCPA, the CPRA and the CORPA in the US, provisions relating to the obligation of data portability from the perspective of policy on competition are also included in the new Digital Markets Act (DMA) proposed in the EU and the (federal-level) ACCESS proposed in the US. This study compares the legal systems of the EU, the US and Japan with regard to data portability and shows the direction of legislation in Japan.

Keywords: Data portability · GDPR · CCPA · CPRA · CORPA · DMA · ACCESS

1 Legal Systems for Data Portability in the EU, TheUS and Japan

1.1 The EU

The General Data Protection Regulation (GDPR)[1] was adopted on 27 April 2016, as a new legislation for protection of personal data replacing the Data Protection Directive

---

[1] Regulation (EU) 2016/679 of the European Parliament and of the Council of 27 April 2016 on the protection of natural persons with regard to the processing of personal data and the free movement of such data (General Data Protection Regulation).

© IFIP International Federation for Information Processing 2022
Published by Springer Nature Switzerland AG 2022
D. Kreps et al. (Eds.): HCC 2022, IFIP AICT 656, pp. 159–169, 2022.
https://doi.org/10.1007/978-3-031-15688-5_14

(Directive); the GDPR came into effect on 25 May 2018, and it stipulates the Right to data portability in Article 20 as one of the rights of data subjects.

Article 20 Right to data portability

1. The data subject shall have the right to receive the personal data concerning him or her, which he or she has provided to a controller, in a structured, commonly used and machine-readable format and have the right to transmit those data to another controller without hindrance from the controller to which the personal data have been provided, where:

(a) the processing is based on consent pursuant to point (a) of Article 6 (1) or point (a) of Article 9 (2) or on a contract pursuant to point (b) of Article 6 (1); and

(b) the processing is carried out by automated means.

2. In exercising his or her right to data portability pursuant to paragraph 1, the data subject shall have the right to have the personal data transmitted directly from one controller to another, where technically feasible.

3. The exercise of the right referred to in paragraph 1 of this Article shall be without prejudice to Article 17. That right shall not apply to processing necessary for the performance of a task carried out in the public interest or in the exercise of official authority vested in the controller.

4. The right referred to in paragraph 1 shall not adversely affect the rights and freedoms of others.

The guidelines developed by the Article 29 Working Group (2017), which was established under the Directive, outline the nature of the right to data portability as follows: [1, pp. 4–5].[2]

Firstly, data portability is a right of the data subject to receive a subset of the personal data processed by a data controller concerning him or her and to store those data for further personal use.

…

For example, a data subject might be interested in retrieving his current playlist (or a history of listened tracks) from a music streaming service, to find out how many times he listened to specific tracks, or to check which music he wants to purchase or listen to on another platform. Similarly, he may also want to retrieve his contact list from his webmail application, for example, to build a wedding list, or get information about purchases using different loyalty cards, or to assess his or her carbon footprint.

Secondly, Article 20 (1) provides data subjects with the right to transmit personal data from one data controller to another data controller without hindrance.

…

---

[2] Also see Ishii (2021) and Komukai (2018) for an explanation of the contents of the guidelines [7] [12].

In addition to providing consumer empowerment by preventing *lock-in*, the right to data portability is expected to foster opportunities for innovation and sharing of personal data between data controllers in a safe and secure manner, under the data subject's control. Data portability can promote the controlled and limited sharing by users of personal data between organisations and thus enrich services and customer experiences. Data portability may facilitate transmission and reuse of personal data concerning users among the various services they are interested in.

As will be described later, all the rights to data portability are discussed as a set with interoperability in the legal systems of each jurisdiction. The guidelines also recommend ensuring the interoperability of data formats in the exercise of the right to data portability [1, p. 3].

As a good practice, data controllers should start developing the means that will contribute to answer data portability requests, such as download tools and Application Programming Interfaces (APIs). They should guarantee that personal data are transmitted in a structured, commonly used and machine-readable format, and they should be encouraged to ensure the interoperability of the data format provided in the exercise of a data portability request.

A lot of issues have been discussed with regard to the right to data portability since they were established as a right of data subjects in the GDPR. Uga (2018) points out the following issues to be dealt with with regard to the right to data portability: (1) measures to counter identity theft; (2) cyberattacks; (3) disincentivises to invest due to loss of *lock-in*; (4) the burden to comply with data portability; (5) passing on the cost to data subjects; (6)difficulty of defining scope of the right to data portability; (7) all-or-nothing approach to data portability; (8) the jurisdiction; (9) illumining the right to data portability [8, pp. 52–61].

The GDPR also stipulates the Right of access by the data subject in Article 15 as a right adjacent to the right to data portability.

The Digital Markets Act (DMA)[3] was proposed by the European Commission on 14 December 2020 as a new business regulation that regulates online platforms in the EU. It proposes to designate the dominant providers in the online platform market as gatekeepers and impose various obligations on them.

The term gatekeeper refers to a provider of core platform services that meets designated criteria. Core platform services include online intermediation services, online search engines, social networking, video sharing platform services, number-independent interpersonal electronic communication services, operating systems, cloud services and advertising services (Article 2 (2)). A core platform service provider will be designated as a gatekeeper by the European Commission if it has a significant impact on the internal market, operates core platform services that are an important gateway for business users to reach end users and has an entrenched and sustainable position in its operations or is predicted to gain such a position in the near future (Article 3 (1)).

---

[3] Regulation of the European Parliament and of the Council on contestable and fair markets in the digital sector (Digital Markets Act).

The obligations imposed on gatekeepers are defined as those that must be imposed on any gatekeepers and those that may be imposed in addition; in the latter category, the obligation of data portability is stipulated in Article 6 (h). And the obligation of interoperability is stipulated in Article 6 (f).

Article 6 Obligations for gatekeepers susceptible of being further specified

In respect of each of its core platform services identified pursuant to Article 3 (7), a gatekeeper shall:

...

(f) allow business users and providers of ancillary services access to and interoperability with the same operating system, hardware or software features that are available or used in the provision by the gatekeeper of any ancillary services;

...

(h) provide effective portability of data generated through the activity of a business user or end user and shall, in particular, provide tools for end users to facilitate the exercise of data portability, in line with Regulation EU 2016/679, including by the provision of continuous and real-time access;

Sasaki (2021) notes their similarities to the regulation of dominant operators in the telecommunications market, in that the DMA designates the dominant providers in the online platform market as a gatekeepers, imposes obligations on them and imposes corrective measures or fines if they fail to fulfil those obligations [14, p. IV-14].

A certain role-sharing can be seen between Article 6 (h) of the DMA and the GDPR with regard to data portability obligations; the GDPR regulates the right to data portability from the perspective of protecting personal information, whereas the DMA aims to do the same from the perspective of regulating business in advance. The latter therefore makes sense as a competition policy.

1.2 The US

The California Consumer Privacy Act of 2018 (CCPA) is the first comprehensive legislation for the protection of personal information in the US, albeit at the state level. The CCPA came into effect on 1 January 2020 and has provisions similar to the GDPR, establishing the rights of access and portability in Section 1798.100 as one of the rights of consumers.

Section 798.100

...

(d) A business that receives a verifiable consumer request from a consumer to access personal information shall promptly take steps to disclose and deliver, free of charge to the consumer, the personal information required by this section. The information may be delivered by mail or electronically, and if provided electronically, the information shall be in a portable and, to the extent technically feasible, readily useable format that allows the consumer to transmit this information to another entity without hindrance. A business may provide personal information to a consumer at any time, but shall not be required to provide personal information to a consumer more than twice in a 12-month period.

The Practical Handbook of the Japan External Trade Organisation (JETRO(2019)) positions the right described above as one of consumers' rights to know about personal information that is collected, disclosed and sold [3, p. 30].

As a right adjacent to the right to data portability, the CCPA can be read as stipulating a right of access in Section 1798.100 (d), as distinguished from the right to portability. Sections 1798.100 (a) and 1798.110 of the CCPA also stipulate a right to request disclosure.

The California Privacy Rights Act of 2020 (CPRA) amends the CCPA to further strengthen consumer rights. The CPRA was passed by a referendum on 3 November 2020, and is scheduled to come into effect in January 2023. As mentioned above, the CCPA has provisions regarding the right to data portability; the CPRA strengthens right and requires businesses more strict measures.

Section 1798.130. Notice, Disclosure, Correction and Deletion Requirements

(a) In order to comply with Sections 1798.100, 1798.105, 1798.106, 1798.110, 1798.115 and 1798.125, a business shall, in a form that is reasonably accessible to consumers:

(3) …

(B) …

(iii) Provide the specific pieces of personal information obtained from the consumer in a format that is easily understandable to the average consumer, and to the extent technically feasible, in a structured, commonly used machine-readable format that may also be transmitted to another entity at the consumer's request without hindrance. 'Specific pieces of information' do not include data generated to help ensure security and integrity or as prescribed by regulation. Personal information is not considered to have been disclosed by a business when a consumer instructs a business to transfer the consumer's personal information from one business to another in the context of switching services.

The International Association of Privacy Professionals (IAPP) states that the right to data portability was already included in the CCPA, but the CPRA has modified the requirement[4]. The CPRA also strengthens the right to request disclosure in Section 1798.110, as a right adjacent to the right to data portability.

The Bill of the Consumer Online Privacy Rights Act of 2019 (CORPA) was introduced in the Congress in 2019 and may become the first comprehensive legislation for the protection of personal information in the US at the federal level.

(a) RIGHT TO DATA PORTABILITY—A covered entity, upon the verified request of an individual, shall export the individual's covered data, except for derived data, without licensing restrictions— (1) in a human-readable format that allows

---

[4] https://iapp.org/news/a/top-10-operational-impacts-of-the-cpra-part-4-other-expanded-rights-and-obligations/.

the individual to understand such covered data of the in dividual; and (2) in a structured, interoperable, and machine readable format that includes all covered data or other information that the covered entity collected to the extent feasible.

The US Federal Data Privacy Bill summary of the Consumer Online Privacy Rights Act (COPRA) (JETRO(2021)) positions the right described above as one of individual's right [4, p. 27].

As a right adjacent to the right to data portability, the COPRA can be read as stipulating a right to access and transparency in Section 102, as distinguished from the right to portability.

The Bill of the Augmenting Compatibility and Competition by Enabling Service Switching Act (ACCESS) was introduced in the Congress in 2021.The legislation, when it passes, will regulate data portability obligations from the perspective of regulating business[5].

SEC. 3. PORTABILITY

(a) IN GENERAL—A covered platform shall maintain a set of transparent, third-party-accessible interfaces (including APIs) to enable the secure transfer of data to a user, or with the affirmative consent of a user, to a business user at the direction of a user, in a structured, commonly used and machine-read-able format that complies with the standards issued pursuant to section 6 (c).

SEC. 4. INTEROPERABILITY

(a) IN GENERAL—A covered platform shall maintain a set of transparent, third-party-accessible interfaces (including APIs) to facilitate and maintain interoperability with a competing business or a potential competing business that complies with the standards issued pursuant to section 6 (c).

Prior to the proposal of this bill, the Subcommittee on Antitrust (2020) recommended interoperability and data portability, requiring dominant platforms to make their services compatible with various networks and to make content and information easily portable between them [11, p. 20].

1.3 Japan

Japan's Act on the Protection of Personal Information (APPI) was promulgated on 30 May 2003 and came into effect on 1 April 2005. A revision of the APPI was promulgated in 2015, taking into account the necessity of facilitating the proper use of big data, including personal data, and the need to provide a response to the globalisation of business activities. The revised APPI came into effect on 30 May 2017. Subsequently, based on the Every-Three-Year Review provision (Article 12 of the Supplementary

---

[5] The bill was proposed as one of five bills on digital platforms, which are: the American Innovation and Choice Online Act, the Platform Competition and Opportunity Act, the Ending Platform Monopolies Act, the Augmenting Compatibility and Competition by Enabling Service Switching (ACCESS) Act and the Merger Filing Fee Modernization Act.

Provisions) of the Act, the draft Act to Partially Revise the Act on the Protection of Personal Information (Act No. 44 of 2020) was enacted on 5 June 2020. This was promulgated on 12 June of the same year and is scheduled to come into effect on 1 April 2022. The following is based on the last mentioned revision (which had not come into effect at the time of writing).

Article 28 thereof stipulates the right to request disclosure of information on the principal (i.e., the data subject), and while the revised APPI of 2020 stipulates that this is principally to be conducted via electronic means, it contains no provisions regarding the right to data portability.

Article 28

(1) A principal may demand a personal information handling business operator to disclose retained personal data in which the principal is identified, and such disclosure shall be implemented by providing an electromagnetic record or by any other method specified by the regulations of the Personal Information Protection Commission.

(2) A personal information handling business operator shall, when having received a demand pursuant to the provisions of the preceding paragraph, disclose retained personal data to a principal without delay pursuant to a method demanded by the principal (or by delivering document(s) in cases where disclosure by the method demanded requires a significant cost or where disclosure by the method demanded is difficult) under the provisions of the preceding paragraph. However, in cases where disclosing such data falls under any of each following item, a whole or part thereof may not be disclosed.

…

Japan also has the Telecommunications Business Act (TBA), which regulates telecommunications operators. However, although digital platforms can be subject to the regulation if they engage in telecommunications as a telecommunications operator, the TBA is not the legislation regarding digital platforms.

In recent years, there has been a series of a new legislation regarding digital platforms in Japan, but all of them have been narrow in their scopes and the obligations that they place on businesses are limited, none of which refer to data portability.

First, the Act on Improving the Transparency and Fairness of Specified Digital Platforms (Specified Digital Platform Act (SDPA)) was enacted in May 2020 and came into effect on 1 February 2021. Secondly, the Act for the Protection of Consumers Who Use Digital Platforms for Transactions (Transactions Digital Platform Act (TDPA)) was enacted on 15 April 2021 and promulgated on 10 May 2021. The SDPA is based on the so-called co-regulation method, which stipulates that the governmental involvement and regulation should be kept to a minimum, premised on voluntary and proactive efforts to improve transparency and fairness implemented by online retail operators and digital platform providers such as app stores. Although the SDPA does stipulate the obligation to disclose information in Article 5 (2), it does not include any data portability obligations [15, p. 140]. The TDPA is a new legislation proposed in response to problems that have arisen in digital transaction platforms such as online retail operators, including the distribution of dangerous products via online and difficulties in resolving disputes because the distributor cannot be identified. The TDPA is intended to respond to these issues and to protect consumer's interests. Article 5 of the TDPA establishes the right for consumers to request the disclosure of the seller's information to the extent necessary in cases such as when a consumer makes a claim for damages; it does not, however, include any data portability obligations.

2 Direction of Legislation in Japan

Above, we have looked at the provisions of the GDPR in the EU, the CCPA, the CPRA and the CORPA in the US for the protection of personal data/information regarding the right to data portability. We have also reviewed the right to request disclosure in Japan's APPI, as is a right most adjacent to it for present. Furthermore, in terms of new movements in relation to the obligation of data portability, we have looked into the two proposed regulations on business, the DMA in the EU and the ACCESS in the US, and summarised the situation in Japan. For example, if we want to transfer our webmail data to another company's service, the obligation of data portability in advance will be imposed on companies on the basis of the DMA in the EU and the ACCESS in the US, and consumers can request data transfer on the basis of GDPR in the EU, CCPA, CRPA and CORPA in the US. On the other hand, the current Japanese legal system only allows for disclosure requests[6]. Let us now consider the direction of legislation in Japan. The following legislation proposals have already been made.

The Personal Information Protection Commission (2019), in its so-called three-year review, stated the following about the introduction of data portability [13, pp. 17–18].

> In relation to data portability, voluntary initiatives in the private sector have already been undertaken by Personal Data Trust Bank, and it is welcome that such initiatives are being undertaken on a voluntary basis in line with the APPI. The voluntary implementation of such initiatives in line with the APPI is to be welcomed. On the other hand, the legal obligation of data portability is not only from the perspective of personal data protection, such as the protection of individual rights and interests, but also from the perspective of industrial policy and competition policy. The EU has introduced new provisions in the GDPR to allow the transfer of personal data directly from one controller to another, but only where it is technically feasible to do so. The need for such a provision in Japan is currently being discussed in various areas, including consumer needs, benefits for operators, practical burdens, etc. Therefore, it is necessary to keep a close eye on the progress of these discussions.

Ishii (2021) identifies the following options for legislation on the right to data portability for personal information: (1) establishing provisions similar to the GDPR; (2)

---

[6] After leaving the paper, the proposal of the Data Act and the REGULATION OF THE EURO-PEAN PARLIAMENT AND OF THE COUNCIL on the European Health Data Space was released in the EU. It is reported that the EU is also considering legislation in individual sectors, such as not only healthcare but also automotive, and the issue of data portability in these individual sectors needs to be considered in Japan as well.

establishing provisions to reinforce current efforts centred on Personal Data Trust Bank[7]; (3) expanding the right to request disclosure; (4) legislating in specialised fields such as finance and medical care. On the basis of these options, Ishii argues that as it is easier to implement legislation by enhancing existing provisions than by establishing a new right to data portability, option (3) is the most realistic choice. Ishii also argues that we should consider mechanisms that can enhance competitiveness separately from considerations on the legal systems relating to personal information protection [7, pp. 169–170][8].

Elsewhere, on 25 June 2021, the Japan Fair Trade Commission (JFTC) and the Competition Policy Research Centre (CPRC) (2021) compiled a *Report of the Study Group on Competition Policy in the Data Market*, which highlighted the importance of ensuring data portability and interoperability. According to the report, specific measures and targets should be considered from the perspective of cost and innovation, in such a way that they do not become a factor that hinders competition. In this regard, the report stated that it will be necessary to carefully consider factors such as the size of business operators, whether the data they hold is industrial data or personal data, and what stage of development the field and markets are in that are to be regulated. The report notes that, especially for digital platforms, ex-post regulations implemented under the existing Antimonopoly Act may not provide a sufficient response and therefore that there may be a need to consider ex-ante regulation as a preferable extra measure. The report also found that it would be beneficial to request various industries to undertake study on a voluntary basis regarding best-practice approaches to formulating regulations on interoperability and data portability and that the government should intervene when necessary [5, pp. 58–61].

Legislation in Japan regarding data portability appears to be moving in two directions: the direction envisaged by Ishii (2021), in which the right to data portability is treated as legislation for protection of the personal information, and the direction proposed by the JFTC and CPRC (2021), in which data portability is mandated through legislation on business regulations.

If Japan is to legislate on the right to data portability as for the protection of personal information, it is important to remember that the new legislation on personal data/information in the EU and the US has adopted a new approach, establishing the right to data portability separately from the conventional right to request access/disclosure.

If Japan is to legislate on the obligation of data portability by way of business regulations, it seems that it will also inevitably have to enact a new legislation for digital platforms in some way. As the JFTC and CPRC (2021) report states, it is conceivable

---

[7] Personal Data Trust Bank is the business of managing personal data based on contracts with individuals or other arrangements, and providing data to third parties based on the instructions of individuals or on pre-specified conditions. In accordance with the *Guidelines for Certification of Information Trust Functions ver1.0* formulated by the Ministry of Internal Affairs and Communications and the Ministry of Economy, Trade and Industry, the Japan Federation of IT Organizations has been conducting the Personal Data Trust Bank certification business since the fall of 2018, and has certified five companies as of March 2020 [9, p.234].

[8] Ishii also notes that the OECD (2021) has highlighted that data portability systems focused on data protection do not always promote competition effectively [10, p.168].For more on the links between the right to request disclosure and the right to data portability as stipulated the current version of the APPI (before its revision in 2020) in Japan, see Itakura (2020) [15].

to enact data portability legislation as either ex-ante regulation or co-regulation[9]. This could be done by either including data portability regulations as a part of comprehensive legislation on digital platforms, in a manner similar to the DMA in the EU, or through legislation that is specific to data portability, such as the ACCESS in the US. There are those who argue from the legislative perspective for the protection of personal data that the right to data portability is both too broad and strict in that it does not specify services, nor take into account the scale of the businesses and also is applicable uniformly, but it seems worth noting that the DMA in the EU designates core platform services that have a certain (not insignificant) degree of influence in the market as gatekeepers. Although Japan's SDPA and TDPA stipulate certain obligations of information disclosure, their legislative purposes are arguably different from the obligation of data portability. To consider where or how to position rights/obligations relating to data portability in our system, it will not suffice to think only of extending one or some conventional rights or obligations; it will be worthwhile to probe into the desirability of designing a new frame for them as Japan develops a full-fledged digital society.

Interoperability is a dependable companion to data portability; data portability would not be as usable a right without it. They were discussed as a set in the course of legislation both in the EU and the US.

Desirably every one of those issues Uga has set out above[10] may be dealt with in legislation rather than in its application if the right to data portability is to be introduced into Japan.

The GDPR will require data controllers to use formats and templates that are structured, commonly used and machine-readable in order to enable data portability, which could place a significant burden on data controllers. There has also been concern that consumer welfare may in fact be hindered because the right to data portability apply to both small-scale new entrants into the market and to monopolies, which may make it difficult for new entrants from the perspective of competition law, incentivising large, well-funded companies to form oligopolies. Whereas there are some who argue along these lines that the right to data portability is both too broad and strict [8, pp. 54–60], others argue that data portability should not be mandatory and should be addressed, where necessary, through the enforcement of competition law [2, p. 10]. In this way, data portability has been discussed not only as an issue of legislation for the protection of personal data/infomation, but also as an issue that spans competition policy [6] [8, pp. 22–29][11].

In the midst of implementing various policies aiming at the digital single market, the EU has positioned the protection of personal data as a basic human right based on

---

[9] The report states that "there is value in requesting various industries to undertake study on a voluntary basis regarding best-practice approaches to formulating regulations on interoperability and data portability and that the government should intervene in when necessary". This is interpreted as referring to *co-regulation*.

[10] See p.3.

[11] Uga (2018) and Ishii (2019) highlight the fact that data portability may be discussed under EU competition law in the context of whether it is unlawful to deny access to data held by an operator under Article 102 of the Treaties of the European Union, or in relation to the Essential Facilities Doctrine. Both Uga and Ishii are cautious about applying the Essential Facilities Doctrine in the context of data portability, given the strictness of its requirements.

the Charter of Fundamental Rights of the EU and has used the GDPR to set out not only obligations for businesses but also various rights for data subjects, such as the right to data portability. The GDPR forms an important part of legislation in regulating digital markets in the EU. As we envision images of a convenient future that allows data to be transferred freely between various services, if we do not make an effort to standardise the format for doing so at a very early stage, individual business operators may proceed with digitisation in their own unique formats. Once this has happened, it will become most difficult to unify those formats. In addition, while it is true that there may be situations where the enclosure of data can be dealt with by enforcing competition law after the fact, by that time it may already be too late to create a competitive environment, as one company may have a monopoly, or several companies may have formed an oligopoly. Thus, enforcement of competition law can only be a remedy after the fact, leaving no room for data portability.

References

1. Article 29 Data Protection Working Party: Guidelines on the right to data portability (2017)
2. Engels, B.: Data portability among online platforms. Internet Policy Rev. 5(2), 1 (2016)
3. Japan External Trade Organization (JETRO): California Consumer Privacy Act (CCPA) Practical Handbook (2019)
4. Japan External Trade Organization (JETRO): The US Federal Data Privacy Bill summary of the Consumer Online Privacy Rights Act (COPRA) (2021)
5. Japan Fair Trade Commission (JFTC) and Competition Policy Research Centre (CPRC): Report of the Study Group on Competition Policy in the Data Market (2021)
6. Ishii, K.: Considerations on peripheral areas of privacy and personal information protection law: focusing on intersection with competition law. J. Inf. Commun. Policy 3(1), IV–1 (2019)
7. Ishii, K.: 'The right to data portability' in terms of personal information. Discl. IR 18, 168 (2021)
8. Uga, K.: On the right to data portability. J. Consum. Law Res. 5, 2 (2018)
9. Ministry of Internal Affairs and Communications: 2020 White Paper on Information and Communications, p. 234 (2020)
10. OECD: Data portability, interoperability and digital platform competition (2021)
11. Subcommittee on Antitrust: Commercial and Administrative Law of the Committee on the Judiciary, Investigation of Competition in Digital Markets: Majority Staff Report and Recommendations (2020)
12. Komukai, T.: Data portability. Jurist 1521, 26 (2018)
13. The Personal Information Protection Commission: The Act on the Protection of Personal Information: Revision in Every 3 Years – Outline of Framework Amendment (2019)
14. Sasaki, T.: Regulation of the online platform market in Europe and the United States: dominant platform regulation approaches. J. Inf. Commun. Policy 5(1), IV-1 (2021)
15. Itakura, Y.: Data portability on digital platforms. Current Consum. Law 46, 135 (2020)

Regulatory Frameworks in Developing Countries: An Integrative Literature Review

Casper Chigwedere[1]([⊠]) [iD], Sam Takavarasha Jr.[2] [iD], and Bonface Chisaka[1]

[1] System, Postgraduate Research Centre, Women's University in Africa, 549, Arcturus Road, Harare, Zimbabwe
casperchigwedere@gmail.com
[2] Department of Information, Women's University in Africa, 549, Arcturus Road, Harare, Zimbabwe

Abstract. In spite of good intentions to develop effective ICT regulatory frameworks that foster universal access, improve competition, drive down access cost, address disputes between stakeholders and create equal opportunities to enter the sector, the outcomes often fail to match their preferences. The development of ICT regulatory frameworks in developing countries is dependent on lessons drawn from industrialised countries. Since the models from different countries have their strengths and weakness, it is imperative to investigate the causes of failure, to compile the strengths and avoid the weaknesses that are documented in literature as a first step to developing any effective ICT regulatory framework.

This paper presents an integrative literature review on regulatory frameworks in developing countries using Habermasian Critical Discourse Analysis (CDA) which views discourse under an Ideal Speech Situation. After a key word selection, Preferred Reporting Items for Systematic Reviews and Meta-Synthesis (PRISMS) model was employed by three researchers and a compilation of 30 papers was drawn from an initial list of 90 papers from AIS, Research4lLife, Googlescholar and Academia.edu data bases. The results present the components of an effective ICT regulatory model for developing countries as a hub and spoke framework with institutionalism as the hub that supports the rest, and all under a common jurisdiction and legislative context.

Keywords: ICT regulation · Frameworks · Comparative analysis · Best practice · Telecommunication

1 Introduction

There is a growing body of literature on ICT regulation in developing countries (José Antonio Gouvêa and de Souza 2020; Galhardo 2020; Walden, and Christou 2018; Palvia et al. 2015; Makoza and Chigona 2013). ICT regulatory frameworks often called telecommunication regulatory frameworks are being discussed in this paper from an Information systems perspective. The literature often draws from a combination of policy studies, ICT law and sectoral regulation studies that are concerned with regulatory frameworks

© IFIP International Federation for Information Processing 2022
Published by Springer Nature Switzerland AG 2022
D. Kreps et al. (Eds.): HCC 2022, IFIP AICT 656, pp. 170–185, 2022.
https://doi.org/10.1007/978-3-031-15688-5_15

of different sectors (Nesti 2018; Brown et al. 2006). We build the background and we critique the ICT regulation corpus on this polymophic approach because other scholars recommend a move beyond monomophic nation, region, or sector (Levi-Faur 2017).

Information systems scholars have noted that as their research area continues to grow it is becoming difficult to have a firm grasp of previous work. This then makes it challenging to advance knowledge in a research area that is increasingly diversified and fragmented, both in terms of its content and methods (Pentland 1995; Ravichandran et al. 2005). This makes it necessary for the writing of review papers, conceptual frameworks, taxonomies, polemics (Rowe 2014; Paré et al. 2015; Okoli 2015). Such work will enable the upcoming scholar to have a quick starting point while at the same time serving as a reference body for regulatory bodies seasoned scholars.

Scholars have lamented that the ICT regulatory systems have failed to deliver as expected. Investors have complained about a lack of fairness while subscribers have claimed to be disenchanted (Brown et al. 2006). Information systems scholars attribute ICT policy regulation failure to the lack of critical research on policy regulation. They further suggest that ICT policy outcomes are affected by the lack of capacity to conduct research that acknowledge the political and economical dimensions of policy reform (Gilwald 2010). Such research on policy is also said to be key to the implementation of information systems at the local level (Thompson and Walsham 2010). Kunyenje and Chigona (2017) suggest that this non-achievement of macro and micro-level ICT policy objectives is to blame for the failure of information systems projects and initiatives.

Due to the foregoing, we argue that research on ICT policy regulation in developing countries need to adopt a critical research theoretical lens. This paper is based on Jürgen Habermas' (1984) Ideal Speech Situation as an emancipatory for the developing world and particularly the post colonial state where ICT design often worsen inequalities. This will help us to go beyond the explaining and understanding phase to the critical questioning of established social structure and norms of ICT regulation and policy making environment. The controversy around conducting critical research from an interpretivist paradigm has already been problematised (McGrath 2005) and rebutted in IS literature (Walsham 2005).

Habermasian Critical Discourse Analysis (CDA) is used for analysing the literature on ICT policy frameworks that are used by developing countries. This paper is motivated by the need to build a knowledge base that the lead author may harness in the context of a PhD research at Women's University in Africa. Their objective is to contribute the IS body of knowledge on ICT regulation by systematically synthesising the body of knowledge on literature on regulatory models in developing countries. The paper therefore takes a conceptual approach which is organised around the main themes and concepts of ICT regulatory topic under review (Torraco 2016). The study endevours to develop an emancipatory model which will enable equal opportunity to communicate, invest and compete in the ICT sector. This objective is addressed by answering a research question which reads, 'What are the components of an effective ICT regulatory model for developing countries?'.

The rest of this paper is organised as follows: this introduction is followed by related work and theoretical grounding. This is followed by a methodology and findings and conclusions.

2 Related Work and Theoretical Framework

The use of systematic literature review is common in ICT policy and regulation research. In a similar endevour to investigate the ICT regulatory process, Galhardo and de Souza (2020) conducted a systematic literature review from a critical perspective and they found that there are opportunities for more Habermasian critiques of ICT regulation processes. This research follows this and earlier work's (Makoza and Chigona 2013) call for more critical work in the conduct of ICT policy and regulatory work in developing countries.

While this literature review project excludes publications by multilateral bodies, it important to acknowledge the outstanding work that also informs the peer reviewed. Zwahr et al. (2005) posits that governments find themselves sharing their power with non-state actors such as Transnational Corporations (TNCs) and Non-Governmental Organizations (NGOs). For instance, World bank's (2013) handbook for evaluating infrastructure regulation which specifies eight factors of a regulatory system. These are, 1) Independence and accountability of the regulator, 2) the need to have a working relationship between policy making bodies and the regulatory authority, 3) the need for regulator to have autonomy, 4) the need for the regulator to exercise transparency in their decision making. 5) the regulator's predictability in decision making. 6) the need for the regulator to have organisational structure and resources available to them, and 8) the need for formal and informal processes for regulatory decision making (Brown et al. 2006).

Space limitations won't allow us to enumerate the vast work done by International Telecommunications Union. The noteworthy is ITU Hand Book of Digital Regulation (2020) which addresses including regulatory independence, Regulatory responses to evolving technologies and technical regulation. Other key non-peer reviewed bodies included the regional bloc-centric bodies like European Commission's (2020) Body of European Regulatory for Electronic Communications, OECD and national bodies like the Ofcom, FCC and the Telecommunication Regulatory Authority of India (TRAI).

Similar to the work by multilateral bodies is work on best practice (Gülen et al. 2007). These authors tend to compile the ideal way of developing and implementing ICT regulatory frameworks. This is usually done as compendiums and evaluations of the components that make up an ideal ICT regulatory framework as discussed below (Palvia et al. 2015).

The regulators in developing countries keep drawing lessons from best practice from multinational bodies and other jurisdictions (Kunyenje and Chigona 2017). The manner in which this is done has awakened the vexed question of whether the developing world is marching to the beat of its own drum, or stuck in eternal mimicry of external agendas. These borrowed models have often been blamed for IS intervention that failed due to their acontextual nature. Avgerou (2010) emphasises the need to avoid the transfer and diffusion model and they advocate for a social embeddedness approach to ICT interventions. The undue influence of external actors was problematised by IS scholars,

(Chiumbu 2008, Kunyenje and Chigona 2017). They found that the influence of external play comes in different ways, e.g. the funding of the process and seconding of experts. The systematic review, however, concludes that the effect remains unknown.

A growing body of literature on ICT regulation in developing countries has tended to focus on the challenges that are faced by developing countries during the policy making process (Chiumbu 2008; Kunyenje and Chigona 2017; Wadhwa and Hallur 2013). Parallel to the above tracks of research also runs a body of comparative works on ICT regulation by different countries (Wadhwa and Hallur 2013; Hallur and Sane 2017). These papers attempt to compare the models in different countries with a view to analysing their differences and commonalities. Such studies often compare two or more countries from developing and/or developed countries. The other key body of literature has focused on the evaluation of existing policy frameworks (Palvia et al 2015). These are evaluated against their ability to enable key policy and regulatory objectives.

A final group of papers tends to focus on rerunning the evaluations using different theoretical frameworks (Palvia et al. 2015; Galhardo and de Souza 2020). Such work is based on the assumptions that different theoretical lenses may extract different policy out comes. These have also been influenced by the effectiveness of the theoretical frameworks in unpacking the research problems they wish to tackle. For instance, Palvia et al. (2015) adopted the design actuality gap with a view to investigating why the intended outcomes are not always realised.

Some of the works on ICT regulation tend to adopt a country specific focus (Kerretts 2004; Mollel 2008a, 2008b). These include papers that also fall into the above categories. This stream of works has the strength of adopting a more context specific approach. Information systems scholars have long emphasised the need for contextualism (Urquhart 2016). Context is the social setting that shapes IS design implementation and intervention at large (Benbasat and Zmud 2003). It is therefore important for best practice work to acknowledge the need for contextualising international best practice to specific jurisdiction. The functionalist approach which embraces universalism of IS solutions has been problematised in literature (Avgerou 2019). There has also been serious debate about the trade-offs between particularism and universalism (Cheng et al. 2016; Davison and Martinsons 2018). Particularism has respected IS design and implementation context at organisational and environmental levels while universalism expect IS to be universally applicable. While agreeing with particularism Cheng et al. (2016) characterise it as the King which is subordinate to generalisation, which the view as the Emperor and ultimate goal of all scientific work. This bergs the question, 'Are there any universally generalisable components and agendas of IS policy in general and ICT regulation in particular?' The jury it out so far.

The post-colonial developing country must adopt an emancipatory focus in order to overcome the disparities that ICTs tend to worsen as digital divides translate to economic divides, and vice-versa. From a feminist epistemological perspective, the IS scholar Alison Adam (2001) posits that '...*the power relations will remain unbalanced if the systems designers* ***do not*** *cast themselves as the liberators or emancipators, with a privileged epistemology based on the new critical IS, storming the barricades of ignorance in emancipating the system users who maybe did not even realize that they were candidates for emancipation* (Adam 2001) p.143'.

2.1 Theoretical Background

A "Regulatory Framework" is real, as articulated by John Dewey's "Theory of Reality" in his Middleworks (Dewey 1899–1924). It, therefore, has metaphysical dimensions and characteristics. He equates the "real-thing" to an organism, which means that the framework is organismic and organistic. The dimensions define the mandate and boundaries of the framework, and the organism has its characteristic behaviour when exposed to stimuli. Andrew Reck presents an accurate account of Dewey's metaphysics based on Experience and Nature (Reck 1993). Since the regulatory framework is real, we need to understand firstly, where it fits in the Universe within which it exists, and secondly, how it communicates/responds to/with adjacent elements. The regulatory framework resides within an institution, as depicted by Williamson's "Institutionalism".

He presents 4 levels of social analysis. The top level includes the norms, customs, morals, tradition, religion, all of which form the informal rules. The second level is the Institutional environment comprising of the polity, judiciary and bureaucracy of government, as well as formal rules. The third level is where the institutions of governance, i.e. where the regulatory organisations are located. Transaction cost economics operates at Levels 3 and 4, which are concerned with resource allocation and employment (prices and quantities, incentive alignment). Level 3 is the main focus of this study, but it can not be looked at in isolation, as it impacts, and is impacted upon by the levels on either side. This will compel us to investigate the whole framework and its inter-relatedness.

Having discussed the regulatory institution as a real organism through the Dewey's (1899–1924) institutionalism lens its components and response to stimuli can be analysed through a Habermasian critical lens. Habermasian CDA perspective proposes that emancipatory discourse should happen under an Ideal speech situation. An Ideal Speech situation refers to a situation where discourse is free from coercive, hegemonic powers. Communicators are therefore free to make assertions and assess the assertions made by others without the influence of either conscious or unconscious hegemonic powers (Cukier et al. 2009; Habermas 1984).

It identifies the veracity of communication through violation of Four key valitidity claims i.e. 1) the communication's comprehensibility, which refers to the technical clarity of the language used; 2) its truthfulness, i.e. the propositional aspects of the communication as depicted by the completeness of the arguments and unbiased assertions and 3) the legitimacy,which refers to the balance in representing the opposite sides of the argument and 4) the speaker's sincerity which is the correspondence between what the communicator says and what she means (Cukier et al. 2009; Wall et al. 2015).

Habermasian CDA is used for analysing the literature on ICT policy frameworks that are adopted by developing countries. According to Myres and Klein (2011), in IS research, critical research deals with social concerns like power, freedom, values, social control, the use and impact of information technology. According to Orlikowski and Baroudi (1991), critical research takes a critical stance against taken-for-granted assumptions on the organisation and IS and its aim is to critique the status-quo by exposing the deep-seated structural contradictions in the social system. It is however problematised for being gender blind and universalistic (Adam 2001).

The Theory of Communicative Action (TCA), which is an extension of Habermas' Ideal Speech Situation, helps us to be critical with the ICT regulatory frameworks that have been deployed in literature. Critical IS research takes on the nature of a cause that aims to critique the wrongs that affect stakeholders in the developing world. Our pro-poor approach to ICT regulation and deployment in developing countries is motivated by the need to foster universal access, improve competition, drive down access cost, address disputes between stakeholders and create equal opportunities to enter the sector.

Habermasian critical theory has been adopted in literature reviews that involve ethical and regulatory aspects of emerging technologies (North-Samardzic 2019; Galhardo 2020).

At the core of critical philosophy is the "Emancipatory" principle (Lyytinen and Klein 1985). It also offers classifications such as "Knowledge Interests" (Habermas Habermas 1972) as "Technical", and "Practical" Three key kinds of social action are associated with these Knowledge Interests i.e. "Social Action" (Habermas 1972b): "Strategic", "Communicative" and "Discursive". In TCA, is his popular rational framework of society, from a "deontological perspective, based on communication driven to a mutual understanding." he also includes the concept of "Valid Norm". (Habermas 1984) from and ethical and moral stance and the concept of "Deliberative Democracy" (Habermas 1987). These concepts are used in several IS research works (Habermas 1984; Habermas 1987; and Mingers and Walsham 2010).

3 Methodology

This study uses an Integrative Literature Review (ILR) for identifying the major publications on ICT policy regulation in developing countries (Torraco 2016). Integrative Literature Review is a qualitative version of the Systematic Literature Review (SLR) which is associated with the positivist or logical empiricist paradigm (Oates 2015). Like SLR, ILR also conducts literature search using a methodological (systematic) manner using pre-specified protocols that are meant to minimise paper select bias. We conduct ILR under a hermeneutic literature search as articulated by Schultze (2015) in order to achieve the rigour of systematic literature search and a flexible hermeneutic engagement with literature. A hermeneutic approach is an iterative process that allows the understanding of texts through ongoing cycles of dialogue between the reader and the text (Rowe 2014).

A integrative literature review aims to identify the most appropriate papers using the Preferred Reporting Items for Systematic Reviews and Meta-Synthesis (PRISMS). We adopt the term PRISMS to deviate from the PRISMA model which employs meta-analysis using quantitative methods. This paper uses meta-synthesis under a qualitative research methods approach. 'Synthesis is a creative act that results in the generation of new knowledge about the topic reviewed in the literature' The approach, therefore, uses syntheses review under an interpretivist paradigm, of a hermeneutic orientation, as opposed to aggregative reviews that are preferred by positivist (Pare et al. 2016). A hermeneutic tradition is preferred for its usefulness in interrogating textual content using an iterative process (Radnizky 1973; Ricoeur 1981; Gadamer 1986; Klein and Myers 1999).

Literature Review Plan: We started by developing a review that laid out how to select the key words, how and where to search the literature from, the selection criteria, the quality assessment process, data extracting process and analysing and interpreting process (Pare et al. 2016).

The search process started with a selection of the data bases i.e. AIS, Research4Life, Googlescholar and Academia.edu using NVIVO's NCapture. NCapture is a tool for importing papers from an online data base to NVIVO. This process was guided by the relevance and the accessibility of the databases to our research team. The final three data bases that were Research4Life, Googlescholar and Academia.edu were selected for their ability search from various publication outlets that contain articles.

This was followed by a key word selection process during which an initial list of papers on ICT regulation was compiled using narrative literature review search methods. The key words were compiled into a lexicon of parent and children hierarchy. See Table 1. The list was augmented by works from expert researchers in the field. A team of three researchers took turns to contribute to the list without being influenced by the others. This was followed by a brain-storming of the relevance of each of the key words on the basis of their appropriateness for addressing the research objectives and for answering the research question. While we acknowledge that this stage was weak on the systematicity front we acknowledge that it was a transparent process which got refined at each iteration. The final list was made up of the following key words; ICT Regulation, Frameworks, comparative analysis, best practice effectiveness, telecommunication, developing countries **The selection criteria** involved that development of an inclusion and exclusion criteria. To refine this stage, we consulted previous review papers in order to evaluate the approaches that were used. Our criteria included peer reviewed journals, conference and book chapters. It, among other varieties, excluded the magazines, unpublished papers, internet sources that fell outside the inclusion criteria.

The quality assessment process, mainly focused on full papers that addressed the subject matter as defined by the key words and research objectives. The extraction process employed NVIVO for compiling nodes of that addressed the theme relevant to the research objectives. Finally, the analysing and interpreting process involved a thorough analysis of the nodes that were identified. It also included the drawing of insights from the themes and the full papers that we read.

Four approaches to systematic reviews were considered for this work, firstly the reviews that describe the phenomena without theory building. Secondly, the reviews that aim at understanding and unpacking phenomena through analysis of concepts investigated in earlier work (Rowe 2014). Thirdly, a positivist genre that endevours to quantitatively test theories through aggregating prior works. Finally, theoretical reviews (Paré et al. 2015) or configurative reviews which combine different streams of work and employ various synthesis approaches and methods (Gough et al. 2012). We adopted the second one because it is amenable to critical IS research and interpretivist approach. This genre, *'Understanding may also refer to examining consistencies and inconsistencies which may be accomplished with the help of various forms of literature reviews, including conceptual and critical reviews.'* (Booth et al. 2012) (Table 2).

Table 1. The keywords lexicon organised as superordinate and subordinate relationship

ICT Regulation	ICT Regulation Frameworks	ICT Best practice	National ICT Policy	Telecommunication regulation	
Regulation	Regulation	Ethics	Convergence	Developing countries	Parent
Developing countries	Transparency	Code of practice	Tool kits	Systematic review	
Systematic review	consistency	Enforcement	legislation	Comparative analysis	
Comparative analysis	Accountability	Developing countries	laws	process	
Process	Competency	Systematic review	Arbitration	National ICT policy	Children
Policy formulation	Independence	Comparative analysis	Developing countries	ICT Governance	
Stakeholders	Competitiveness	Process	Systematic review	Investment	
Other	Enforcement	Effectiveness	Comparative analysis		
	Funding	International	National ICT policy		
	Investment		conflict		

Table 2. Cluster analysis

Initial cluster	Articles			Re-clustering
	Iteration 1	Iteration 2	Iteration 3	
Policy for conflict/competition/investment	7	21	8	International Best Practices for inclusive growth
International Best Practices for inclusive growth	19			
ICT Governance and policy	36	8	5	ICT Governance and policy
Policy Appraisal and reforms for stimulating investment and funding;	25	15	14	Policy Appraisal and reforms
Investment and tariff management	3	8	3	Tariff management
TOTAL	90	52	30	

In Fig. 1 below we present the Preferred Reporting Items for Systematic Reviews and Meta-Synthesis flow chart showing the articles screening process which selected 30 article out of an initial 147 papers extracted from four databases.

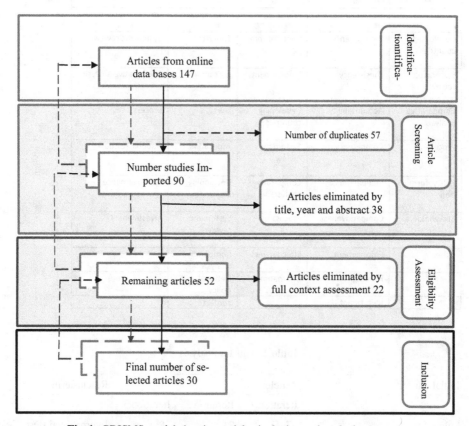

Fig. 1. PRISMS model showing articles inclusion and exclusion process

4 Findings

Table 3 presents the findings from the systematic review. It lists the publications categorised by factor as well as well as the comments on the findings on each of the key regulatory factor.

Table 3. Literature review findings categorized by regulatory factor

Factor	Article	Comment
Independence	Wadhwa and Hallur (2013); Xiuqiing et al. (2014); Robert Herian (2018); Li and Lyons (2008)	The regulator must have financial independence from government and stakeholders such as business, regulatory,
Regulatory Transparency	Xiuqiing et al. (2014); (Mone 1996a 1996b, 1997; Thatcher and Stone Sweet 2003, 4; Gilardi 2008, 30); (Bert-Jaap Koops et al. (2006)	The openness and predictability of the policies allows for investors and the market to plan accordingly, with full knowledge of the impact of their decisions
Pro-competitiveness	Xiuqiing et al. (2014); Joseph Schumpeter; Jose Antonio Gouvea and Cesar Aexandre de Souza	A regulator should create an environment that allows fair competition, limits powers of any individual stakeholder, protects all stakeholders, and still leave room for innovation and possibility of realising profit, in order to attract investment
Enforcement powers	Xiuqiing et al. (2014); (Bert-Jaap Koops et al. (2006); (Stuart Biegel 2003)	The regulatory intervention's success is dependant upon the regulator's capacity to enforce its laws and decisions
Consistency	Anita Bramford-Wade and Cheryle Moss (2010); McCubbins et al. (1987)	The regulatory body must use the same principles and act consistently and predictably on similar situations
Competency	Nguyen Hai Thi Thanh (2007); Pujan Ziaie (2013); (Majone 1996a, 1996b, 1997; Thatcher and Stone Sweet (2003, 4); Gilardi (2008)	The regulator's Human Resources, Leadership, and interventions must exude competency on the policy, arbitration and technical realms
Policy research capacity	Majone (1996a, 1996b, 1997); Thatcher and Stone Sweet (2003, 4); Gilardi (2008); Nesti (2018)	The ICT industry is fast moving, therefore continuous adaptation of policies in order to remain competent and current
Accountability	Nesti (2018); Righettini and Nesti (2018); Majone (1996a, 1996b, 1997); Thatcher and Stone Sweet (2003, 4); Gilardi (2008); Nesti (2018)	The institutional environment, and clearly articulated responsibilities, will determine respective ownership

(*continued*)

Table 3. (*continued*)

Factor	Article	Comment
Financial autonomy	Xiuqiing et al (2014)	The regulator must be financially independent to avoid being constrained and conflicted by relationship with government and local and international funding bodies who may want to control the sector
Political & Legal	Pujan Ziaie (2013); Roger Brownsword (2008); Bert-Jaap Koops et al. (2006)	The political and legal instruments determine commitment, and provide oversight and enforcement powers of the regulator
Institutionalism	Ziaie (2013); Williamson (1998)	The institutional space within which the regulatory framework will operate, is the determining factor for its success

5 Discussion and Conclusions

These findings are meaningless if they end without a model that can inform future research and practice and build a better word with the power of ICTs. Critical IS focuses on an emancipatory epistemology. Webster and Watson (2002) posit that literature review must develop models that guide future research and provide conclusions and implications that will inform researchers and practitioners. Consequently, we have developed the hub and spoke conceptual model that presents the an emancipatory ICT regulatory framework in developing countries. See Fig. 1.

Harbarmas' Ideal Speech Situation depicts the nature of the play field that the ICT regulator aims to establish in post colonial developing countries that are affected by inequalities of ICT access, influence and ICT enabled opportunities. It prepossess that the participants are free to communicate. There should be no hindrances due to lack of effective regulatory regime and no conscious or unconscious cohesive forces that constrain citizens' ability to express themselves thorough ICT platforms. The Ideal speech situation consists of 1) the communication's comprehensibility, 2) truthfulness, 3) the legitimacy, 4) the speaker's sincerity (Cukier et al. 2009; Wall et al. 2015). The following section we will discuss the factors of a regulatory framework in the context if the four valid claims of an Ideal Speech Situation.

1) The communication's comprehensibility: Under the first of the four valid claims i.e. communication's comprehensibility, three spokes of the regulatory model link the institutional hub to the regulatory context. These are Competency, Policy research capacity, and the Political & Legal parameter. Habermas' (1984) Comprehensibility

refers to the technical clarity of the language. We operationalised this to conceptu-alise the need for clarity in the regulator's implicit and tacit messages to and from the ICT sector. The sector needs to receive coherent messages, technically correct and research based policy from the regulator. The lack of research capacity has been blamed for poor policy outcomes in developing countries (Kunyenje and Chigona 2017; Gilwald 2010). The second spoke from literature is competency. This is closely related to research capacity in that it calls for training and experience though it can also draw from multi national bodies that seek to inform grant receiving develop-ing countries (Kunyenje and Chigona 2017). The third spoke refers to political and legal factors. These tend to affect the implementation of otherwise plausible regu-latory frameworks developed by the most competent consultants. The weaknesses on this front often lead to the hinderance of an emancipatory environment in the post-colonial developing country.

2) Truthfulness: Habermas (1984) posits that "Truthfulness refers to the propositional content of communication as represented by complete arguments and unbiased assertions" (Cukier et al. 2009); the propositional aspects of the communication as depicted by the completeness of the arguments and unbiased assertions. Regula-tory Transparency, Pro-competitiveness (Limeasia 2007). Various inequalities that prevail in the developing world are often masked by opaque processes of regulatory decision making. There is a crying call for a fair playing field where stakeholders compete fairly, calls for both transparency and pro-competitiveness. The incom-pleteness of the arguments that are presented as justification for an uncompetitive environment are often caused by the need to avoid scrutiny for the regulatory pro-cesses. As a result the existence of such an environment will fuel the furtherance of inequality and partiality and an ineffective regulatory environment which will not emancipate the weak stakeholder who, according to Adams (2001), may not realise that they are candidates for emancipation (Fig. 2).

3) The legitimacy: The regulatory climate's legitimacy refers to which refers to the bal-ance in representing the opposite sides of the argument. Refers to the representation of different perspectives; all perspectives should be heard and considered (Cukier et al. 2009; Habermas 1984). We operationalise the regulatory environment's legit-imacy as its Independence, Enforcement powers and Financial autonomy. In devel-oping countries, the regulators may be cognisant of the need to be accountable to its stakeholders but this is not always the case due to weak institutions that characterise the developing and emerging economies. This tends to tilt the play field in favour of the executive branch which is often undifferentiable from legislature.

The same challenge is experienced with regards to the regulator's Independence, and Financial autonomy. The independence and autonomy are compromised by the weak-ness of the governing institutions one which is the ICT regulator itself. The stakeholder that includes the executive branch and business often impose undue disproportionate influence at the expense of other actors interests. Scholars have advocated for elimina-tion of monopolies and privatisation of telecommunication giants (Wadwa and Hallur 2013). Toward this end, Wallsten (2003) further argues for the establishment of the reg-ulator before privatisation because investors were found to invest more in countries were regulatory reforms proceeded.

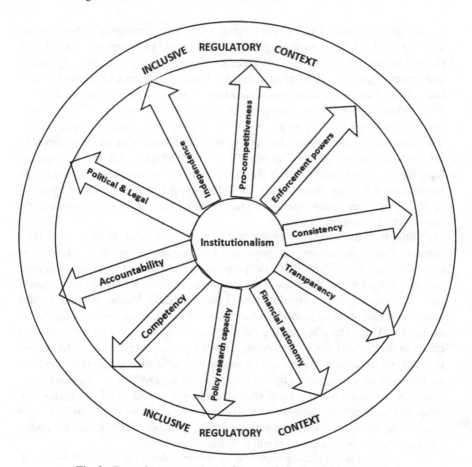

Fig. 2. Emancipatory regulatory framework for developing countries

The SPEAKEr's Sincerity: Lastly we use Harbaermas's (1984) speaker's sincerity to conceptualise the stakeholders participation in an Ideal speech situation consisting of Consistency and Accountability. Sincerity is 'the correspondence between what the communicator says and what she means' The stakeholders in the sector are given to tactics that serve inconsistent ends that favour the current situation. The body of literature showed the need for consistency in the regulator's activities (Cukier et al. 2009). While scholars from developing countries such as Nesti (2018) argue that the neutrality of the regulator from politics and democratic values weakens its accountability, however, the developing world stakeholder laments its politicisation as the source of inequality (Ziaie 2013). As a result, they advocate for privatisation as a way of removing the executive's bias towards state-owned enterprises.

Institutionalism: At the centre of the hub and spoke model is the concept of institutionalism as articulated by (Williamson 1990). The implemantation of the above regulatory factors are dependant on institutional capacity. According to scholars of Institutionalism, cultural, normative and cognitive factors are key. They suggest that external institutional pressures shape the organisational structures and practices (Scott 1992, 95, 2001; Baxter and Chua 2003). These may take the form of partisan politics The post colonial developing country is often bedeviled by weak institutions which lack the capacity to withstand pressures that impede regulatory decision.

6 Conclusion

Due to the finding of this study, it must be concluded that an effective regulatory framework for the developing country must firstly be context-specific. The contextual issues of concern in developing countries include the disenchantment of the consumer and the uneven business climate that do not allow free competition. The weak institutions in the post-colonial developing state tend to be weak and unfit for dispute resolution. It is therefore key to note that the prescription of conventional regulatory factors presented by multilateral bodies like the World bank will not achieve effective regulatory environment in the absence of context specific research findings implemented by strong institutions.

References

Adam, A.: Gender, emancipation and critical information systems. In: The 9th European Conference on Information Systems Bled, Slovenia, 27–29 June 2001 (2001). https://aisel.aisnet.org/cgi/viewcontent.cgi?article=1000&context=ecis2001

Benbasat, I., Zmud, R.W.: The identity crisis within the is discipline: defining and communicating the discipline's core properties. MIS Q. **27**(2), 183–194 (2003)

Boell, S.K., Cecez-Kecmanovic, D.: A hermeneutic approach for conducting literature reviews and literature searches. Commun. Assoc. Inf. Syst. **34** (2014). Article 12. http://aisel.aisnet.org/cais/vol34/iss1/12

Brownn, A.C., Stern, J., Tenenbaum, B.: Handbook for Evaluating Infrastructure Regulatory Systems (2006). chrome-extension://efaidnbmnnnibpcajpcglclefindmkaj/viewer.html?pdfurl=https%3A%2F%2Fppp.worldbank.org%2Fpublic-private-partnership%2Fsites%2Fppp.worldbank.org%2Ffiles%2Fdocuments%2Fworld_bank-_ppiaf-_handbook_for_evaluating_infrastructure_regulatory_systems_2006_english.pdf&chunk=true

Cheng, Z.A., Dimoka, A., Pavlou, P.A.: Context may be king, but generalizability is the Emperor! J. Inf. Technol. **31**(3), 257–264 (2016). https://doi.org/10.1057/s41265-016-0005-7

Chen, Y., Zahedi, F.M.: Individuals' internet security perceptions and behaviors: polycontextual contrasts between the United States and China. MIS Q. **40**(1), 205–222 (2016)

Chiumbu, S.H.: Understanding the role and influence of external actors and ideas in African information, communication and technology policies: the African information society initiative. Ph.D. thesis. University of Oslo, Oslo, 1 February 2008

Davison, R.M., Martinsons, M.G.: Context is king! Considering particularism in research design and reporting. J. Inf. Technol. **31**(3), 241–249 (2018)

Gadamer, H.-G.: Truth and Method. The Continuing Publishing Corporation, New York (1986)

Galhardo, J.A.G.: ICT regulation process in a civil law, peripheral, and multilevel administration country: Habermas' deliberative paradigm revisited. In: Kommers, P., Viana, A.B.N., Issa, T., Isaías, P., Issa, T. (eds.) IADIS International Conference Internet Technologies and Society 2020, pp. 105–109. International Association for Development of the Information Society, São Paulo (2020). http://www.iadisportal.org/digital-library/ict-regulationprocess-in-a-civil-law-peripheral-and-multilevel-administration-country-habermas-deliberativeparadigm-revisited

Galhardo, J.A.G., de Souza, C.A.: ICT regulation process: Habermas meets the multiple streams framework. In: AMCIS 2020 Proceedings, 16 (2020). https://aisel.aisnet.org/amcis2020/adv_info_systems_research/adv_info_systems_research/16

Geeling, S., Brown, I., Weimann, P.: Information systems and culture - a systematic hermeneutic literature review. In: CONF-IRM 2016 Proceedings, Paper 40 (2016). http://aisel.aisnet.org/confirm2016/40

Gülen, G., Makaryan, R., Volkov, D., Foss, M.: Improving regulatory agency efficiency and effectiveness best practices, processes and organizational structures. In: Proceedings, 11th Annual Conference of the International Society for New Institutional Economics, Reykjavik, Iceland, vol. 23 (2007)

Habermas, J.: Knowledge and Human Interests. Beacon Press, Boston (1972a)

Habermas, J.: Toward a Rational Society: Student Protest, Science, and Politics. Shapiro, J.J. (Trans.). Heinemann, London (1972b)

Habermas, J.: The Theory of Communicative Action: Reasons and Rationalization of Society. Mccarthy, T. (Trans.). Beacon Press, Boston (1984)

Habermas, J.: The Theory of Communicative Action: Lifewolrd and Social System. Mccarthy, T. (Trans.). Beacon Press, Boston (1987)

Wadhwa, D., Hallur, G.: Comparative analysis of ICT regulation frameworks: a study of seven countries (2013)

Hallur, G.G., Sane, V.S.: Indian telecom regulatory framework in comparison with five countries: structure, role description and funding. Digit. Policy Regul. Gov. **20**(1), 62–77 (2017). https://doi.org/10.1108/DPRG-06-2017-0035

José Antonio Gouvêa, G., de Souza, C.A.: ICT regulation process: Habermas meets the multiple streams framework. In: AMCIS 2020 Proceedings 16 (2020)

Klein, H., Myers, M.A.: Set of principals for conducting and evaluating interpretive field studies in information systems. MIS Q. **23**(1), 67–94 (1999)

Kunyenje, G., Chigona, W.: External actors' influence on national ICT policy in developing countries: a literature review. In: ACIST 2017, pp. 1–10. ACIST, Cape Town (2017)

Levi-Faur, D.: The odyssey of the regulatory state: from a 'Thin' monomorphic concept to a 'Thick' and polymorphic concept article in law & policy, April 2013. https://doi.org/10.1111/lapo.12000

Makoza, F., Chigona, W.: How gender is embedded in the national ICT policy of Malawi. In: Proceedings for CPRsouth8/CPRafrica 2013 Conference, Mysore, India, 5–7 September, 2013, pp. 1–20 (2013). SSRN: https://ssrn.com/abstract=2531859. https://doi.org/10.2139/ssrn.2531859

Mingers, J., Walsham, G.: Toward ethical information systems: the contribution of discourse ethics. MIS Q. **34**(4), 833–854 (2010). https://www.jstor.org/stable/25750707

Mollel, A.: The legal and regulatory framework for ICT in developing countries: case study of ICT and the law of evidence in Tanzania. A paper delivered at IPID ICT4D PG/PhD Symposium (2008)

Mollel, A.: The legal and regulatory framework for ICT in developing countries: case study of ICT and the law of evidence in Tanzania. A paper delivered at IPID ICT4D PG/PhD Symposium, 7–9 September 2008 (2008)

Nesti, G.: Strengthening the accountability of independent regulatory agencies: from performance back to democracy. Comp. Eur. Polit. **16**, 464–481 (2018). https://doi.org/10.1057/cep.2016.24

North-Samardzic, A.: Biometric technology and ethics: beyond security applications. J. Bus. Ethics **167**(3), 433–450 (2019). https://doi.org/10.1007/s10551-019-04143-6

Okoli, C.: A guide to conducting a standalone systematic literature review. Commun. Assoc. Inf. Syst. **37**, 43 (2015)

Palvia, P., Baqir, N., Nemati, H.: ICT policies in developing countries: an evaluation with the extended design-actuality gaps framework. Electron. J. Inf. Syst. Dev. Countries **71**(1), 1–34 (2015)

Paré, G., Trudel, M.C., Jaana, M., Kitsiou, S.: Synthesizing information systems knowledge: a typology of literature reviews. Inf. Manag. **52**(2), 183–199 (2015)

Pare, G., Tate, M., Johnstone, D., Kitsiou, S.: Contextualizing the twin concepts of systematicity and transparency in information systems literature reviews. Eur. J. Inf. Syst. **25**(6), 493–508 (2016). https://doi.org/10.1057/s41303-016-0020-3

Pentland, B.T.: Information systems and organizational learning: the social epistemology of organizational knowledge systems. Account. Manag. Inf. Technol. **5**(1), 1–21 (1995)

Radnitzky, G.: Contemporary Schools of Metascience. Humanities Press/Henry Regnery Company, Chicago (1973)

Ricoeur, P.: Hermeneutics and the Human Science. Cambridge University Press, Cambridge (1981)

Ravichandran, T., Lertwongsatien, C., Lertwongsatien, C.: Effect of information systems resources and capabilities on firm performance: a resource-based perspective. J. Manag. Inf. Syst. **21**(4), 237–276 (2005)

Rowe, F.: What literature review is not: diversity, boundaries and recommendations. Eur. J. Inf. Syst. **23**(3), 241–255 (2014)

Torraco, R.J.: Writing integrative literature reviews: using the past and present to explore the future. Hum. Resour. Dev. Rev. **15**(4), 404–428 (2016)

Walden, I., Christou, T.A.: Legal and regulatory implications of disruptive technologies in emerging market economies. SSRN Electron. J. 2018. https://doi.org/10.2139/ssrn.3230674

Wall, J.D., Stahl, B.C., Salam, A.F.: Critical discourse analysis as a review methodology: an empirical example. Commun. Assoc. Inf. Syst. **37** (2015). Article 11. https://doi.org/10.17705/1CAIS.03711

Williamson, O.E.: The institutions of governance. Am. Econ. Rev. **88**(2), 75–79 (1998)

Ziaie, P.: Challenges and issue of ICT industries in developing countries. In: International Conference on Computer Applications Technology, Sousse, Tunisiam 20–22 January 2013. IEEE Xplore (2013)

Zwahr, T., Rossel, P., Finger, M.: Towards electronic governance: a case study of ICT in local government governance. In: The National Conference on Digital Government Research (dg. o2005) (No. CONF) (2005)

Application of International Law to Cyber Conflicts Outline of Japan's Legal Response Against Low-Intensity Cyber Conflicts Through Countermeasures

Tetsunosuke Jinnai(✉)

Institute of Information Security, Yokohama, Japan
dgs213101@iisec.ac.jp

Abstract. Cyber conflicts are an important security challenge, but the applicable legal regime remains ambiguous. Especially, low-intensity cyber conflicts, which do not amount to armed conflicts under international law, are difficult to handle legally because the boundary between conflicts and crimes is ambiguous. Domestic debates on the legal response to such cyber conflicts so far have mainly focused on the applicability of self-defense under Japan's extreme pacifist constitution. However, applying self-defense to low-intensity conflicts is quite difficult under the constitution, and further progress in the debate is unlikely. This study proposes specific ways to respond to cyber conflicts by utilizing countermeasures as a new legal framework. In the first part, after touching on an overview of the application of international law in cyberspace, this study will show the advantages of countermeasures under low-intensity cyber conflicts. In the latter part, through some scenario analyses, this study will clarify concrete ways of how to apply countermeasures, foreseeable problems, and how to respond to them as conclusions. The rationale for this study was mainly based on a literature review, including previous studies, and the scenario study method was also used to draft the conclusions.

Keywords: Cyber conflicts · Law of international responsibility · Countermeasures

1 Current Status and Perception of the Problems in Cyber Conflicts

The intensification of cyber conflicts in recent years has become a serious security concern for Japan. Japan's new cyber security strategy [1] released in 2021, expresses the sense of crisis in its situational awareness; "As such, the situation in cyberspace, while not amounting to national emergency per se, can no longer be deemed purely in peacetime." From the perspective of international law, cyber conflicts have various characteristics that differ from conventional international conflicts, such as diversity of legal entities, anonymity, and dilution of the concept of national borders. The most important characteristic is that most cyber conflicts are conducted below the threshold of armed conflicts, and the boundary between conflicts and crimes is obscure, which makes

D. Kreps et al. (Eds.): HCC 2022, IFIP AICT 656, pp. 186–199, 2022.
https://doi.org/10.1007/978-3-031-15688-5_16

it difficult to determine the applicable legal framework. Figure 1 explains an example of the legal classification of cyber conflicts. To effectively deal with cyber conflicts, Japan is required to make its legal position clear against cyber incidents and respond to the situation immediately.

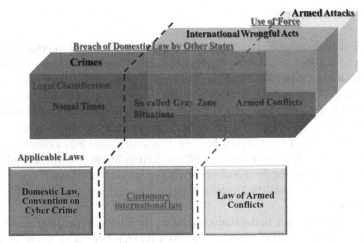

Fig. 1. Schematic of the legal classification of cyber conflicts. (This figure shows an example of the legal classification of cyber conflicts. Use of force and breach of domestic law straddle over the boundary of each category.)

However, Japan's current situation shows that the development of cyber protection capability lags that of neighboring countries partially because legislations to deal with cyber conflicts have not been sufficiently studied [2].[1] In particular, the severe restrictions on administrative agencies originated from the "renunciation of war" and "secrecy of communications" stipulated in Japan's constitution,[2] as well as the unclear role of each ministry and agency in the security in the cyber domain as seen in the Basic Act on Cybersecurity,[3] are hindering effective responses.

Still, seeing the situation of academic studies in this field, the mainstream of discussions domestically on cyber conflicts seemed to be on the application of self-defense so far. However, the debate on the application of self-defense to low-intensity cyber conflicts[4] easily leads to the one lowering the threshold of the use of force, which is quite challenging under Japan's pacifist constitution. These discussions do not seem to be

---

[1] The International Institute for Strategic Studies (U.K.) produced a report that assessed 15 countries' cyber power. It ranks a country's cyber capacity and effectiveness and ranks Japan in the lowest layer, tier.3, due to the delay in developing effective domestic legislation for cyber operations.

[2] The Constitution of Japan, articles 9 and 22.

[3] The Basic Act on Cybersecurity, article 18, provides that "The national government is to provide necessary measures with the intention to.... clarify the division of roles among relevant bodies as actions to address threats which may critically affect the country's safety concerning Cybersecurity-related incidents," which means that those have not been clarified yet.

[4] Here, "low-intensity cyber conflicts" means the cyber conflicts which don't achieve the threshold of armed conflicts.

progressing realistically. Therefore, the focus of this paper is to recommend responses to low-intensity cyber conflicts by creating a new framework using countermeasures under international law.

2   Previous Research

In the field of international law, discussions on the application of international law to cyberspace have been held at the Government Experts' Group at the United Nations and the United Nations Open-ended Working Group on Cybersecurity. Both submitted their final report documents in 2021 [3, 4]. In addition, there are many previous studies on the application of international law to cyber conflicts. In particular, the Tallinn Manual [5], which is a compilation of expert opinions on international law, seems to have a strong influence even though it is not legally binding. Especially speaking of countermeasures, Michael N. Schmitt [6], the proponent of the Tallinn Manual, and the leader of its compilation has argued for the use of countermeasures, and Jeff Kosseff [7] of the U.S. Naval War College has published a paper strongly arguing for the necessity of collective countermeasures.

However, looking back to the studies in Japan, the number is not large, furthermore, most of them focus on self-defense such as [8]. Little has been done to the application of countermeasures to cyber conflicts with considering unique Japanese legal policy situations.[5] Given this situation, it can be considered that this paper has novelty in this field.

3   Internationally Wrongful Cyber Acts

3.1   Overview of International Wrongful Cyber Acts

First, it is necessary to clarify what are lawful and unlawful acts in cyberspace under international law. The Article of State Responsibility [9] provides the elements of an act of violation of international law by a State, which consist of acts or omissions that are attributable to States under international law and constitute a breach of the state's international obligations.[6] The requirements are clearly stated in the Tallinn Manual 2.0 [5] to be applicable in cyberspace as well. The following is a discussion of the specific application of each requirement, considering the characteristics of cyberspace.

3.2   Attribution to the State

In principle, only sovereign States can be legal entities in international law, and the status of legal entities of individuals and international organizations is mainly created

---

[5] For example, there are several studies about self-defense in cyberspace that are done by Japanese researchers, but it is difficult to find the works related to the application of countermeasures to cyber conflicts considering specific Japanese situations.

[6] Draft Articles on Responsibility of States for Internationally Wrongful Acts, article 2.

by treaties between States.[7] In other words, to hold someone responsible for an illegal act, it is necessary to attribute it to States. The cases in which a State can be held responsible generally fall into two categories: (1) acts of State organs and (2) acts of private individuals [10]. The second case is further divided into the following categories: acts of private individuals under the directions of States, State endorsement of the acts of private individuals, and violation of the principle of due diligence. In cyber conflicts, many indirect cyber operations are using non-State actors as proxies, so the attribution of private acts to States becomes a major issue.

3.3 Breach of the State's International Obligations

Regarding the second requirement, breach of international obligations, the Articles of State Responsibility [9] provide that "a breach of an international obligation by a State exists if the conduct of the State is not consistent with that required of the State by the international obligation, regardless of the origin or nature of the obligation."[8] In general, obligations regarding the context of cyber conflicts include (1) the principle of State sovereignty, (2) the prohibition of intervention, (3) the prohibition of the use of force, and (4) due diligence.

The Principle of State Sovereignty. It can be said that States have generally established a consensus that the principle of State sovereignty applies to cyberspace. Malicious cyber activities by a State against another State's cyberinfrastructure without the latter's consent may be a violation of sovereignty. However, there is no consensus on the lawfulness of cyber espionage or unauthorized remote access from outside the State's territory [5].

The Prohibition of Intervention. The prohibition of intervention is a principle that States refrain from intervening in the domestic jurisdiction of other States, and there is no discussion on the application of this principle in cyberspace [5]. However, there is no established agreement on what the specific components of domestic jurisdiction are [10]. In general, whether an act violates the prohibition of intervention is determined by whether it relates to the above-mentioned domestic jurisdiction and whether it is inherently coercive. Intervention without a coercive element does not constitute unlawful intervention [11]. For example, a large-scale DDoS attack on a government agency to force the country to withdraw from a military alliance, or an attempt to hack into another country's election system to falsify the results of a particular election would be a violation of this rule.

The Prohibition of the Use of Force. Regarding the obligation to refrain from the use of force, while article 2 of the UN Charter[9] prohibits it, article 51 permits the exercise of individual or collective self-defense only in the event of an armed attack. Although there are various arguments about the difference between the use of force and armed

---

[7] Therefore, in principle, non-State actors cannot owe the responsibility of international wrongful cyber acts.

[8] Draft Articles on Responsibility of States for Internationally Wrongful Acts, article 12.

[9] Charter of the United Nations, article 2 paragraph 4 and Article 51.

attacks, in the Nicaragua case judgment [11], the court described armed attacks as the "most grave forms of the use of force" and expressed the idea of distinguishing between the two. Additionally in the judgment, the court adopted the scale and effects test as criteria to determine whether a specific act constitutes an armed attack.[10] Given the fact, Tallinn Manual 2.0 [5] applies the test as criteria to judge whether a cyber act meets the threshold of use of force. Although the difference between the use of force and armed attacks in cyberspace and the detail of the test are still unclear, it has been established from the past discussions that a cyber act that causes physical damage such as death or injury to a person or destruction of property would at least meet the criteria of the use of force. On the other hand, there is no consensus on whether non-physical damage such as data destruction can be satisfied with the threshold of the use of force or not [5].

Due Diligence. "Due diligence" is an obligation that States must exercise due diligence in ensuring territory and objects over which they enjoy sovereignty are not used to harm other States [12]. This obligation seems to be widely recognized as a general law principle, however, the scope of actions required is quite ambiguous [5]. In the context of cyber conflicts, a territorial state is obliged to crack down on illegal cyber activities conducted from within its territory against other countries. If the territorial State is aware of the fact but does not take any action, the injured State can pursue the violation of due diligence of the territorial State. It is noticeable that Japan's Ministry of Foreign Affairs has expressed the same idea [13].

4 Response to Internationally Wrongful Cyber Acts

Next, this paper will describe the legal frameworks for dealing with international wrongful cyber acts. To solve international disputes, UN Charter provides peaceful resolutions such as negotiation, enquiry, mediation, etc.[11] In addition, retaliatory measures such as economic sanctions, freezing assets, and blocking communications also can be taken. However, both are often ineffective in real cyber conflicts and more effective means are required. The Articles of State Responsibility [9] provide various circumstances precluding wrongfulness and those can be strong tools for responding to internationally wrongful acts.[12] Among those, there seem to be three considerable approaches for low-intensity cyber conflicts: "self-defense", "necessity", and "countermeasures."

4.1 Self-defense

Self-defense allows for powerful counterattacks and collective responses including the use of force which might end conflicts soon and minimize damage. In addition, it can be

---

[10] *Ibid,* paras. 194–195. The court said, "the prohibition of armed attacks may apply to the sending by a State of armed bands to the territory of another State, if such an operation, because of its scale and effects, would have been classified as an armed attack rather than as a mere frontier incident had it been carried out by regular armed forces."

[11] Charter of the United Nations, article 33.

[12] Draft Articles on Responsibility of States for Internationally Wrongful Acts, article 20–25.

exercised against non-State actors without worrying about attribution. However, to exert self-defense against cyber acts below the threshold of armed conflicts will be against the mainstream interpretation of international law, which claims that self-defense can be applied only against armed attacks [11].[13] Also, it seems difficult to apply self-defense to the situation considering the extreme pacifist constitution and foreseeable intense backlash from domestic and international public opinion. Furthermore, there is a high possibility of escalation into a full-scale armed conflict, because taking self-defense meagers means giving the other party justification for the use of force automatically. Although there are arguments [14] in Japan that self-defense should be recognized in low-intensity cyber conflicts,[14] it seems unrealistic under the situation above noted.

4.2 Necessity

An advantage of applying necessity to low-intensity cyber conflicts is that it does not require attribution, and there is a possibility that it can resort to the use of force as a response measure even in low-intensity cyber conflicts.[15] However, the applicable conditions for applying it in cyber conflicts are unclear, especially it is difficult to imagine the situation in low-intensity cyber conflicts meeting the condition of "it is the only way for the State to safeguard an essential interest against a grave and imminent peril" which is provided in the Articles of State Responsibility [9]. Therefore, necessity seems not to be a promising measure in the circumstance, and it should be applied as supplemental means in case both self-defense and countermeasures are not applicable.

4.3 Countermeasures

Compared to the former two means, countermeasures may be able to deter the escalation of conflicts well by negotiating with the other party while appropriately counterattacking through the minimum and adequate forces. The U.S. strategy of persistent engagement policy seems to adopt a similar approach [15]. In addition, the range of situations that countermeasures can deal with is wider, from "use of force" to "violation of sovereignty", making them easy to apply. In Japan, another positive reason is that it is easier to harmonize with domestic laws. However, unlike self-defense, responses that include the use of force cannot be taken and strict proportionality is required, which may result in insufficient coercive effects to bring the responsible State back to its duty. Especially, if collective countermeasures cannot be used, although some studies strongly insist on the necessity of them [6, 7, 16–18],[16] Japan will have to respond alone, which means

---

[13] There are a few opinions that self-defense can be applied to the use of force that does not meet the threshold of an armed attack, such as the USA, but they are in the minority.

[14] For example, the Liberal Democratic Party's "First Proposal of the Liberal Democratic Party Cyber Security Task Force" (April 24, 2018) advocates "cyber self-defense."

[15] According to Tallinn Manual2.0, there still has been discussion as to whether to include the use of force as a means of necessity.

[16] A number of international legal scholars, including Michael N. Schmitt, Jeff Kosseff, Gary Corn, and Sean Watts, have expressed their views on the need for collective countermeasures, and the perceptions of countries appear to be changing. For example, Estonian President Kersti

a lack of implementation power. Furthermore, the biggest issue is attribution, and it is necessary not only to identify the perpetrator of the act but also to attribute the act to some State.

As described above, although countermeasures still have various challenges, overall, they seem to be suitable to prevent escalation of conflict and are easier to apply to Japan due to few restrictions under domestic laws. Regarding the lack of coercive power, there are some possible ways to supplement the drawbacks. First, from the short-term perspective, setting a relatively high threshold for the interpretation of the use of force leads to the consequence that there is wider room by the threshold of use of force, which means Japan can implement stronger means as countermeasures. Besides that, avoiding attribution problems by actively utilizing due diligence is promising. Second, From the long-term perspective, it is preferable to actively advocate the legalization of collective countermeasures. Also, it would be effective to consider enhancing collective attribution schemes through international cooperation. Table 1 summarizes the advantages and disadvantages of each legal response measure.

Table 1. Comparison of legal response measures

	Self-defense	Countermesures	Necessity
Requirement	➤ The existence of an armed attack. (in the general interpretation) ➤ Necessity(imminence) ➤ Proportionality	➤ The existence of preceding internationally wrongful acts. ➤ Attribution to a State ➤ Proportionality	➤ State's essential interest faces grave and imminent peril. ➤ The sole means of averting that peril.
Advantage	➤ The use of force is available. ➤ Collective responses are available.	➤ Can respond to a wide variety of malicious acts from abroad. ➤ Easy to fit Japan's domestic laws.	➤ There is no need to prove the preceding internationally wrongful acts and attribution to a State.
Disadvantage	➤ Against the mainstream of interpretations of international law. ➤ High possibility of the escalation of disputes. ➤ Antipathies of public opinion at home and abroad. ➤ Difficult to fit Japan's domestic laws.	➤ The use of force is not available. ➤ Attribution to a State is required. ➤ Proof of continuity of wrongful activities is required. ➤ Collective responses are not allowed.	➤ The threshold of invocation is extremely high in low-intensity cyber conflicts. ➤ Requirements are highly ambiguous.

5 Scenario Analysis: Application and Challenges of Countermeasures to the Low-Intensity Cyber Conflicts

As mentioned earlier, countermeasures seem to be the most effective legal mechanism in the response to low-intensity cyber conflicts, but it is foreseeable that several issues will occur in actual situations. This paper clarifies the details and how to handle them

---

Kaljulaid made a positive affirmation of collective countermeasures in her keynote speech at the 2019 CyCon.

through specific scenario analysis. The following three scenarios shown in Table 2 are typical cases of low-intensity cyber conflicts that Japan might encounter in near future.

Table 2. Hypothetical cases of low-intensity cyber conflicts.

Case	Situation
Case1	Functional damage to military assets and facilities
Case2	Functional damage to critical infrastructures
Case3	Political turmoil and social unrest by Information Operation

5.1 Assumed Situation

This section explains the premise in common with each scenario. The location of each State is shown in Figure 2[17]. Japan and State C have had a territorial dispute regarding a small Island in the East China Sea for many years. One day, an accidental public vessels collision happened in the disputed area, which resulted in several casualties on the State C side. State C demanded an apology and compensation from Japan, but Japan refused. Both States dispatched more public vessels and aircraft including military assets to the area, and tensions have been rising.

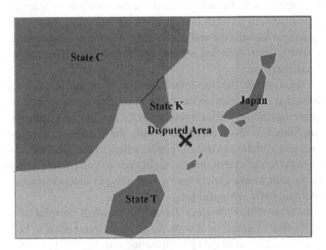

Fig. 2. The locations of each state

5.2 Case 1: Functional Damage to Military Assets and Facilities

Assumption. State C invaded Japan Self-Defense Force's (JSDF) C4ISR (Command, Control, Communication, Computer, Intelligence, Surveillance, and Reconnaissance)

[17] Please note that the scenarios and premises are fictional.

system by installing malware. The exploitation caused serious data loss and temporal suspension of the system. The incident was caused by the installation of malware in JSDF's internal system via USB through an internal informant, and the malware spread immediately via internal email communication. Eventually, the data in the contaminated terminals was lost, and communications were temporarily cut off. Additionally, during the incident, numerous other unauthorized remote accesses to JSDF's external systems, mainly came from State C, had been confirmed.

Regarding specific damage, JSDF's activities were inactive for several days and many assets had to withdraw from the area. Additionally, the fact of enemy penetration of C4ISR system protection degraded the credibility of the security of the system, and existing of betrayers gave serious damage to the soldier's morale. However, there was no physical damage.

Response. This part discusses how to apply countermeasures to the situation specifically. First, let's see the requirements. Regarding the existence of prior international wrongful cyber acts, the damage that Japan received should be assessed. In this assumption, armed attacks cannot be recognized because physical damage has not occurred. However, since the target is JSDF facilities, there is a military context, and the use of force might be recognized even without any physical damage. In addition, hindering JSDF's effective response would fall under the category of a violation of sovereignty. Furthermore, if State C's involvement and intention to advantageously solve the territorial dispute are clear, it may deserve unlawful intervention.

In this case, Japan might be able to attribute the incident to State C by obtaining evidence of its involvement through investigation of the insider, analyzing the malware code, detecting unique signatures, and identifying IP addresses regarding the unauthorized accesses. The tension between State C and Japan just before the incident should be taken into consideration.

However, to demonstrate that the internationally wrongful acts are continuing, it is necessary to show that the incident in the system is not a single, isolated act, but a series of complex actions together with the remote accesses, and that recurrence is highly likely. Without proving State C's involvement in it, only the remote access from its territory would be pursued as a violation of due diligence, which means that countermeasures can only be implemented to the extent that its negligence to control its territory effectively. Therefore, it is difficult to implement enough effective countermeasures to force State C to stop its internationally wrongful acts.

Next, the question is how degrees Japan can conduct harmful countermeasures against State C. In this assumption, a wide range of options seems to be possible from deleting or exposing confidential data by infiltrating into State C's governmental system as an equivalent mean to directly take down the C&C servers in State C related to the incident. However, it is necessary to avoid being regarded as the use of force.

What are the Challenges? There seem to be three challenges in this scenario. The biggest one is how to prove the continuity of international wrongful cyber acts and their attribution. To do that, consideration should be given to enhancing attribution capabilities including cooperation with allies such as the USA [19][18] and revising domestic laws to enable more effective intelligence activities. Another one is which organization takes responsibility to conduct the countermeasure operations and what kind of specific procedures in the government is required to integrate the efforts of many organizations, as well as the laws that provide the basis of taking such actions. The last one is the foreseeable lack of coerciveness to stop State C's wrongful acts, especially in the case of due diligence. From the legal perspective, it is necessary to consider what effective measures can be taken below the threshold of use of force to conduct effective cyber operations giving reasonable damage against State C. To do so, enhancing cyber intelligence capability and identifying State C's COG[19] is necessary. Besides that, considering the Japanese current technological level, collective countermeasures seem to be indispensable to conducting effective cyber countermeasure operations, even though the legality of it is uncertain for now [18, 20].[20]

5.3   Case 2: Functional Damage to Critical Infrastructures

Assumption. Aiming for political turmoil and social unrest in Japan, State C hacked into the industrial control system of power generation and transmission facilities owned by a private company that supplies electricity to the metropolitan area in Japan, and remotely shut down the power supply, causing a large-scale blackout. The incident was triggered by the exploitation of an employee's computer with a spear-phishing mail attack in a power company that mainly provides electricity to the area. After the exploitation, malware spread rapidly and finally reached the power control system. Immediately after then, the power supply to the center area of Tokyo was cut off by remote access. About 6 million households in the 23 wards of Tokyo, including government offices and various companies, were affected by the blackout, and it took about three days for the power to be restored. Despite no major disruption to government agencies and medical facilities due to the backup power systems and priority restoration, the economic damage was awful. Part of the source code of the malware was written in State C language, and the IP address of the attacker's C&C servers was identified to the area in State C, K, and T territories. However, no new damage has been confirmed since the recovery.

Response. Although the incident does not clear the threshold of armed attacks because of the lack of physical damage, there is a possibility that the use of force can be recognized depending on the scale and effect of the economic damage. In addition, an attack on

---

[18] The Guidelines for Japan-U.S. Defense Cooperation (April 27, 2015) says "To help ensure the safe and stable use of cyberspace, the two governments will share information on threats and vulnerabilities in cyberspace in a timely and routine manner, as appropriate."

[19] COG: Center of Gravity. Identifying the enemy's COG and attacking it enable countermeasures to be more effective with causing less damage.

[20] Concerning self-defense, the U.S.–Japan Security Consultative Committee affirmed that collective self-defense will be applied to a cyber-attack in certain circumstances, based on the U.S.-Japan Security Treaty. However, there is no such agreement regarding international wrongful cyber acts below the threshold of armed attack.

critical infrastructure, including governmental institutions, may constitute a violation of sovereignty as in Case I.

However, the fact that the power outage was promptly restored, and no new damage was caused might be regarded as the end of the internationally wrongful act. To take countermeasures, the possibility of continued violation of international law by the same entity must be explained. As for the attribution, it might be possible to prove State C's violation of the due diligence principle by the fact it was remotely operated from C&C servers in State C's territory, even though there was no concrete evidence to demonstrate State C's involvement in the incident. As in Case I, proportionality and being under the threshold of the use of force are necessary for the implementation of countermeasures.

What Are the Challenges? In this scenario, the biggest challenge would be attribution, because of the suspension of State C's international wrongful cyber acts. How can Japan explain the remaining threats of furthermore attacks? What kind of evidence is required to demonstrate it? Additionally, when Japan takes countermeasures against State C's violation of the due diligence principle, is it possible to aim at State C's critical infrastructure? Can the proportionality rule be cleared considering the damage Japan received? Furthermore, if State C has declared that it regards malicious cyber acts against its critical infrastructure as the use of force, do Japanese countermeasures breach the prohibition of "use of force?" Those are still open questions.

5.4   Case 3: Creating Political Turmoil and Social Unrest by Information Operation

Assumption. State C launched a negative campaign against Japan's government on the Internet by falsifying the websites of the Japanese government and private companies, spreading fake news, exposing secrets, etc., intending to lower support for the current government in Japan. Since the collision in the disputed area, there have been several cases of tampering with the websites of celebrities. On those websites, many opinions supporting State C have been posted, and a lot of information related to the regime scandal has been posted on the Internet. Some of them turned out to be fake news. As a result, the current approval rate for the government dropped significantly. Most of the IP addresses were routed through public proxy servers located in State K and T. However, a part of them was found to be routed through State C's territory, but the State C government denied any involvement. As for the fake news, there were some errors in characters which are common in the sentences of translation from State C's language to Japanese.

Response. Infiltrating and falsifying government websites will deserve to violation of sovereignty, but the legal perspective of doing the same things against private ones is ambiguous. In short, countermeasures can't be applied to the latter acts because countermeasures require internationally wrongful acts. Although such acts can be against the domestic laws of each State, international law mentions nothing about a State's violation of another State's domestic laws. So, in this scenario, Japan can apply the countermeasures only within the limits that State C did against the government websites in terms of the proportionality rule.

What are the Challenges? The challenge in this scenario is the legal character of the infringement against private systems. Nowadays Information Operations have a strong influence on governments' policies and societies around the world. However international law doesn't say anything about the wrongfulness of those as far as the operations are aimed at only private systems and do not cause any physical damage. More discussions seem to be required about this matter. Besides that, the Attribution of wrongful cyber acts through third States will be also a big issue.

6 Proposals

Finally, this paper suggests some proposals that Japan should consider conducting effective countermeasure operations in low-intensity cyber conflicts. So far, this paper has explained an overview of the international law applicable to low-intensity cyber conflicts and demonstrates that countermeasures can be a powerful tool in the situation, of Japan. And then, this paper clarifies how to apply countermeasures to concrete cases through the scenario analysis, and several challenges are also identified during the analysis. To conquer them, this paper proposes the following realistic policies which Japan should take; (1) clarifying the responsible organization and establishing domestic legislation about cyber countermeasures (2) taking initiative in the campaign for the legalization of collective countermeasures, (3) improving attribution capability including collective ways with allies, and (4) developing ethical and legal norm to prohibit the malicious cyber acts against private enterprises.

6.1 Clarifying the Responsible Organization and Establishing Domestic Legislations about Cyber Countermeasures

To conduct cyber countermeasure operations, it is imperative to clarify a responsible organization and establish proper domestic legislation to provide legitimacy to the operation. For now, Japan does not have clear domestic laws to provide such operations with a concrete legal basis. It means that Japan cannot react to the immediate cyber threats with countermeasures, so this matter should have the biggest priority.

6.2 Taking Initiative for Legalization of Collective Countermeasures

A drawback of countermeasures is the possible lack of enough power to persuade a responsible State to stop conducting its malicious cyber acts. In that case, collective countermeasures are highly lucrative. Indeed, there are still many negative opinions about its legality of it, however, many international law experts have recognized and insisted on the necessity of establishing a new legal framework that enables States can take collective countermeasures.Japan should express clear support for the idea and lead the argument.

6.3 Improving Attribution Capability Including Collective One with Allies

Regarding the improvement of the attribution capability, it will be important for Japan not only to enhance its capacity but also to cooperate with other countries, including mutual exchanging technical support and intelligence. To do so, the criteria and legal requirements enough to attribute malicious cyber activity to a responsible State should be clarified. Especially it is necessary to consider what kind of evidence is required and how deep accountability an injured State owes to attribute.

6.4 Developing Ethical and Legal Norm to Prohibit the Malicious Cyber Acts Against Private Entities

The biggest defect of countermeasures is that the malicious cyber acts against private entities will be out of their scope, whereas the most common cyber incidents fall in this category. Particularly disinformation activities are becoming formidable threats due to the development of technology and change in social structures. To deal with this issue, the new ethical and legal norm seems to have to be considered. Japan should try to construct those norms by cooperating with other States. It can also be considered an effective way that Japan insists on the continuation of a framework such as the UN Groupe of Government Experts and taking leadership.

7 Conclusion

Responding to low-intensity cyber disputes is a major challenge for the international community as a whole, and various studies and discussions have been conducted on the use of countermeasures. In Japan, however, discussions have been weak and no concrete progress has been seen. Given Japan's unique circumstances, countermeasures have the potential to be an effective means of response, and further research is expected. The proposals made in this paper are realistic and do not require a constitutional amendment, and they can be the first step for Japan to take a leadership role in establishing norms in cyberspace.

References

1. The Government of Japan: Cyber Security Strategy. https://www.nisc.go.jp/materials/index.html. Accessed 12 May 2022
2. International Institute for Strategic Studies (IISS): Cyber Capabilities and National Power: A Net Assessment (2021). https://www.iiss.org/blogs/research-paper/2021/06/cyber-capabilities-national-power. Accessed 12 May 2022
3. Report of the Group of Governmental Experts on Advancing Responsible State Behaviour in Cyberspace in the Context of International Security, U.N. Doc. A/76/135 (2021)
4. Open-ended working group on developments in the field of information and telecommunications in the context of international security: Final Substantive Report, U.N. Doc. A/AC.290/2021/CRP.2 (2021)
5. Schmitt, M. (ed.): Tallinn Manual 2.0 on the International Law Applicable to Cyber Operations. Cambridge University Press, Cambridge (2017)

6. Schmitt, M.: "Below the threshold" cyber operations: the countermeasures response option and international law. Va. J. Int. Law **54**, 697–732 (2014)

7. Kosseff, J.: Collective countermeasures in cyberspace. Notre Dame J. Int. Comp. Law **10**, 18–34 (2020)

8. Keiko, K.: Invoking the right of self-defense against cyber-attacks. In: Eto, J. (ed.) Aspects of International Law Studies Reaching: The Point and Looking Ahead: Mr. Murase Shinya's Rare Memories, pp. 847–862. Shinzan-sha, Tokyo (2015)

9. Draft Articles on Responsibility of States for Internationally Wrongful Acts, in Report of the International Law Commission on the Work of its Fifty-third Session, UN GAOR 56th Sess., Supp. No. 10, at 43, U.N. Doc. A/56/10 (2001)

10. Sugihara, T.: Lectures on International Law. 2nd edn. Yuhikaku, Tokyo (2013)

11. Case Concerning Military and Paramilitary Activities in and against Nicaragua, 1986 I.C.J.14,181, Merits, Judgement, 27 June

12. Case The Corfu Channel (United Kingdom of Great Britain and Northern Ireland v. Albania), 1949 I.C.J. 105, Merits, Judgement, 9 April

13. Ministry of Foreign Affairs of Japan.: Basic Position of the Government of Japan on International Law Applicable to Cyber Operations. https://www.mofa.go.jp/policy/page3e_001114.html. Accessed 12 May 2022

14. The Liberal Democratic Party: First Proposal of the Liberal Democratic Party Cyber Security Task Force, 24 April 2018. https://www.jimin.jp/news/policy/137263.html. Accessed 12 May 2022

15. Fischerkeller, M., Harknett, R.: Persistent engagement, agreed competition, and cyberspace interaction dynamics and escalation. In: The Cyber Defense Review, Special Edition, International Conference on Cyber Conflict (CYCON U.S.), 14–15 November 2018, Cyber Conflict During Competition, pp. 267–287. Army Cyber Institute, New York (2019)

16. Corn, G., Jensen, E.: The use of force and cyber countermeasures. Temple Int. Comp. Law J. **32**(2), 127–133 (2018)

17. Schmitt, M., Watts, S.: Collective cyber countermeasures? Harvard Nat. Secur. J. **12**(2), 373–411 (2021)

18. Roguski, P.: Collective countermeasures in cyberspace: Lex Lata, progressive development or a bad idea? In: The 12th Annual International Conference on Cyber Conflict (Cycon 2020), pp. 25–42. NATO CCDCOE Publications, Tallinn (2020)

19. The Government of Japan.: The Guidelines for Japan-U.S. Defense Cooperation, 27 April 2015. https://www.mofa.go.jp/region/n-america/us/security/scc/index.html. Accessed 12 May 2022

20. Ministry of Foreign Affairs of Japan: Joint Statement of the Security Consultative Committee (2019). https://www.mofa.go.jp/mofaj/files/000470738.pdf. Accessed 21 Dec 2021

Privacy Protection During Criminal Investigations of Personal Data Held by Third Parties

Taro Komukai(✉)

Faculty of Global Informatics, Chuo University, Tokyo, Japan
komukai@tamacc.chuo-u.ac.jp

Abstract. This study focuses on privacy issues concerning personal data held by third parties during criminal investigations. The development of information technology has made it possible to collect and store vast amounts of information. Since data held by third parties are often provided to investigating authorities without the data subject's knowledge, serious privacy issues are a concern. There are two possible approaches to protecting the rights of the individual in such a situation. One relates to the restriction of investigating authorities and the other concerns the confidentiality obligations of data controllers. This study compares the relevant legislation on the privacy of personal data held by third parties and criminal investigations in the United States, the European Union, and Japan to propose appropriate solutions to address data privacy concerns. Specifically, the main recommendations of this study are that investigating authorities should be subject to certain restrictions and greater transparency requirements when processing personal data and that data controllers should be subject to greater confidentiality obligations.

Keywords: Criminal investigation · Privacy · Data protection · Due process · Third party doctrine

1 Criminal Investigations of Data

1.1 Investigations of Third Parties

At present, various data on people are collected via networks and processed by computer systems, even more so now with the development of the Internet of Things. This information is stored and processed by big data and AI technologies, which continuously generates new data [1]. The use of data is expected to grow exponentially in the future [2].

The growth in data use has resulted in the accumulation of vast amounts of personal data to which investigating authorities have access [3]. When a crime is committed, investigating authorities use a variety of methods to look for clues and gather information on people they believe to be connected to the crime. Some of these data are generated using new technologies. For example, it is now a widespread practice to review CCTV

© IFIP International Federation for Information Processing 2022
Published by Springer Nature Switzerland AG 2022
D. Kreps et al. (Eds.): HCC 2022, IFIP AICT 656, pp. 200–212, 2022.
https://doi.org/10.1007/978-3-031-15688-5_17

footage and dashboard cameras for criminal investigations. In addition, many tracers are stored in information systems such as emails, social network messages, web services, shopping histories, location data, and access logs. It is very useful for investigators to collate this information to create lists of likely offenders, examine their behavioural history, and track down suspects [4]. The use of information to improve the sophistication and efficiency of criminal investigations is desirable for society. However, as an increasing amount of information is collected in a variety of fields and its content is becoming increasingly diverse, new problems are arising because those who have an interest in the information and those who hold it do not always coincide [5].

If an investigating authority requests a person to provide their information, they can decide whether to accept or refuse the request after considering the implications. If the person refuses to cooperate with the investigation, the investigating authorities may still carry out the search with a warrant if they consider the information as necessary for the investigation. In this case, the investigating authority must present the warrant to the concerned person. This presentation enables the person to know the extent of the search to be carried out. If the person considers the procedure or scope of the search as inappropriate, they can lodge an objection with a court. The court will then re-examine whether the warrant is appropriate based on the person's arguments.

By contrast, if a third party such as a service provider is asked to provide data, protecting the privacy of the data subject is not necessarily important for this third party. The third-party data controller may voluntarily comply with a request from the investigating authority as long as they are not exposed to any legal liability. In this case, the fact that this data controller has provided information to the investigating authorities will not, in principle, be communicated to the data subject. They will only learn that the investigating authority has such information after it has been presented as evidence in court, and even then it may not be clear by what means the investigating authority has obtained the information (see Fig. 1).

If this third party refuses the request for cooperation, the investigating authorities may still conduct the search with a warrant. In this case, the search warrant is presented to the data controller and not to the data subject. Therefore, the data subject cannot object to this compulsory search when it takes place. In this case too, they can only raise their objections after the data have been submitted as evidence in court.

While there are different views and debates on how the right to privacy should be defined, it is widely agreed that there are cases where a person can object to state forces accessing their information on the basis of their right to privacy [6]. The question here is whether the rights of the individual are sufficiently protected during investigations of this nature into data held by third parties. There are two possible approaches to protecting the rights of the individual:

(i) Restrictions on the Investigating Authorities
(ii) Confidentiality Obligations of the Data Controllers

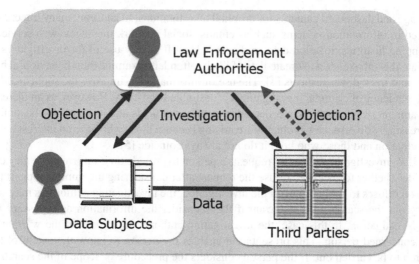

Fig. 1. Privacy problems in investigations of third-party records.

1.2 Restrictions on Investigating Authorities

When there is a concern that a search carried out by the investigating authority may be infringing on fundamental human rights, the authority must generally follow the statutory procedure. Arrests and seizures are typical violations of human rights, and such compulsory searches should, in principle, be carried out by the investigating authorities with a warrant issued by a judge in accordance with the law. The process and warrant principle is enshrined in the Fourth Amendment to the US Constitution, Article 8 of the European Convention for the Protection of Human Rights and Fundamental Freedoms, and Article 35 of the Japanese Constitution as essential to the protection of fundamental human rights.

Regarding searches on data held by third parties, the first question is whether an investigating authority may request data from a third party without a warrant. A warrant is required for a compulsory search because it restricts fundamental human rights, whereas a search can be carried out without a warrant if it does not infringe on fundamental human rights. Therefore, the question is whether the request for cooperation from a third party infringes on the fundamental human rights of the person concerned. Even if the investigating authority obtains personal data from a third party with a warrant, the warrant will only be presented to the third-party data controller. The question then arises whether fundamental human rights can be said to be protected when the data subject is not informed about the warrant.

1.3 Confidentiality Obligations of Data Controllers

If the investigating authority asks the data controller to cooperate in an investigation on a voluntary basis, it is the data controller who decides whether to cooperate. If the data controller is legally obliged to maintain confidentiality or there is a risk that the data controller may be sued by the data subject for damages on the grounds of invasion of privacy, then the data controller will exercise caution. However, if the likelihood of such liability is low, it is not surprising that the data controller will cooperate with the investigating authorities. Therefore, it is important to know the confidentiality obligations of data controllers.

The rapidly growing importance of personal data for the right to privacy has led to the introduction of data protection legislation in many countries over the past few decades [7]. Personal data protection schemes often require data controllers to clarify the purposes for which personal data will be used to ensure transparency of processing. However, the provision of information to investigating authorities for criminal investigations is often permissible to comply with a legal obligation.

Special confidentiality obligations are imposed on those who handle personal data that are particularly sensitive and require strict protection. In some sectors such as telecommunications and medical services, there is a statutory obligation of confidentiality regarding the sensitive information handled during business, the breach of which is subject to sanctions. However, cooperation with investigating authorities is often an acceptable exception to such confidentiality obligations.

In addition, a large amount of information about users is collected and used by various operators, including tech giants such as Alphabet, Amazon, Apple, Meta, and Microsoft. These operators are not always under a special obligation of confidentiality in general and do not have a strong incentive to refuse requests from the investigating authorities from a legal perspective.

2 Comparison of Legal Systems

2.1 United States

Restrictions on Investigating Authorities. In the United States, fundamental human rights in criminal investigations are protected by the Fourth Amendment of the US Constitution [8]. The Fourth Amendment prohibits unreasonable searches and seizures and states the requirements for the issuance of a warrant. However, it does not say anything about when a warrant is required.

It is not assumed that a warrant is required for every collection of information conducted by an investigating authority and there is disagreement as to what types of searches require warrants [9]. A significant number of warrantless searches are conducted as 'consent searches'. In some cases, a search may be permitted based on the consent of a third party who has actual control over the object to be searched such as a joint owner of the premise [10].

On the question of when a warrant is required, it was initially thought that intrusions into 'persons, houses, papers, and effects' were problematic, and that a warrant was required for searches that threatened freedom of action and private property rights in particular [11]. However, the development of technology has made it possible to obtain information about the privacy of the subject without such intrusion. In the case of Katz v. US [12], the Supreme Court reversed a conviction based on the warrantless interception of a conversation by placing an electronic listening device outside the telephone booth used by the suspect for the conversation, holding that the prior justification procedure at the heart of the Fourth Amendment was lacking. It held that intrusion was no longer determinative because the importance of physical invasion had relatively diminished such that investigators could intercept conversations without physically entering the home and that the Fourth Amendment protects a 'reasonable expectation of privacy'.

After Katz v. US, the idea that a reasonable expectation of privacy was protected by the Fourth Amendment was established. However, the Supreme Court has long applied the 'third party doctrine' in a variety of contexts, holding that individuals do not have a 'reasonable expectation of privacy' in information they 'voluntarily convey' to third parties [13].

In 2018, the Supreme Court ruled that cell site location records held by wireless carriers were protected by the Fourth Amendment [14]. The case involved a court order requiring a mobile phone operator to submit location information (base station information) to the investigating authority. The 'reasonable grounds' requirement for issuing a court order is less strict than the probable cause for issuing a warrant. The court has ruled that the location information must be based on a warrant before it can be filed, as it also protects reasonable expectations of privacy. However, this judgement does not deny the third-party doctrine itself. The court has emphasised that cell site location information is 'unique' in terms of its power to reveal an 'exhaustive chronicle' of a person's daily life and its intimate details, which is the reason for not being applicable to the third-party doctrine.

Investigating authorities can also access the data held by third parties based on a subpoena. The issuance of a subpoena does not require a 'probable cause', but rather a much more moderate 'reasonableness' and the procedure is very simple [15]. A grand jury subpoena, for example, can be drafted by the public prosecutors themselves for books, documents, materials, data, and other objects. It is even permissible to call for a subpoena to ensure that 'the law has not been violated' [16]. In addition, objections to subpoenas are rarely effective.

Furthermore, the principle of the exclusion of unlawful collection is not very effective in protecting privacy, as there are insufficient penalties for disregarding the Fourth Amendment [17]. This is because even if the information collected is excluded from evidence in a trial, the privacy of the subject has already been violated and the exclusion of such evidence often has no effect on the conclusion of the judgement.

Confidentiality Obligations of Data Controllers. The United States does not have a comprehensive data protection federal law such as the General Data Protection Regulation (GDPR) in the European Union [18]. There are various laws protecting personal data in different sectors, including individual industries and public authorities. However, in most cases, the provision of personal data to investigating authorities is permitted. For some special categories of data such as telecommunications, the law imposes a duty of confidentiality on the business and the provision of data to the investigating authorities is restricted.

The Stored Communications Act in the United States (SCA, 18 U.S.C. §§ 2701–2712) requires the investigating authority to make requests to telecommunications operators providing public telecommunications services only in accordance with statutory procedures. The required procedure depends on the type of information being processed. To obtain content data such as unopened email messages, a search and seizure warrant is required if the data have been stored for less than 90 days, while a subpoena or judicial order is required if the storage period is longer or if the data have already been accessed. Subpoenas and judicial orders of this kind require notice to the user. However, such notice may be excluded or delayed if there is reason to believe that it will have an adverse effect.

With respect to no-content data, which include a user's name, address, telephone number, network address, contractual information, and payment information, the SCA holds that the government may access such information with a subpoena from an administrative agency or grand jury without any obligation to notify the user. Nonetheless, it states that investigating authorities must obtain a warrant or court order to access, for example, addresses sent by email or information about sites visited, without requiring notice to the user. Further, while the SCA requires the user to be notified in some proceedings, its provisions only cover providers of public telecoms services and not tech giants, which are major players in handling information stored on the Internet.

In areas other than telecommunications such as medical institutions, there is a duty to protect patient confidentiality. In a case where a patient was arrested after reporting to the police that a urine test carried out at a national hospital had tested positive for cocaine, the Supreme Court ruled that this constituted an unreasonable search without the patient's consent [19].

2.2 European Union

Restrictions on Investigating Authorities. Article 8 of the European Convention of Human Rights stipulates that '[e]veryone has the right to respect for his private and family life, his home and his correspondence' [20]. Legal procedures are required for investigations that may violate fundamental human rights in member countries of the Council of Europe.

The European Union also adopted the Law Enforcement Directive [DIRECTIVE (EU) 2016/68] [21] in 2016 regarding processing personal data by investigating authorities and others. The Directive is designed to protect human rights in relation to processing personal data by investigating authorities for the prevention, investigation, detection, and prosecution of criminal offences and execution of criminal penalties. It requires member states to establish a system requiring that personal data collected by investigating authorities be used for clearly specified purposes, be used only to the extent appropriate in relation to those purposes, and not be retained for longer than necessary. The data subject must be able to know which investigating authority is processing the information, what data they are processing, and under what authority they are processing the information (Articles 13 and 14). The investigating authorities must create records of data processing (Article 24). Establishing a supervisory authority for data processing in this area and granting appropriate powers are also required (Articles 45–49) [21].

Confidentiality of the Data Controller. In the European Union, data protection is guaranteed as a fundamental human right. Paragraph 2 of Article 8 of the Charter of Fundamental Rights of the European Union provides that personal data 'must be processed fairly for specified purposes and on the basis of the consent of the person concerned or some other legitimate basis laid down by law' and that '[e]veryone has the right of access to data which has been collected concerning him or her, and the right to have it rectified' [22].

To achieve protection, the GDPR requires a lawful basis [Article 6(1)] for processing personal data in general. Providing information to investigating authorities may be justified as a 'legal obligation' with the provision that it is only recognized as a 'legal obligation' if it is based on the law of an EU member state. Although there are considerable differences between the national laws of member states, the specific procedures required of the investigating authorities must be based on clear and specific provisions of legal obligation [23].

If an investigating authority requests cooperation on a voluntary basis, rather than through such a mandatory procedure, the provision of the data could be justified if it was 'for the purposes of the legitimate interests'. For a data controller to provide data based on a 'purpose of the legitimate interests', they must assess whether the information is necessary for the investigation and whether the scope of the information provided is proportionate to the purpose of the investigation. They must then be convinced that the provision of the information is indeed for 'the purpose of the legitimate interests'.

In the case of information relating to telecommunications, the legislation in most member states provides enhanced protection for the subject of the investigation. For example, special warrants are required in cases where investigations are carried out with respect to the interception of communications or communication records.

2.3 Japan

Restrictions on Investigating Authorities. Article 35 of the Constitution of Japan provides that, except in the case of a legitimate arrest, '[t]he right of all persons to be secure in their homes, papers and effects against entries, searches and seizures shall not be impaired except upon warrant issued for adequate cause and particularly describing the place to be searched and things to be seized' [24]. Article 197 of the Code of Criminal Procedure stipulates that a 'compulsory search shall not be applied unless otherwise provided for in this Act'. Therefore, when the investigating authority imposes a compulsory search, it must do so based on a warrant or other statutory procedure.

The Japanese Supreme Court has ruled that a 'compulsory search' means not only 'the way involving the use of tangible force', but also 'the way which it would be inappropriate to tolerate in the absence of special ground rules, such as acts of suppressing the will of an individual and realizing the purpose of an investigation forcibly by imposing restrictions on their body, residence or property' [25]. Although some may view the acquisition of personal data against the will of the individual as a compulsory measure, a request by the investigating authority for information from a third party is not generally considered as such a measure. Article 197(2) of the Code of Criminal Procedure states that '[p]ublic offices or public or private organizations may be asked to make a report on necessary particulars relating to the investigation' and investigating authorities may make 'written inquiries on investigative matters' (so-called 'enquiry sheets'). However, this is a voluntary request for cooperation and there is no penalty for refusing the request. Indeed, investigating authorities request companies to provide information such as customers' names, addresses, telephone numbers, their usage history of services, purchase history of products, usage history of points, and GPS location information obtained from online games only on a voluntary basis [26].

In Japanese criminal investigations, the principle of voluntary investigation has been adopted [27] based on the belief that a compulsory search that violates or restricts human rights should be avoided as much as possible. Based on this principle, the voluntary cooperation of citizens with the investigating authorities has been considered as desirable by the Japanese authorities. It is not considered as problematic, at least in Japan, for investigating authorities to ask organisations to provide information about their customers or for organisations to respond voluntarily unless the information includes the secrecy of communications. The courts have often found the provision of information to the investigating authorities to be appropriate [28]. Thus, the fear of being held liable for an invasion of privacy by the person concerned is little deterrent in such cases.

The Act on the Protection of Personal Information (APPI) in Japan was amended in May 2021 and enacted in April 2022, which subjected investigating authorities to the supervision of the Personal Information Protection Commission. However, there are many provisions where criminal investigations are exempted, such as the provision for the restriction of use (Article 69 of the amended Act) and provision for ensuring transparency (Article 74 of the amended Act).

Confidentiality Obligations of Data Controllers. In Japan, Article 27 of the APPI generally prohibits data controllers from providing personal data to third parties without prior consent from the data subject. However, in cases where the investigating authorities request the provision of such data for an investigation, it can be provided without the consent of the data subject since it is a 'case based on laws and regulations'. The voluntary provision of information, including in response to an enquiry sheet from the investigating authority, also falls under the category of 'cases based on laws and regulations'. As long as the procedure is carried out properly, no infringement of the APPI will be an issue [29].

Regarding the secrecy of communications, voluntary cooperation with the investigating authorities is strictly prohibited. Article 21(2) of the Constitution of Japan prohibits the violation of 'the secrecy of any means of communication'. The Telecommunications Business Act provides for the prohibition (Article 4) and punishment (Article 179) of violating the secrecy of communications handled by a telecommunications carrier. Communication secrets include traffic and content data. A warrant issued by a judge is required for the investigating authorities to obtain information under the category of the secrecy of communications handled by a telecommunications carrier and a warrant is required for the investigating authority to obtain the location data held by a mobile phone operator [30]. The Ministry of Internal Affairs and Communications has supervisory authority over the secrecy of communications handled by telecommunications carriers and administrative sanctions may be imposed for infringing the secrecy of communications.

There are other areas in which legal obligations for confidentiality are imposed. For example, doctors and other medical staff are prohibited from divulging to third parties the confidential information that they have acquired during their profession and there are penalties for breaching this (e.g. Article 134 of the Penal Code provides a penalty for physicians, pharmacists, pharmaceuticals distributors, midwives, and so on when disclosing their patients' confidential information). However, it is generally accepted that there is no breach of duty for cooperating with voluntary investigations, as it is considered as a justifiable reason [31].

3 Discussion

3.1 Due Process and Data Protection

Regarding criminal investigations, the protection of fundamental human rights has been ensured by the guarantee of due process. There is a view that the warrant principle should be more strictly enforced to cope with the fact that new technological developments allow investigating authorities to collect large amounts of information [32]. It is true that if the investigating authorities require the submission of data, due process must be carried out. The courts must also check whether the human rights of the subject have been unjustifiably infringed by the investigation. However, a warrant is not required when the data controller under investigation cooperates with the investigating authorities voluntarily and the courts will only check such warrantless searches if evidence obtained in the search is presented during a trial and the defendant questions the legality of the evidence.

The development of information technology has made it possible to collect and store vast amounts of information and the individual's concern about information held by third parties is much greater than before. Personal data protection systems have evolved in response to these concerns. For this reason, data protection legislation provides rules for transparency and individual involvement.

However, other aspects of data protection legislation also cause friction with the traditional approach to criminal investigations. In the field of criminal investigation, the gradual collection of information is a basic procedure and the request for investigative cooperation from third parties in possession of information is an extension of traditional investigations such as stakeouts and interviews. It is difficult to align criminal investigation with the concept of personal data protection, which limits the scope of data use by clarifying the purpose of use in advance. Regarding transparency, it is also undesirable for suspects to know what information the investigating authorities have about them.

However, it is possible to limit the use of personal data to the purposes necessary for criminal investigations and increase transparency to the extent that this does not hinder criminal investigations. The EU Law Enforcement Directive presupposes that the protection of personal data is limited for purposes such as criminal investigations and this difficulty has been considered during the development of the system. For example, it is assumed that the right to information and access may be restricted for reasons of investigative necessity or public safety.

It is not desirable for criminal investigations to be unduly curtailed and for public safety to be compromised. To strike a balance between the need for criminal investigations and fundamental human rights, it is desirable to establish rules for the proper handling of information to the extent that it does not interfere with law enforcement and to ensure a certain level of transparency.

3.2 Duty of the Confidentiality of the Data Controller

Companies are increasingly aware that they should protect their customers' privacy. Some of the largest companies have adopted a policy of only providing information to law enforcement agencies when they are legally obliged to do so. They also publish transparency reports on their cooperation with law enforcement agencies. However, in many regions outside the European Union, it is up to individual companies to decide whether to take such actions.

If the data controller is obliged to maintain the confidentiality of the information, they will carefully consider whether to provide it. If there is a risk of penalties or sanctions for providing information in response to a request from an investigating authority, they will be reluctant to submit to a voluntary investigation. They will also be cautious about cooperating in a voluntary investigation if they are likely to be sued for damages due to the invasion of the person's privacy.

However, there may be cases where it is reasonable and socially acceptable to provide information voluntarily in response to a request from an investigating authority. For example, the GDPR requires that processing personal data in general, including its provision to investigating authorities, is justified. Cooperation with voluntary investigations is only permitted if it falls under the purpose of legitimate interests. If information is to be provided under this provision, the data controller must assess the necessity and proportionality of the provision and decide that it is appropriate. This is an example of a rule that strikes a balance between the need for investigation and protection of the individual's human rights.

Apart from personal data in general, special confidentiality obligations are imposed on data controllers with respect to information requiring particularly strong confidentiality, such as confidential communications and medical information. Nonetheless, the voluntary provision of information to cooperate with the investigating authorities may be excluded from the confidentiality obligation. However, given the sensitive nature of this information, it is advisable for investigators to seek a warrant when obtaining it and the provision of such information should generally still be prohibited without a warrant or other due process.

3.3 Ensuring Effectiveness

As already noted, the court review process does not function adequately when the investigating authority collects information from a third-party data controller. The courts reviewing what information is being collected and stored by the investigating authority and whether it is necessary and appropriate to do so is also difficult. Further, the confidentiality obligations of data controllers require a supervisory body independent of the investigating authority. For example, if the investigating authority supervises breaches of confidentiality, it is not possible to prosecute and punish those who cooperate in providing information requested by the same investigating authority.

In the European Union, data protection supervisory authorities are expected to fulfil this role. In Japan, a warrant is strictly required for the submission of confidential communications to an investigating authority because the Ministry of Internal Affairs and Communications supervises telecommunications operators and regulates any infringements on the secrecy of communications, not the criminal investigating authorities.

4 Conclusion

In light of the foregoing, it is desirable that, in general, the following legislation be put in place in relation to criminal investigations concerning the personal data held by third parties:

(1) Restrictions to investigating authorities.
- The investigating authority should be obliged to ensure that their processing of personal data is appropriate for the purposes for which it is used and that there is a degree of transparency by allowing access to data protection authorities.
- The processing of personal data by investigating authorities should be supervised by a data protection authority which is independent of the investigating authority.

(2) Confidentiality obligations of data controllers
- Data controllers should be prohibited from providing personal data to investigating authorities unless they are under an enforceable legal obligation or consider it appropriate in terms of necessity and proportionality.
- Information requiring a particularly strong duty of confidentiality, such as confidential communications and medical-related information, should not be provided unless there is a warrant.
- The confidentiality obligations of data controllers should be regulated by a supervisory body independent of the investigating authorities.

Table 1 compares the current systems in the United States, the European Union, and Japan from these perspectives.

Table 1. Restriction on investigating authorities and data controllers.

	Investigating authorities		Data controllers	
	Restriction	Safeguard	Restriction	Safeguard
US	Due Process (Amendment 4)	Judge (warrant)	Confidentiality Obligation	Private Action
EU	Due Process (ECHR* 8) Data Protection	Judge (warrant) DPA**	Data Protection	DPA**
Japan	Due Process (Constitution 35) Data Protection	Judge (warrant) DPA**	Secrecy of Communications	MIC***

* European Convention of Human Rights.
** Data Protection Authority.
*** Ministry of Internal Affairs and Communications.

In the United States, the courts must supervise whether investigating authorities are conducting proper investigations. However, as it is difficult for the courts to supervise the processing of data by investigating authorities, a data protection authority should supervise it. In addition, there is no independent supervisory body for the confidentiality obligations of data controllers. In the United States, data subjects sue data controllers for the breach of confidentiality and investigating authorities for the illegal collection of information more often than in other countries, but there must be a clear basis in law for the plaintiff's claims to be recognised. Therefore, the legal restrictions on investigating authorities and confidentiality obligations of data controllers should be strengthened.

The European Union has made the most progress on protecting data subjects in this area, both in terms of restrictions on investigating authorities and in terms of the confidentiality obligations of data controllers, which are supervised by independent data protection authorities. However, it is up to the systems of each member state to ensure that data protection agencies are adequately informed by investigating authorities. It is thus necessary to constantly check whether the regulations are being properly implemented.

In Japan, investigating authorities are also subject to supervision by the data protection authority under the recently amended law, although many provisions exempt investigating authorities from restrictions. This needs to be amended so that appropriate supervision can take place. In addition, the confidentiality obligations of data controllers are not sufficiently enforced, except for information containing the secrecy of communications. Therefore, the confidentiality obligations of data controllers need to be strengthened.

Further studies are necessary for to propose more specific law reform in each area and country.

Acknowledgements. This work was supported by JSPS KAKENHI (Grant Number JP18K01393).

References

1. Dos Falcon, A.: Cyber Privacy: Who Has Your Data and Why You Should Care. BenBella Books, Dallas (2020)
2. Schneier, B.: Data and Goliath. Norton, New York (2015)
3. Cate, H., Dempsey, J. (eds.): Bulk Collection. Oxford University Press, New York (2017)
4. Ferguson, A.: The Rise of Big Data Policing. New York University Press, New York (2017)
5. Komukai, T.: Access to personal data held by third parties by investigating authorities and protection of the individual. J. Inf. Commun. Policy 4(1), 63–80 (2020)
6. Solove, D.: Understanding Privacy. Harvard University Press, Cambridge (2008)
7. Fuster, G.: The Emergence of Personal Data Protection as a Fundamental Right of the EU. Springer, Cham (2014). https://doi.org/10.1007/978-3-319-05023-2
8. United States Senate Webpage, Constitution of the United States. https://www.senate.gov/civics/constitution_item/constitution.htm. Accessed 30 Jan 2022
9. Davies, T.: Recovering the original Fourth Amendment. Mich. Law Rev. **98**(3), 547 (1999)
10. Dressler, J., Michaels, A., Simmons, R.: Understanding Criminal Procedure. Carolina Academic Press, Durham (2017)
11. Boyd v. United States, 116 U.S. 616, 627: Olmstead v. United States, 277 U.S. 438, Goldman v. United States, 316 US 129, 134–136 (1886)
12. Katz v. US, 389 U.S. 347 (1967)
13. United States v Miller, 425 U.S. 435, 442 (1976)

14. Carpenter v. United States, 138 S. Ct. 2206, 2221 (2018)
15. Taslitz, A., Henderson, S.: Reforming the grand jury to protect privacy in third party records. Am. Univ. Law Rev. **64**, 195 (2014)
16. United States v Morton Salt Co, 338 U.S. 632, 643 (1950)
17. Michael, P.: Taking data. Univ. Chicago Law Rev. **86**, 77–141 (2019)
18. European Union: Regulation 2016/679 of the European Parliament and of the Council of 27 April 2016 on the protection of natural persons with regard to the processing of personal data and on the free movement of such data, and repealing Directive 95/46/EC (2016). https://eur-lex.europa.eu/eli/reg/2016/679/oj. Accessed 30 Jan 2022
19. Ferguson v. City of Charleston, 532 U.S. 67 (2001)
20. Council of Europe, European Convention on Human Rights and Fundamental Freedoms. https://www.echr.coe.int/Documents/Convention_ENG.pdf. Accessed 30 Jan 2022
21. European Union: Directive 2016/680 of the European Parliament and of the Council of 27 April 2016 on the protection of natural persons with regard to the processing of personal data by competent authorities for the purposes of the prevention, investigation, detection or prosecution of criminal offences or the execution of criminal penalties, and on the free movement of such data, and repealing Council Framework Decision 2008/977/JHA (2016). https://eur-lex.europa.eu/legal-content/EN/TXT/?uri=celex%3A32016L0680. Accessed 30 Jan 2022
22. Charter of Fundamental Rights of the European Union, 7 December 2000. https://www.europarl.europa.eu/charter/pdf/text_en.pdf. Accessed 30 Jan 2022
23. Voigt, P., von dem Bussche, A.: The EU General Data Protection Regulation (GDPR): A Practical Guide. Springer, Cham (2017). https://doi.org/10.1007/978-3-319-57959-7
24. Prime Minister of Japan and His Cabinet webpage, The Constitution of Japan. https://japan.kantei.go.jp/constitution_and_government_of_japan/constitution_e.html. Accessed 30 Jan 2022
25. Judgment of Supreme Court, 16 March, Japan (1976). https://www.courts.go.jp/app/hanrei_en/detail?id=47. Accessed 30 Jan 2022
26. Kyodo News: Denuded private life, Sekai No. 921, pp. 106–114 (2019)
27. The Code of Criminal Investigations, Rules of the National Public Safety Commission No. 2, Article 99 (1957)
28. Judgment of Nagoya District Court, 16 July 2004, Japan (2004). https://www.courts.go.jp/app/hanrei_jp/detail4?id=7540. Accessed 30 Jan 2022
29. Uga, K.: A Commentary of the Act on the Protection of Personal Information (APPI), 6th edn. Yuhikaku, Tokyo (2018)
30. Ministry of Internal Affairs and Communications (MIC): Commentary for guidelines For Protection Of Personal Information In Telecommunications Business, MIC Notice No. 152 of 2017; Last Amendment: MIC Notice No. 297 of 2017, September 2017 (Updated in February 2021). https://www.soumu.go.jp/main_content/000744055.pdf. Accessed 30 Jan 2022
31. Yonemura, S.: Lectures on Medical Law. Nippon Hyoron Sha, Tokyo (2016)
32. Gray, D.: The Fourth Amendment in an Age of Surveillance. Cambridge University Press, Cambridge (2017)

Author Index

Printed in the United States
by Baker & Taylor Publisher Services